Leading for Change

This book offers new theoretical ground for thinking about, and transforming, leadership and higher education worldwide. Through an examination of the construct of intimacy and "nearness", including emotional, spiritual, psychic, intellectual and physical closeness, Jonathan Jansen demonstrates its power to influence positive leadership in young people. He argues that sensory leadership, which includes but extends beyond the power of touch, represents a fresh and effective approach to progressive transformation of long-divided institutions.

Considering richly textured narratives, chapters explore complex intimacies among black and white university students in South Africa, post-apartheid and in the aftermath of a major racial atrocity. The stories reveal the students' transformation in the process of "leadership for change", interweaving concepts of racism, human relationships and intimacy, and in turn expanding the knowledge base of social and institutional improvement. This book explores how, when different kinds of nearness come together in leadership change, young people respond in ways that would not be possible through conventional instruments such as policy, legislation and the appeal to moral sensibilities alone.

Leading for Change will be critical reading for academics, researchers and postgraduate students in the fields of education, educational justice, higher education, educational leadership and change, and social and/or racial justice. This book will also be of interest to those working in the fields of anthropology, social psychology and South African contemporary politics, policy and institutional practices.

Jonathan Jansen is Vice Chancellor and Rector of the University of the Free State, South Africa, and President of the South African Institute of Race Relations. He is a Fellow of the American Educational Research Association and a Fellow of the Academy of Science of the Developing World. In 2013 he was awarded the Education Africa Lifetime Achiever Award in New York and the Spendlove Award from the University of California, USA, for his contributions to tolerance, democracy and human rights.

Routledge Research in Educational Leadership series

Books in this series:

Political Philosophy, Educational Administration and Educative Leadership
Reynold Macpherson

Educational Administration and Leadership
Theoretical Foundations
Edited by David Burgess and Paul Newton

Indigenous Leadership in Higher Education
Edited by Robin Starr Minthorn and Alicia Fedelina Chávez

Student Voice and School Governance
Distributing Leadership to Youth and Adults
Mark Brasof

Leading for Change
Race, intimacy and leadership on divided university campuses
Jonathan Jansen

Leading for Change
Race, intimacy and leadership on divided university campuses

Jonathan Jansen

LONDON AND NEW YORK

First published 2016
by Routledge
2 Park Square, Milton Park, Abingdon, Oxon OX14 4RN

and by Routledge
711 Third Avenue, New York, NY 10017

Routledge is an imprint of the Taylor & Francis Group, an informa business

© 2016 J. Jansen

The right of J. Jansen to be identified as author of this work has been asserted by him in accordance with sections 77 and 78 of the Copyright, Designs and Patents Act 1988.

All rights reserved. No part of this book may be reprinted or reproduced or utilised in any form or by any electronic, mechanical, or other means, now known or hereafter invented, including photocopying and recording, or in any information storage or retrieval system, without permission in writing from the publishers.

Trademark notice: Product or corporate names may be trademarks or registered trademarks, and are used only for identification and explanation without intent to infringe.

British Library Cataloguing in Publication Data
A catalogue record for this book is available from the British Library

Library of Congress Cataloging in Publication Data
Jansen, Jonathan D.
  Leading for change race, intimacy and leadership on divided university campuses/Jonathan Jansen.
  pages cm
  Includes bibliographical references and index.
  1. Universities and colleges – South Africa – Administration.
  2. Education, Higher – Social aspects – South Africa. 3. Education, Higher – Aims and objectives – South Africa. 4. College students – South Africa – Attitudes. 5. College integration – South Africa.
  6. Educational equalization – South Africa. I. Title.
  LB2341.8.S6J36 2016
  378.1'010968 – dc23
  2015008198

ISBN: 978-1-138-89026-8 (hbk)
ISBN: 978-1-315-71251-2 (ebk)

Typeset in Galliard
by Florence Production Ltd, Stoodleigh, Devon, UK

Contents

Poem: "Somehow we survive"   vii
Acknowledgements   ix
Preface   xiii

1. A researcher's guide to intimate storytelling   1
2. Dangerous intimacies: explaining the Reitz scandal   17
3. "The misnamed free state"   39
4. Intimacy   57
5. The resident swastika   73
6. Intimacy demands a common language   83
7. The labour of intimacy   91
8. Intimate knowledges   105
9. Portraits of intimacy   123
10. From intimacy to nearness   133
11. A near and present danger   153
12. The intimate observer   173
13. Nearness in leadership   201

Index   221

SOMEHOW WE SURVIVE[1]

Dennis Brutus

Somehow we survive
and tenderness, frustrated, does not wither.

Investigating searchlights rake
our naked unprotected contours,

over our heads the monolithic decalogue
of fascist prohibition glowers
and teeters for a catastrophic fall;

boots club the peeling door.

But somehow we survive
severance, deprivation, loss.

Patrols uncoil along the asphalt dark
hissing their menace to our lives,

most cruel, all our land is scarred with terror,
rendered unlovely and unlovable;
surrendered are we and all our passionate surrender

but somehow tenderness survives

NOTE

1   Special thanks to Tony Brutus who, on behalf of the family, provided the permission to use the poem.

Acknowledgements

It is almost impossible to run a university as well as research and write a book. Unless, of course, you have family and friends who make this possible, and colleagues who understand the revitalising benefits that result from going between reflecting on and doing leadership in challenging circumstances.

I begin by thanking my energetic, smart and committed research assistant, Nicoleen Snyman, for working through nights without regard for time differences between Bloemfontein in the Free State and Palo Alto, California. The general research support was outstanding but the hard labour of toiling through the archives of the *Volksblad* in search of missing "letters" in order to generate the first draft of a basic content analysis is deeply appreciated.

It would not have been possible to do this research, travel to and live for three months in the stimulating intellectual environment of Stanford University without the financial support of the Oppenheimer Memorial Trust. The Chairman of the University of the Free State (UFS) Council, Justice Ian van der Merwe, was always supportive of my intellectual work as well as my public duties, and I thank him and Council for the three-month break between my two-term appointments as university principal.

The Stanford University librarian Karen Fung and the University of the Free State librarian Hesma van Tonder made sure that there was no lag between the request for special items and their receipt on my desktop and, for such excellent service and guidance, I am very grateful. In this regard my outstanding secretary, Rhoda Grobler, made sure that an excellent communication system was maintained between the home office and my Stanford location so that books and other resources would arrive at great speed via courier, email or person-to-person delivery.

I especially thank Professor Martin Carnoy from the Stanford University Graduate School of Education for the invitation as Visiting Scholar; the Stanford Center for the Humanities for office space; and Professor Richard Roberts and his staff from the Center for African Studies for tremendous generosity throughout the visit to ensure that there was physical accommodation, intellectual support and friendship at all times. Professor Joel Samoff and Rachel Samoff have been pillars of support since my anxious days as a beginning graduate student at Stanford through this recent stint as Visiting Scholar; their friendship and support to me, my family and generations of African students passing through their home in Palo Alto cannot be overstated.

I was greatly privileged to present the rough ideas for this book to academic colleagues in various parts of the world; their comments and criticism, and directions to literary resources, have refined and altered some of my arguments and strengthened the book overall. At Stanford University – and especially that unforgettable Faculty Seminar – I thank Joel Samoff, Richard Roberts, Laura Hubbard, David Abernethy, Grant Parker, Robert Seegal, Larry Diamond, Jim Campbell and Martin Carnoy; as well as Hans Weiler, Ann Lieberman, Lee Shulman, Judy Shulman, Linda Darling Hammond and Arnetha Ball. At Indiana University, Alex Lichtenstein, Erna Alant and Bob Arnove; at the Pennsylvania State University, Charles Dumas and Tracey Beckett; at UCLA, Bill Worger and Carlos Torres; at the UFS, Andre Keet, Lis Lange, JC van der Merwe, Pumla Gobodo-Madikizela, Helene Strauss, Andre Wessels, Neil Roos, Rudi Buys, Ian Phimister, Melanie Walker, Dionne van Reneen and many other colleagues; at The University of Humanistic Studies, in the Netherlands, Caroline Suransky-Dekker; at the University of KwaZulu Natal, Betty Govinden and Michael Samuel; at the University of Cape Town, Crain Soudien and Rob Sieborger.

There are many friends holding various stations in public and professional life who continue to challenge and encourage me in the conduct of leadership in South African society; their friendship and commitment to the human project have kept me going through the difficult times of leadership on- and off-campus. In this respect I thank Simon Morilly, Leon Wessels, Lorenzo Davids, Brand Pretorius, Thebe Ikalefeng, Louise Grantham, Clare Digby, Phumzile Mlambo Ngcuka, Don Gips, Liz Berry Gips, Nancy Christie, John Christie, David Christie, Kobus Maree, Zakes Mda, John Sama, John Pearson, Gail Weldon and Jonathan Berk.

Then there is my expanded team who have actually done the hard work of conciliatory leadership on campus and whom far too often are not recognised given the visibility of the team leader. And so I thank the competent and committed senior leaders in my Rectorate team – Nicky Morgan, Choice Makhetha, Lis Lange and Corli Witthuhn; the world-class team in Student Affairs led by Rudi Buys, Cornelia Faasen, Yeki Mosomothane, Hetsie Veitch and Renee Pelser; the deans of the faculties and their heads of departments; the SRC presidents and their teams from Moses Masitha, Phiwe Mathe and Mosa Leteane; and that beacon of decency, Professor Teuns Verschoor, who led the UFS as Acting Rector in the aftermath of Reitz, and whose chronology of events in his manuscript *"The Mapping of Reitz"* became a valuable factual resource for my book.

My family once again gifted me the physical, emotional and intellectual space away from home to do this writing and this work would, like all the rest, remain undone were it not for the support, criticism and encouragement of my wife, Grace. I love you, and thank you for making this work of intimacy possible.

The family understands that my sanity depends on having multiple opportunities for reflection and writing on difficult subjects in difficult times.

The heart of this book is about young people, those undergraduate university students from the University of the Free State who continue to teach, motivate and inspire me as a leader on campus and in the larger society. I would have given up a long time ago had I not witnessed your capacity for love, forgiveness and bridge-building despite the hardship you all had to bear, black and white, as pioneers of a model of reconciliation and justice now widely admired around the world.

To the students: this is your doing and I am so privileged to be able to walk among you and learn from you as the next generation of Mandelian leaders.

Preface

The television crew arrived at my Cape Town hotel dead on time. We bonded immediately, the black middle-aged rector (university president) from the University of the Free State and the white, Afrikaans-speaking team of mostly young, energetic TV people. The plan was long in the making, to isolate me from my busy schedule as the leader of a once-troubled university in middle South Africa to be followed for a day to the places where I spent my childhood. A "journey into the past" was something this television programme aired every week on Afrikaans television focused on one or other well-known public figure or celebrity.

At first I tried to duck out of this commitment; I simply could not spend hours of a working day visiting my past haunts a thousand kilometres away. But my colleagues in "strategic communication" convinced me that telling my story was important in our ongoing efforts to build support from the broader community of especially white Afrikaans parents and alumni, many of whom still remained sceptical of this thing called "transformation" at our 100-year old university which I was privileged to lead. So I agreed.

It is difficult to explain to outsiders but as a black person in South Africa, even a self-confident black rector, you approach every encounter with white strangers with a measure of reserve. Deep inside your memory bank there are records of unpleasant encounters with white people, when they were in charge, and a fair recollection of pain. With time, I got better at these first encounters and so I quickly connected with the very pleasant crew and enjoyed the meaningless banter and the free flow of jokes in their language, Afrikaans. "What a nice group of optimistic South Africans," I thought; "there is hope for our country."

My guard down, we now rolled along the streets of Cape Town towards the high school in District Six where I taught Biology to the senior grades. The minute television cameras were positioned all over the large, comfortable van to capture the drive, the surrounding environment, as well as the exchange between the driver – a well-known Afrikaans singer – and myself on the passenger side. Every now and again the car behind us would call for a stop, through the driver's earphones, to make some adjustment to the cameras or to ask for a question or response to be repeated; the technicians in the other car could hear and see everything in this high-tech, mobile studio.

"This place reminds me of a difficult time in my life," I told the driver-interviewer. While I taught the life sciences to black students, the last of their houses were being flattened by very large bulldozers of the apartheid government since the area had been declared for "whites only"; the students and their families would be shunted many miles away to the windswept Cape Flats to restart their lives. In one of the teaching rooms, the students could see directly through the windows of the classroom how their homes came down in rubble and dust. I was beyond angry and many of the students were radicalised into protest action.

One or two buildings in District Six would not be moved, including a mosque, a church and where we were now headed, Trafalgar High School. This school had a proud history of resistance to apartheid and several teachers were demoted, banned or driven into exile for defying the restrictions placed on teaching, curricula and political association. To this day Trafalgar carries that political badge of honour with great pride.

As I rambled on about the struggle history of the school, I got the distinct impression that my interviewer-cum-driver had very little interest in the politics of education; so I changed the subject to more pleasant issues. We arrived at the school, on short notice, but as is South African custom with strangers, you lay on the best. Tea was served with familiar Malay dishes from these quarters, such as the obligatory plate of samosas. My salivary glands worked overtime and I felt proud of my former colleagues for their warmth and open-heartedness towards the familiar strangers in my company; strangers whose forefathers brought down their homes. But this was a time to enjoy intimate company as laughter filled the room.

Suddenly, everything changed. The older man in the group, faced with the plate of samosas, said calmly, "*ek eet nie Coolie-koekies nie*" (I do not eat Coolie cookies). My heart sank. I felt my mouth dry and for a moment I could not swallow. The instinct to respond immediately in the face of an act of racism simply was not there; I was in shock and did not have the capacity for response at that moment. *Coolie*, the derogatory reference to an Indian, was not only out of place in a geographic sense (the colleagues were not Indians but descendants of Malay slaves from South East Asia) but deeply offensive in a racist sense.

I thought long and hard about what happened. What stunned me was not so much the racism; it was the assumption of intimacy. Less than 30 minutes earlier this same man had greeted me warmly outside the hotel and said that I was his hero, that he looked up to me and enjoyed following my "*uitsprake*" (pronouncements) on matters of education. I appreciated his warmth, and his embrace. We were closer in age and I genuinely enjoyed his company. Then the drop, the unexpected let-down, and the absolute despair that followed. I nervously followed the eyes of my Muslim-Malay friends, the alleged *Coolies*, and with restraint and grace they continued to serve as if nothing happened.

This is the dilemma that lies at the heart of this book. Can racism and intimacy coexist? In other words, is it possible to be physically and emotionally close to others, such as historical enemies, and yet be the subject of racial hurt and humiliation? Why is it that the perpetrator can move so easily between intimacy and racism without even recognising the slippage? How do victims arrange their lives around and within such dangerous intimacies in ways that cushion harm? What does it mean when perpetrators claim ignorance of the offence as in "I did not know"? What does this mean for racial integration on university campuses in the aftermath of apartheid or slavery – especially in that most intimate of spaces – the student residences? And how can leadership, especially affected leadership, transform the hurt of intimacy into hope and healing?

1 A researcher's guide to intimate storytelling

Introduction

I had always wanted to write an academic book that was a work of scholarship and yet easily readable by non-specialists in the field. The theory binding the book should be immediately evident to the trained academic eye and yet not be an obstacle to fluency of communication. An accomplished historian friend compares this ambition to installing the scaffolding for building a new house and then, when done, to remove these external support structures leaving only the beautiful home in view.

This quest to be accessible through writing might be a function of reaching a season of academic seniority, and therefore little to prove as a scholar, or maybe it is the abiding instincts of a professional teacher that values simplicity. Or perhaps it derives from my earliest reprimand trying to write at high school; to this day I remember the cutting remarks of my Grade 12 English teacher, an old Greek educator called Cockinis: "just say what you want to say and stop using big words." That comment hurt at the time but it is the best feedback I ever received on an essay or "composition" as it was called in South African schools in those days.

I therefore do not appreciate bombastic language parading as academic writing; frankly, it irritates me. This kind of impenetrable writing precedes but certainly became worse with the postmodern or poststructuralist moment in the social sciences, humanities and even education. Despite solid training in "post" – ways of thinking and doing academic work – I could not grasp why such convoluted language needed to be used. The question I would keep asking of the journal articles and books written in this vein was simply: "What are you trying to say?" There is no question that writing in obscure and complex ways comes from the socialisation of young academics in their disciplines. Through university seminars and academic conferences, you learn acceptable and completely non-natural ways of talking once you enter those communities. You certainly do not talk that way at home.

In South African academic tradition these non-natural ways of talking are reinforced by training researchers to write in the third person. This obviously makes "natural talk" difficult if not impossible; "the researcher believes" is not only odd and unnecessary, it feeds into the kind of distant writing that separates the writer from their own emotions, history and participation in the research process from design to conduct to outcomes. Fortunately, social research in the qualitative tradition has come a long way since the narrow, positivist thinking that tries to apply an outdated notion of scientific objectivity to human studies. The research for this monograph works inside such advances in qualitative research[1] by drawing on intimate encounters between white and black students over a period of five years at the University of the Free State in middle South Africa.

In the book *Coming Close*, Jane Mead makes the pertinent observation that: "One of the great privileges of teaching, of having students, is the way it puts you in people's lives just as they are open to learning, and perhaps even open to how that learning might change them."[2] From this vantage point, many of the stories I tell rely largely on my direct experiences with, observations of, and discussions among students in which I was present, observing how they learn and change. What follows, therefore, is not simply research on intimacy but intimacy in research in which "the rhythm, smell, sense, tension and pleasure that go into producing data" should be evident in the stories told.[3]

Some of these intimate encounters were recorded instantly and appear – without theoretical commentary – in my *Times* columns on Thursdays and in the popular collections of these same pieces in the books *We Need to Talk* and *We Need to Act*.[4]

There is a sensible criticism of "mere stories" in some of the literature and this is why the narration of student lives and experiences in this book is hooked onto theories of closeness, intimacy and nearness, primarily in the field of social psychology but also history, curriculum theory and politics. A story in itself can be passed off as anecdote unless, as attempted in this book, it is placed in social and intellectual contexts that assign those stories structure, meaning and significance.[5] For those who cannot resist placing the book somewhere within the changing taxonomies of qualitative methods, this particular approach to storied writing comes closest to what Norman Denzin calls interpretive auto-ethnography.[6]

One of the core concepts from new ways of doing auto-ethnography, and that shows up in the stories that frame this book, is that it "shifts the focus from authority to vulnerability".[7] The people in the stories, the writer and the students, are therefore presented as imperfect human beings struggling to create intimate community on difficult terrain. To be vulnerable, in this context, means "to be fragile, to be susceptible to wounding (Latin, *vulnus* or wound) and to suffering"[8] as will become evident in the narration. It is this state of fragility and the risk it carries that makes intimacy possible, for "vulnerability and dependency are intertwined".[9]

There is a rich tradition of writing stories in this way when it comes to particular kinds of scholarly writing, as in American scholar Beverley Daniel Tatum's celebrated monograph *Why Are All the Black Kids Sitting Together in the Cafeteria?*[10] And, more recently, the edited South African book, *Being at*

'Home': Race, Institutional Culture and Transformation at South African Higher Education Institutions.[11]

But this is not simply a narrative analysis of student stories; it is also an attempt to tell the story of institutions, principally this century-old university with its rich store of memories, history and tradition. The analytical task, as will be seen, was to connect stories of individuals and groups to the stories of the institution. Student experiences, and how they come to voice them, hang together with the overhead institutional story either as reinforcement of, or resistance to, what the young people already know. At the heart of the institutional story is of course the curriculum as an institution[12] and how unsettling that codification of knowledge challenges and conflicts with received stories held by black and white students alike.

Even the university as an institutional story is embedded within other social institutions such as schools, homes and churches. I deliberately did not dwell too much on these other interlocking institutions since that was done in my predecessor book, *Knowledge in the Blood*.[13] Suffice to say in this work that students come into university not only with intellectual knowledge but emotional knowledge from powerful institutions; again, those incoming stories are told more fleetingly here because they appear elsewhere.

Stories are always contested and conflictual, and in saying that I locate my work broadly within the critical theory tradition without being overly constrained or orthodox about one theoretical disposition. The stories told in this book are about power, but not one-dimensional power. I avoid therefore the simple narratives of evil white/good black or powerful oppressor and powerless victims, the easy binaries of both popular literature, as well as academic writing on two of race's most troubled institutions, slavery and domestic labour.

The stories shared are on the lookout for exceptions, for intimacies that do not make sense and that are avoided, dismissed or sneered at in mainstream social science research. I examine, in other words, opportunities opened up by complex intimacies that offer glimmers of hope and healing rather than the pessimism of the regnant literatures on the subject.

I take advantage of my training as a comparativist to draw out comparison between stories about individuals and institutions in South Africa and the United States of America. More than a few scholars have been attracted to the utility of comparison between these two countries with their parallel histories of chattel slavery, white supremacy and racial segregation, and the common and divergent ways in which these phenomena were expressed on either side of the Atlantic.[14] Both novels about the past and real stories from the present in the two countries demonstrate the enduring effects of race and racism which, in turn, raise questions about claims that we have actually achieved post-racial (in the USA) or post-apartheid (South Africa) community.

How then were the stories compiled? Next to my office desk is a large brown box. Every time I received an angry or gracious letter on transformation, I would slip it into that box. Now and again the letter would be so inflammatory, even deadly, I would call in my secretary and read it to her; she would shake her head in disgust and I would tear up the derogatory piece. Surely even social research must have its limits on what counts as data when it comes to such demeaning and degrading sources? So instead of landing up in the big brown box on my right for later analysis, it would end up in the dirt bin on my left as garbage. As indicated, many of the stories were immediately written up as columns for *The Times*, though without the kind of academic commentary allowed for in this book.

Throughout the telling of the stories in the book I have guarded against unfounded optimism. I wanted of course to tell stories of progress but also of recidivism; of students experiencing transformation and those who, sadly, do not; of dangerous intimacies alongside loving affection which "sees the other in oneself", or nearness as I coined it. More than anything I wanted to convey the messiness of change and that transformation in large and complex organisations is never a straight line going forward.

How does one bring these stories to light in a vivid and memorable way that writing in words, alone, cannot? This is particularly important for those reading about a place they will never visit and human faces they will never encounter. We accumulated more than one thousand photographs of students, and of students in interaction with leadership, and each other, to convey the dynamism of campus life and the intimacies of human connection over the five-year period. The selection of photographs for the book was carefully chosen to capture the arrhythmia of transformation impulses in the heart of a fast-changing, conservative university. In these portraits I wanted to, moreover, capture stories of trauma and triumph, hurt and healing, hopelessness and hope.

Photographs are not innocent, though, as Monica Moreno Figueroa tells in the text *Looking Emotionally: Photography, racism and intimacy in research*.[15] A photograph has no context to a neutral observer; it is interpreted. It might mean different things to "sitters" and takers of the image. It is manufactured by photographer and subject alike, a point Karina Simonson demonstrates in *How to Photograph Nelson Mandela*.[16] As Figueroa puts it:

> Photographs, discourses of race and beauty, and experiences of racism can be easily entangled with the pleasure of looking, forgetting their histories of formation and the material and symbolic meanings they have accumulated.[17]

The evidence for ocular misrepresentation is particularly disturbing in historical images of race and race relations, such as in period photographs of melon-eating blacks "under which condition no darkey boy could help looking happy".[18] And yet photographs – not only of suffering – offer "an intimacy unrivalled by other images" with the power to convey emotion, spur action and distil hope.[19]

Conscious of the threat of misrepresentation, and yet alert to the hopefulness of selected images, I placed each of the photographs in the narrative run of the book offering context and explanation, including a sense of time and place, so that the reader is provided some measure of interpretation for what is being observed even as I recognise that such meaning-making ultimately resides with those who will "read" these pictures.

It should now be clear that I deliberately chose for the introductory pages of this book the playful ambiguities presented in the unlikely photograph of two young girls, believed to have been taken inside one of the Boer War concentration camps more than one hundred years ago.

What is going on here? How is it possible that a black hand, on top, holds a white hand at a time when racial subjugation was already firmly fixed through colonial conquest? How "real" is the image, therefore, as a reflection of race relations at the time or is this photograph staged – notice the matching of the colours of the umbrellas with the skin tones of the girls.[20] And what are those puzzling anklets around the feet of the black girl – female adornment or controlling attachment? It is these ambiguities of intimacy represented in this photograph that thread through the book and which I hope will keep interpretation on the edge as the most intimate of human relationships are examined on a university campus.

Transformation and its reactions play out in real time and I wanted to therefore capture the raw, human emotions that responded to shifts in racial demographics, institutional culture and curriculum change from the primary commentator on these events, the local Afrikaans newspaper called *Volksblad*. For this purpose we conducted a detailed content analysis of every "Letter to the Editor" about the university published in this newspaper since my appointment in 2009 over the five-year period to 2014. There must be few places in the world where so much argument, anxiety, anger and assault against a university are condensed into one section of a newspaper (the *Letters* section), often in response to persistent criticisms leveraged by the editors and their writers.

We began by examining the frequency of university-directed letters on a daily, monthly and annual basis; clear trends were observable over any year, the slow months and the busy months. We of course also identified thematic concerns that run through these correspondences over time such as: "What do readers write about? Whom do they write about? What is the tone of the writing? Who is the author responding to?" From the thematic analyses I generated a narrative analysis that brings together a fairly strong and consistent story about the intimate relationship between community and campus – or town and gown in another idiom.

The concept of entanglement

My conceptual starting point for both the visual and written forms of narrative was the notion of *entanglement*. It is a word that came to me unforgettably during a visit of professors and their students from a university in the Netherlands. Almost all of the members of the group were first-time visitors to the University of the Free State and to South Africa. While some of their number were Dutch, most of the students came from various Asian and other European countries, and some were Africans. Just before I delivered a lecture to the group I went around the table and asked each visitor to name one thing that puzzled them, or that stood out in their experiences, over the first few days of their encounter with South Africa. Of course, "one thing" was too much to ask the excited party of students to name and reflect on. But when it came to the turn of one of the professors in the group, an erudite scholar from India, he uttered two words to convey this striking observation of country and campus: "Your entanglements."

I love that word. Sarah Nuttall describes entanglement as the state "of being twisted together ... an intimacy gained even if it was resisted, or ignored or uninvited".[21] Here is South Africa's dilemma writ large. We were bound together under apartheid and stuck together after that cataclysm. Dependent on each other for labour and wages, skills and training, mission and mercy, nobody can or wants to leave. Speaking of these troubled entanglements between white and black South Africans, the social historian Charles van Onselen makes the crucial point that

> [...] what analysts sometimes fail to understand is that without prior compassion, dignity, love or a feeling of trust – no matter how small, poorly or unevenly developed – there could have been no anger, betrayal, hatred or humiliation.[22]

In the course of time the settler would become the native; the white native, the co-inhabitant of suburbs and boardrooms, classrooms and factories, shopping aisles and farms. There are no longer separate lines for queuing at banks, the post office or checkout counters; like it or not, we now stand and sweat alongside each other in that rarest of entanglements in post-colonial Africa.[23]

Where the settlers either left after independence or were too small in number to ignite the friction of proximity, the post-independence threats of entanglement were minimal. In a few places it turned dangerous, as in Zimbabwe's land occupations,[24] but even there the white numbers were too few to cause a lasting problem. It is in South Africa where large numbers of perpetrators and victims, and their children with inflammable second-generation memories, are still entwined together trying to find ways of living, learning and loving together. There could therefore be no more appropriate metaphor for these stories than entanglement.

Central to "the narrative turn" in qualitative research is the duty to declare one's own place in this entangled story. I am not innocent.

One of the endearing and yet misleading questions my students sometimes ask me is: "How do you remain so calm after that crisis?" If only they knew the anger I sometimes have to subdue and the racial insults I have to swallow, all in the interests of demonstrating another way of leading in difficult times. Their perception of calm, of course, allows me to be able to speak to students when they explode – and this I understand – when they experience either white racism or black prejudice. I am not sure they would listen if I was part of the tumult.

So I declare my entanglement in the daily and intimate tussles with white and black colleagues, with the racial attacks from those in the black press who point an accusatory finger of not doing enough to stem racism and those in the white conservative press whose modus operandi is to demean your very person for trying to transform "their" heritage. Sometimes I do explode but it is mostly managed, a controlled detonation such as when buildings are carefully wired so that at a planned moment they collapse in one place, hopefully doing no harm to surrounding properties.

Nandi (not her real name) was furious that a busload of whites from the outside had come onto campus on a drive-through tour after an end-of-year function; it is safe to assume some of them were intoxicated. Security granted them permission since some of the visitors claimed to be alumni who had a working association with the university. Halfway through the campus ice was thrown from (in their words, miraculously fell from) an open window onto one of the cars of the black students, doing some damage. When the black student complained, one of the men from the bus allegedly confronted the student and a violent altercation ensued.

Nandi was furious. She posted a personal attack against the university leadership on Facebook and claimed this is what happens when the rector wants to reconcile with whites. In her telling of the story, these whites from the outside are now whites on the inside for which the university management bears responsibility. I saw the postings, with a short video of the entanglement, and was furious that these people could come onto a calm campus and undo the hard work of conciliation achieved among students. So I asked Nandi via Facebook to please explain to me what happened. Eventually she came back to me, and I assured her of my full support, an immediate investigation and results.

But I wanted Nandi, as I remind all students, to consider herself a leader. She was being prepared for a country and a world in which such challenges, sadly, would face her, and if she used such intemperate language and wild accusation, it would undermine her capacity to lead in crises. I put it softly, and she responded with disarming grace:

> Thank you, Prof. I respect and honour you and always have; there was no disrespect intended in my comment. It's almost a sense of frustration to have us get to a place where we recognise each other as divine creations, beyond the boundaries of skin colour . . . I love you.

I understood that "sense of frustration" so deeply. But Nandi was not finished as yet: "Forgive me. Perhaps I wrote in a state of impulse. Surely I will do better next time. Thank you Prof. Proverbs 12:15." I was busy talking with colleagues about the incident through text messaging between California and

Bloemfontein so I did not have time to look up the scripture. Did we have enough counselling and medical support, if needed, for the students affected by this incident? Did we ensure the campus security and police had solid statements from both parties to the conflict? Do we know who these outsiders were, and do they, as claimed, have any working relationship with the university? Are they in fact former students? (Turns out, their claims were false as far as the main aggressor was concerned, and I can only speculate what these outsiders really came to do on campus, and why).

A day later I looked up Proverbs 12:15. Nandi had taken me far too seriously in this self-castigating scripture: "The way of a fool is right in his own eyes but a wise man listens to advice." I responded on Facebook: "lol I just read the Proverbs advice; don't be too hard on yourself." She concluded the string: "lol ... Thank you Prof, I won't, but have definitely learnt from this."

Of course these kinds of entanglements in daily life on campus, with outsiders and insiders, have deep roots, and for me the most troubling origins of my own vulnerability as a university leader inside these stories come not from white racism but from much closer to home.

An inconvenient closeness

I was, to many in my church, the admired product of a rough neighbourhood. I was a devout young Christian and preacher in the church, on street corners and on trains. I was among the very first from our Cape Flats neighbourhood to progress past school to university. I was a leader of youth. In our evangelical community of lay preachers I was often asked to speak at the other "assemblies" as they were named, a call-up that happened more frequently after my adult baptism. It was on one of these Sunday evening missions to speak at a branch church, on the invitation of a serious but kind elder, that I first saw my future wife.

We became friends and, as was the custom at the time, you asked the parents for permission to date their daughter. It so happens that the 20-year-old-plus daughter was the child of the elder who had invited me. Since he knew me, I thought there would be no need for elaborate introductions. My girlfriend made the arrangements and I arrived at their home early one evening to seek the parents' support for our continued and now public dating.

On arrival at the house, I got the shock of my life. Gone was the warm brotherly greeting. The parents sat on the couch, opposite my single chair, as if they had seen a ghost; a black one, it turns out. I popped the question and then, to my horror and confusion, the elder got up and said· "I am going to the prayer meeting now [...]" (a regular Monday night event in this church) "[...] and by the time I am back, you both should be out of this house." He walked out of the living room with his wife hurrying behind him. It was easily the worst moment in my life – not simply because he walked out on the planned meeting but because I had no idea why.

It soon became clear. His daughter is fair-skinned and her hair is straight. I am dark-skinned and my hair refuses to budge. While both families were classified Coloured, and therefore oppressed as one group within the black community, her phenotype showed up favouring their Scottish ancestors while mine favoured our Khoi/Malay ancestry rather than my Dutch forebears. Another elder's wife, from the same church, put the issue more crisply to my future wife: "You should think about what your children would look like."

That was the first time I became ill in my life. I had become adept at anticipating and managing white racism; I was floored by this incident, inept at handling black racism – and that among people who did not see themselves as black to begin with. The frequent episodes of hyperventilation led to medications that altered my physical body. My public confidence took a hammering. And worst of all, I started to rage against the hypocrisy of our segregated churches and the false prophets who lead us. By the time he returned from, ironically, the prayer meeting, we had cleared out of the house, in compliance with his command, and without a place for my fiancée to sleep.

Late one night I slid a letter under the front door of my future father-in-law explaining very graphically what the Bible says about people like him.

Of course he did not show up at the wedding, nor give a cent towards the proceedings; at that time the tradition was that the bride's family pays for the wedding. Some family members avoided us like the plague; others were clearly awkward. My family and many, many friends inside and outside the church came to support us in what was a soft stand against the racism we had experienced.

This book therefore acknowledges my vulnerability inside these stories. I am not a perfect leader and, in my own estimation, I am not a good leader. These are not stories from the pen of a political eunuch; I am deeply moved, to anger and love, even I as try to show my students a better way. I make mistakes and I hope they are forgiven. The methodology underlying this research is not, therefore, the clean and crispy kind of the experiment-control type or that yields untainted evidence of the randomised control trial. Both concept and method is, rather, part of a messy, narrative account of human encounters shot through with pain and (com)passion and committed to hope and healing.

It is, in the final analysis, humane research, that takes its form from where and when it is conducted.

A sense of place and time

The drama of race and intimacy reported in this book takes place on the old, original campus of the University of the Free State in the city of Bloemfontein; in other words, the former white campus founded in 1904. There are, however, two other campuses of the UFS.

The one in the Eastern Free State, about 330 km away, is called "the Qwa Qwa campus" after the name of the former apartheid homeland serving the

Basotho ethnic group. The democratic government under its second Minister of Education, Kader Asmal, required that the UFS "incorporate" this campus, which was transferred from its home institution at the time, the University of the North, then renamed in its current designation as the University of Limpopo. One of the reasons for giving this University of the North Qwa Qwa campus (UNIQWA) to the UFS was because the latter was the closer by half the distance of the two big institutions but also because, as a former white university, the UFS would be expected to use its relative position of strength in terms of resources and capacity to raise the profile and performance of this deep rural campus.

The third campus lies in the south of Bloemfontein, a mere 20-minute drive from the original or main campus. This facility was once the VISTA University Bloemfontein Campus, one of several such campuses spread around the major cities of South Africa to serve "urban Africans" under apartheid; that is, those who did not attend the homeland universities for rural Africans, such as UNIQWA. The Vista Campus was also incorporated under Minister Asmal into the University of the Free State.

In short, two smaller black campuses were incorporated into the larger white campus, which together formed the single University of the Free State. Given racial and resource sensitivities with the two smaller campuses, and their perception of not being taken as seriously by the old campus in terms of resource allocations and curricular diversity, it was decided to refer to the main campus as the Bloemfontein Campus, the Vista Campus as the South Campus, and the UNIQWA Campus as simply the Qwa Qwa Campus of the UFS.

The race/intimacy drama would naturally play out on the theatre of the Bloemfontein Campus since the other two were in reality black campuses, notwithstanding the small numbers of white students on South Campus as a result of recent programmatic shifts. The old campus is after all where the white students are enrolled, where the memories of previous generations of white students were formed in and outside of the residences, and where the sharpest changes in racial demographics were taking place.

In one sense the Reitz scandal (see Chapter 2) was not simply a violent reaction to a few black students being integrated into white residences. It was that the campus "no longer felt white" as one colleague put it. Reitz, I would argue, was in part a response to demographic pressures in which, unlike any other traditional Afrikaans campus,[25] whites had become a minority on campus as they always were off campus.

In 1994 there were 8,057 (84.28 per cent) white students on the original campus and only 1,503 (or 15.72 per cent) black students, yielding a total of 9,560 registrations ahead of the incorporation of the other two campuses.[26]

Ten years later, in 2004, the white student numbers had increased to 8,707 but the proportion stood at 40.17 per cent – less than half the 1994 percentage – because the black student numbers had risen sharply to 12,971 (or 59.83 per cent), with a total registration figure of 21,678 students.

Another decade later and the white student numbers stayed more or less the same (8,641) but because of the small but continuing rise in black numbers to 13,656 students (61.25 per cent), white students as a percentage of total enrolments had also dropped slightly (38.75). In the larger university – that is, including the two incorporated campuses – total registrations stood at 31,243 in 2014 with black: white enrolments at 22,099 (70.3 per cent): 9,144 (29.27 per cent).

In short, while the number of white students had actually increased by 13.5 per cent since 1994, the first year of democracy, the black student numbers had exploded so that the racial dynamics on the old campus were expected, and predicted from research,[27] to impact on the sense of place among conservative white students. By the time Reitz happened, black students were already in a solid majority on the historic campus. And in a race-sensitive community, changes in racial demographics were felt long before they were counted.

But increasing the numbers of excluded groups is not enough for purposes of integration and, as will be demonstrated in the chapters that follow, "sheer contact"[28] could be downright dangerous. The entire emotional, educational and to some extent physical infrastructure of the campus had to be recast in order to convey to both black and white students a sense of mutual belonging as well as a sense of justice. In reflecting on this "paradox of integration", Eve Fairbanks, who studied the UFS over a three year period, asks the question: "How can it be that minority students [in the USA] seem unhappier when they have a larger presence within institutions that once excluded them?" Something deeper within the institutional culture had to change as well, which she claims has happened at the UFS to become – in the words of a black student – "a public space for all who live in it".[29] Together.

The case for integration

I need now to state clearly where I stand on the central plot of the book, togetherness, or integration. The crux of the racial conflict on the historic main campus had to do with arrangements for black and white students to live together and the explosive centre of this drama was the white residences. At one stage in the days leading up to the Reitz incident black and white students found common ground – they insisted on staying in racially segregated residences. For the white students it was a simple racist move camouflaged as a matter of cultural choice; for black students it was about conflict avoidance, a desire to simply stay out the way of abusive and sometimes violent behaviour by white seniors. And so, in a bizarre turn of events, both black and white students set up tents and camped outside the main building from where they launched bricks into the windows of the administration building.

Why not simply allow these South African students to live in separate residences? I must say that in years past my Black Consciousness orientation would have pushed me in that proud direction – why on earth make all this effort to reach out to people who think they're better than black folk? "Black man you are on your own" was once a powerful rallying call of one of South Africa's foremost intellectual activists[30] of the 1970s, Steve Biko, when as young undergraduate students we were conflicted about ideological direction in those boiling pot years of the struggle.

There is, however, grave danger in segregation given the great divides of economics, education and social status that continue to plague post-apartheid society. An angry black majority segregated in education and society from a privileged white minority when in fact they shave up daily against each other, as they always have, with such visible inequalities on display, is a recipe for disaster. More so when the *expectation* of democracy was that their lot would improve, racial separation resolves nothing other than to steadily build an ignitable resentment among black youth.

On the positive side of the ledger, however, there is now compelling evidence of the advantages of integration pulled together in Elizabeth Anderson's award-winning book, *The Imperative of Integration*.[31] I focus on the evidence marshalled only as it relates to education.

Integration opens up access to resources which privileged groups try to protect through "social closure" (segregation).[32] Integration gives students access to cultural capital, knowledge of how to relate to others, and the cultural habits required to succeed in the open market place.[33] Integration breaks down stigma and stereotypes thereby interrupting the reproductive cycles of prejudice and the continued infliction of injury and harm.[34] Integration demands that different groups find ways of working together and learning the habits of democracy such as mutual respect.[35]

The Anderson evidence fits with my own observations of how integration works to benefit students but there is one issue that she does not spend much time on. Integration benefits white students; as a cultural minority their chances of "fitting in/to" an increasingly black-dominated economy and society depend on unlearning bad habits (such as to assume control when blacks are present, to speak down to people, and to adopt a facial scowl under pressure) and learning the corresponding good habits (such as respect, tolerance and cooperation from a position of equal status). Integration helps black students discover their own social and academic worth in competition thus overcoming one of the most pernicious myths of white supremacy – the intellectual inferiority of black people. And most of all, in a country that made a legal and policy fetish out of differences, integration enables white and black students to discover the many things they have in common at the level of values and aspirations, but also in relation to their mutual vulnerabilities.

For these reasons and more this book is premised on the notion of integration as an invaluable resource not only for social cohesion, educational progression and economic well-being but as a bulwark against interracial conflict fuelled by still unresolved inequalities. In this context the university might be the last place in which black and white youth, the next-generation leaders of the country, still have an opportunity to learn togetherness in intimate community.

It is one thing however to make the ideal case for integration in school and society, it is a completely different matter considering its potential for harm when advanced without consideration of attendant conditions.

Notes

1 Clandinin, D.J. and Connelly, F.M. 2000. *Narrative Inquiry: Experience and story in qualitative research.* San Francisco: Jossey-Bass publishers; Reismann, C.K. 2008. *Narrative Methods for the Human Sciences.* London and Thousand Oaks: SAGE Publications; and Sandalowski, M. 1991. Telling Stories: Narrative approaches in qualitative research. *Journal of Nursing Scholarship* 23(3), 161–6.
2 Mead, J. 2013. Introduction. In L'Esperance, M. and More, T.G. (eds) *Coming Close: Forty essays on Philip Levine.* Iowa City: Prairie Light Books, distributed by University of Iowa Press, p. xvii.
3 This quote, and the distinction between research "on and in" intimacy, is from: Fraser, M. and Puwar, N. 2008. Introduction: Intimacy in research. *History of the Human Sciences* 21(4), 1–16 (p. 2).
4 Jansen, J.D. 2011. *We Need to Talk.* Johannesburg: Bookstorm and Pan Macmillan; Jansen, J.D. 2014. *We Need to Act.* Northcliff: Bookstorm.
5 Vincent, L. 2015. "Tell us a new story": A proposal for the transformatory potential of collective memory stories. In Tabensky, P. and Matthews, S. (eds) *Being at Home: Race, institutional culture and transformation at South African higher education institutions.* South Africa: UKZN Press, pp. 21–44; see endnote #2.
6 Denzin, N.K. 2014. *Interpretive Autoethnography.* 2nd edition. Thousand Oaks, California: SAGE. Auto-ethnographies, holds Denzin, are narrative expressions of life experiences structured by conventions which assume "the existence of others; the influence and importance of race, gender and class; family beginnings; turning points; known authors and observers; objective life markers; real persons with real lives; turning-point experiences; and truthful statements" (p. 7).
7 Conquergood, D. 1991. Rethinking Ethnography: Towards a critical cultural politics. *Communication Monographs* 58, 179–84 (p. 183).
8 Mackenzie, C., Rogers, W. and Dodds, S. 2014. Introduction: What is vulnerability, and why does it matter for moral theory? In Mackenzie, C., Rogers, W. and Dodds, S. (eds) *Vulnerability: New essays in ethics and feminist philosophy.* New York: Oxford University Press, pp. 1–29 (p. 4). The Latin and translation, in parentheses, is added.
9 Ibid.
10 Tatum, B.D. 1997. *"Why Are All the Black Kids Sitting Together in the Cafeteria?" And other conversations about race.* New York: Basic Books.
11 Dass, M. 2015. Making Room for the Unexpected: The university and the ethical imperative of unconditional hospitality. Chapter 4 in Tabensky, P. and Matthews, S. (eds) *Being at Home: Race, institutional culture and transformation at South African higher education institutions.* South Africa: UKZN Press, pp. 99–115; Njovane, T. 2015. The Violence beneath the Veil of Politeness: Reflections on race and power in the academy. Chapter 5 in Tabensky, P. and Matthews, S. (eds) *Being at Home: Race, institutional culture and transformation at South African higher education institutions.* South Africa: UKZN Press, pp. 116–29; Tabensky, P. and Matthews, S. 2015. (eds) *Being at Home: Race, institutional culture and transformation at South African higher education institutions.* South Africa: UKZN Press.
12 See the chapter on curriculum as an institution in my earlier work: Jansen, J.D. 2009. *Knowledge in the Blood: Confronting race and the apartheid past.* Stanford, CA: Stanford University Press.

14 *Researcher's guide: intimate storytelling*

13 Jansen, J.D. 2009. *Knowledge in the Blood: Confronting race and the apartheid past.* Stanford, CA: Stanford University Press.
14 Three prominent works of comparison are Frederickson, G.M. 1981. *White Supremacy: A comparative study of American and South African history.* New York: Oxford University Press; Marx, A.W. 1998. *Making Race and Nation: A comparison of the United States, South Africa and Brazil.* Cambridge, UK: Cambridge University Press; and Evans, I. 2011. *Cultures of Violence: Racial violence and the origins of segregation in South Africa and the American South.* Manchester, UK: Manchester University Press.
15 Figueroa, M.G.M. 2008. Looking Emotionally: Photography, racism and intimacy in research. *History of the Human Sciences* 21(4), 68–85.
16 Simonson, K. 2014. Litvaks in South Africa: How to photograph Nelson Mandela? *UFAHAMA: A Journal of African Studies* 38(1), 55–68. Available from: http://escholarship.org/uc/item/0fw830ps
17 Figueroa, M.G.M. 2008. Looking Emotionally: Photography, racism and intimacy in research. *History of the Human Sciences* 21(4): 68–85 (p. 75).
18 Sheeman, T. 2014. Looking Pleasant, Feeling White: The social politics of the photographic smile. In Brown, E.H. and Phu, T. (eds) *Feeling Photography.* Durham and London: Duke University Press. pp. 127–57 (p. 141).
19 See: Abel, E. 2014. Skin, flesh, and the Affective Wrinkles of Civil Rights Photography. In Brown, E.H. and Phu, T. (eds) *Feeling Photography.* Durham and London: Duke University Press, pp. 93–123.
20 I am grateful to the distinguished Boer War historian Albert Grundlingh from the University of Stellenbosch for his comments on, and evaluation of, this photograph.
21 Nuttall, S. 2009. *Entanglement: Literary and cultural reflections on post-apartheid South Africa.* Johannesburg: Wits University Press, p. 1.
22 van Onselen, C. 1996. *The Seed is Mine: The life of Kas Maine, a South African sharecropper, 1894–1985.* Oxford: James Currey, p. 4.
23 It was Mahmood Mamdani who, in his inaugural address at the University of Cape Town in 1998, famously posed the question: When does the settler become a native? Available from: http://citizenshiprightsinafrica.org/docs/mamdani%201998%20inaugural%20lecture.pdf
24 An engaging read on this subject is: Godwin, P. 2008. *When a Crocodile Eats the Sun: A memoir of Africa.* New York: Little, Brown & Company.
25 I exclude the University of Johannesburg because it resulted from a merger between the traditional Afrikaans campus, the Rand Afrikaans University (RAU), with a former white Technikon and a black teachers' college in Soweto. It became known as a Comprehensive University given the offering of technical and academic programmes, and overnight became a black campus without any fuss. RAU was a much more recent white Afrikaans campus established in the 1960s and, for all the above reasons, had a very different historical and political meaning in Afrikaner memory and identity than the century-old campuses like Pretoria, Stellenbosch, Potchefstroom and, of course, the Free State.
26 All the data in this section were kindly provided by colleagues in the university's Directorate for Institutional Research and Planning (DIRAP).
27 Long ago, Gordon Allport recorded his observations about the impact of "the size and density of minority groups" within majority populations as a threat proposition; see, Allport, G.W. 1979. *The Nature of Prejudice.* Boston, MA: Addison-Wesley Publishing Company, p. 261 (original publication 1954), p. 227.
28 From the work of Allport, G.W. 1979. *The Nature of Prejudice.* Boston, MA: Addison-Wesley Publishing Company, p. 261 (original publication 1954).
29 Fairbanks, E. 2014. Paradox of Integration. *The New York Times,* 17 October. Available from: www.nytimes.com/2014/10/19/opinion/sunday/a-paradox-of-integration.html?_r=0

30 I count the only other person of that period as a rival activist intellect to Steve Biko to be the Pan-Africanist Congress leader, Robert Sobukwe.
31 Anderson, E. 2010. *The Imperative of Integration*. Princeton, NJ: Princeton University Press.
32 Ibid., p. 7.
33 Ibid., p. 35.
34 Ibid., p. 44.
35 Ibid., p. 109.

2 Dangerous intimacies
Explaining the Reitz scandal

Introduction

It started off as a game. Four white male students and five black workers, one a man. The white boys called the four women "*squeezas*" (something to be squeezed) and the man "*Maljan*" (Mad John), an unflattering reference to diminished mental capacity. The black workers were two to three times the ages of the white students, but it did not matter. They knew each other well, especially the four black women and the four white men. They also trusted each other, so that drinking alcohol and playing games together during official work or class time bothered neither the workers nor the students.

At first glance, the video recording of the games comes across as innocent fun, for the most part. Until you stand closer, for then the crushing weight of history and culture, race and class, memory and identity, overwhelm the viewer of this recording of the single most horrific act of racism ever to be perpetrated on a university campus. Because of this incident in one residence on one campus, it would be the first time since the end of legal apartheid that a Minister of Education would launch a full-scale investigation into racism covering all 23 public universities by a burdensomely named Ministerial Committee on Transformation and Social Cohesion and the Elimination of Discrimination in Public Higher Education Institutions.

The students produced the video for one purpose only – to protest intimacy or, in their words, the racial integration of the residences. They simply did not want to live with black students in their male residence called Reitz, so named after Francis William Reitz, President of the Boer Republic, then called the Orange Free State, from 1889 to 1895. This Renaissance man – poet, statesmen, jurist and Boer War propagandist – would surely not have foreseen that one day his name, Reitz, would become shorthand for a racist atrocity in a university student residence once named to honour him.

But the four white students had a particularly perverse way of showing their contempt for what was at the time (2007) a rather moderate university policy on integrating the residences. They would humiliate the black workers through a series of first-year (freshmen) initiation rituals common to the Reitz residence culture; in other words, the four boys would treat the senior black workers of the university as if they were first-year students.

They made them drink strong liquor, encouraging the workers to gulp down bottles of the strong stuff while sitting on high chairs at the bar for senior Reitz students. They had the workers line up for athletic sprints with *Chariots of Fire* music playing in the background. They made the workers dance to music, and even joined in, as the senior citizens tried to stay upright. And then the act that turned stomachs all over the world – they urinated into a pot of food, and gave this to the workers to ingest while these older black people were on their knees. The workers try to spit out the disgusting brew; one of the boys calls one of the women a *"hoer"* (whore). Throughout this macabre event the white boys are relaxed, laughing and clearly making fun of the black workers in the process and whom themselves *appear* to be having a ball.

The video was entered into an annual residence competition, the Reitz Cultural Evening, and won. A few months later the video was leaked to the press, shown on campus and loaded onto YouTube. All hell broke loose and a little-known university in the rural heartland of South Africa would make headlines across the world for all the wrong reasons.

The senior leadership of the university scrambled, and their very diverse responses at an emergency sitting were revealing signs of the incapacity of the team to understand and manage, let alone anticipate, the crisis:

> Early the next day, 26 February 2008, the video was already circulating amongst members of the South African Parliament and in the hands of international press agencies.
>
> At about 10h00 that morning all the available members of the Executive Committee of Senate at the University of the Free State (UFS) were summoned to the Council Chamber to watch the video and to decide on how to respond thereto.
>
> We sat watching this video in stunned silence and at the end thereof some of us were softly crying, some were cursing, and whispering: "Close down this bloody hostel," some were smiling nervously, and saying "This was only a student prank, right? The workers looked like they enjoyed it, right?"[1]

This was no longer a game.

"Innocently racist"

Amid the cacophony that followed, it was South Africa's most distinguished education scholar who would quietly make the pertinent observation that:

> [...] very little is known about what really happened. How the video was conceived and what went into its conceptualisation is not known. The students were not asked the obvious question: "what were you thinking when you constructed this scene?" One has no access to what was in their heads. There is, likewise, no sense of the workers' own involvement in the incident ... One has no idea of the state of their own complicity.[2]

In the days following video revelations of the atrocity, the country would hear from civil and criminal lawyers, university officials, parents, human rights experts, academic talking heads, union leaders, alumni including Reitz old boys, journalists and the general public; not once from the students and only much later through carefully managed, clipped voices, from the workers.[3]

Now, for the first time, one of the male students in the video hands me an unpublished manuscript on the cover of which he scribbles this note in Afrikaans: "Prof Jansen! My attempt to tell my side of the story."[4] I dropped everything, cancelled a meeting and sped through the 112 pages like an out-of-control speed reader. Many of us had waited a long time to hear "their side of the story" and knew it would have to come, as for the workers, on their own time.

The title was already perplexing: "The Reitz Video: Innocently racist" and the opening lines make it clear: "This book is based on [my] perceptions." As I started to read this first-ever account in the voice of one of the perpetrators, I found myself responding in my head to a conversation we would still need to have in the future; what follows, therefore, is both the former student's account of what happened, and my imaginary conversation (in italics, to highlight the story–response sequence) with him *as if he were near*.

Sitting immediately under the title came the first defence of what was widely regarded as the most offensive of all the initiation rituals involving the workers:

> The mixture contained water, bread, coffee, protein powder, raw garlic and milk – the impression could be created that someone had urinated into it, but it never happened.
>
> (A, the student author)

> *But it does not matter, A. The fact that one of you showed on video the action of urinating into the food conveys what you wanted the viewers to believe you actually did. What happened after that does not matter; here the symbolism is the reality. You might not like the analogy but it's like a gunman firing a blank into the head of a blindfolded rival in a mock execution. From the point of view of the victim, it does not matter that there was no bullet in the chamber. Not knowing is probably worse.*
>
> (J, me)

Then he quotes Pierre de Vos, a university academic with impeccable credentials as a critical scholar in one of his more unusual statements:

> I do believe that this situation was blown completely out of proportion. It was a media goldmine that probably rivalled the Waterkloof-4.[5] The fact is that there were no signs of trauma until it became a public spectacle.
>
> (A quoting de Vos)

> *A, understand that Pierre de Vos is a constitutional lawyer and not a psychologist. Furthermore, the fact that he could not see "signs of trauma" from*

his offices in Cape Town on the faces of the workers in Bloemfontein 1000 kilometres away does not mean there was no trauma. Trauma seldom wears its consequences on the face. The most normal looking people in the world could be the most traumatised. This cannot, therefore, be of any comfort to you or the other three Reitz boys.

(J)

"2007 was a great year," starts Chapter One, of studying hard for a degree, training for and playing rugby with the goal of making the provincial team, and exciting dreams about the future. These were not your typically lazy jocks who see university as a cooling off period before working for their fathers on the farm. They were serious students, some in honours programmes and at least one of them making the top 15 per cent of academic students admitted to the Golden Key International Society. The self-description in the book certainly does not reveal a bunch of ruthless bigots waiting to spring a racist act on some unsuspecting black people.

The boys from Bungalow 12 of the Reitz Hostel – the only one with a kitchen and reserved for the very senior students – had a problem. The next night was the Annual Reitz Culture Evening and the four were not prepared. A typical routine was for a group of students to jump on stage and engage in a singing or dancing routine in search of a prize.

> We're seniors so we can make a video instead of putting ourselves on the stage! Yes! Yes! B and C (B and C, two of the other Reitz students) did not like the idea of making fools of themselves on stage (A). If we make a video . . . then we will be able to cut scenes, edit or even re-film a section if we want to (C) . . . Great idea! Also, we won't have to be at every filming session. What'll the video be about? [This is the planning conversation the night before the Culture Evening]

(A)

> *This is very interesting, A. So the idea was not planned way in advance but almost spontaneously the night before. So I understand the motivation for going the video-route was that you did not want to embarrass yourselves on the stage. Did you not realise, however, that you would be making fools out of these "much older than you" workers of the university? Did you not realise that they would feel humiliated if they knew they would be paraded in this way across the stage? Help me, please, for this is what so many people simply do not understand. I am not judging you; I simply want to know – did you not see these workers as dignified, older people demanding respect just as any other older human being? I know you. You have always been respectful in my dealings with you. Did these adult workers not deserve the same?*

(J)

B told us about his dad, who had done something similar when he was studying. . . . [B speaking]: "I'm not sure exactly why, but my dad and some friends asked the cleaners in their hostel to act as though they were boxing. He says everyone laughed and cheered, and they got a standing ovation. I think the event was rather similar to our annual culture evening."

(B)

Okay A, so you were simply repeating what you had heard done before, thus keeping the tradition alive of using workers in this play-acting situation for the enjoyment of others. So at this stage, if at all, does it hit you that the actors being recruited are black older workers and the audience young white students? Are you aware of the racialised meanings that would be attached to such an act from outside – even if you and the workers were supposedly having fun? In other words, is there any sense of history here, of black people being paraded for the fun of white people?

(J)

[A]: [. . .] [O]ur Reitz culture has been part of this UFS campus forever. You know my friend Jean Venter? Well her father was here at Reitz, and he can't face an egg. He had to eat thirty raw eggs when he was in his first year. [B, C and D laugh; D is the fourth Reitz student]. We'd all drunk that horrible Reitz juggy concoction, which every member of Reitz has to drink at the beginning of his second year in order to be recognised as a fully-fledged member of Reitz.

(A)

And we can include our rugby games, our beers, our dancing, and the whole lot.

(B)

Yip, and we'll show a mock juggy episode so that we mess with the minds of these 2007 first years. Then they'll be intimidated and need lots of courage, when they face drinking it next year.

(D)

So the intention is to intimidate the 2007 first years when their time comes due for this initiation. I must tell you that many South Africans would find great cruelty in these initiation ceremonies, such as the example of having a young student eat 30 raw eggs to the extent that he cannot face an egg in his adult life. Quick question: why would someone laugh about this? Again, my aim is not to judge you but to try to fathom why destroying a man's eating habits, perhaps permanently, would be remembered with laughter? And then, are you aware of the possibility that such extreme acts of initiation could lead to death? In fact, did you know that one of our students actually died once as a result of initiation?

(J)

We can ask the squeezas to help us by acting in the video. I don't even like my photo being taken never mind seeing myself in a video. I just don't have that sort of guts (C) [We all burst into laughter, D] If they agree, that'll be great . . . and they can act in our place. I hope they want to. (A) And the cleaners are part of Reitz. They're good sports, I'm sure they'll do it.

(B)

I see. So in your minds the involvement of the women is optional. There are three issues here, A. One, why do you call these senior women "squeezas"? Is there any sense on your part of how demeaning it is to speak of older women, the ages of your mothers, by this term – something to be squeezed? Does that not reflect an underlying racial contempt for black people? Two, can their participation really be optional? You realise you are white men, the "base" (masters) and "kleinbase" (little masters) from the past and, in some parts of the country, the present; surely you are aware of the fact that they would not respond to you in the same way they would respond to black youth your ages? Is this something you even considered? And three, surely they would not go through with what you planned so far, especially with the raw eggs and concoction (juggy) tale in mind – unless, of course, you did not tell them exactly what you were going to do?

(J)

The students then go off to request the participation of some of the more influential workers to participate in their scheme, and to find others. This, according to A, is how they responded:

Good old E (one of the black women workers) didn't disappoint. She dropped her broom and pretended to be very angry and with her hands on her hips.

(A)

You want to talk to me? I'm very busy and I don't have time to talk to you . . . You're wasting my time B. Say what you want to say and go to class. That's why you're here, isn't it? . . . What you four want? I've known you for four years and . . . You want to make a video? With a camera? You want me to be in the video? Like a TV actor? . . . You want me to play rugby? You'll have to pay me a lot of money before someone throws me on the ground! . . . Maybe I will. But then you keep your room clean, okay?

(E)

Okay, A. So now I see you've pleaded with the initially reluctant workers to become involved in your scheme. One is more easily coaxed than another, but they seem to leave open the possibility of participating. But so far there is no information about abuse. You simply give information about the video and the games though you mention "drink juggy" in your book. Did they know what "drink juggy" means and what you would do over that brew?

(J)

At this point A shares some important information about the pre-existing relationship with two of the workers:

I knew E always liked B. I think it's because he's gentle and polite but he always brought her meat and milk from his father's farms so she said ... I really loved F (another black woman worker). I knew about some of her problems. I knew her son was about my size, and occasionally I gave her a shirt or a pair of trousers for him. We talked about transport costs and the pain she sometimes had in her leg and things like that.

(A)

I was aware of how B helped E in the past when she needed money, and he, for instance, had brought two 50 kg bags full of mealies to her, because she'd told him: "I can sell mealies near my home for R2 or R3 each." He'd said, "E you can give me R1 each per mealie, and sell them for whatever you can get."

(A)

So this, A, is where many people stumble. You declare love and kindness towards the workers. You speak of affection and the sharing of material goods to aid the workers. They took you into their confidence, according to your record of the event, about personal health problems, and so on. So given this relationship, how could you do these things to these older people? How can you love them, and then give these adults a concoction of food, in which you pretend to urinate? How are both these things possible at the same time – love and abuse?

There is another dilemma I should point out. You know that in white Afrikaans culture you dare not call an older person by their first names; yet you do this so easily in your account of the bargaining with the workers. You would even, in your culture, call a complete stranger "Meneer of Mevrou" (Sir or Madam) and, even more commonly, "Oom of Tannie" (uncle or aunt). So explain this: why are these older people called on their first names? Surely the only possible reason is because they're black and therefore your playmates, not mature adults?

(J)

So the workers show up for the video and, according to the students, agree and ask for some kind of compensation for their participation.

You know that if you're part of Reitz you have to be able to drink a beer without stopping ... We chanted the "down, down, down" chorus, we cheered them on, and we each had a beer.

(A)

Okay, let's freeze this moment. The workers are on the job. You are telling them, in effect, to drink a full bottle of beer and not to rest between gulps. Do you by this time understand the many problems here – that these are workers on the job and they are likely to walk away drunk? And that these are your seniors, adult human beings, being instructed to gulp down beer by what in all our cultures would be called children? Do these questions make any sense to you?

(J)

I'll do it. I know you'll give me something (worker G, black male worker) ... We'll act in this video, but what can you give us? What about a bottle of whiskey? (worker E) E was bargaining the way we bargain in Africa.

(A)

I must say, A, that this might look innocent but obviously it is poor workers, who are black, asking for things they could hardly afford given their low wages. Surely you are aware of the fact that this is not bargaining as between students but between poor black people and middle class white people; are you aware at this stage of the unequal relationship and how your "asking" for participation could be read as exploiting the workers?

(J)

Looking back on that day I can only remember all of us having fun and laughing loudly as we ran and kicked the ball, and our cleaner friends tried to act just like the Reitz guys. I could see that the cleaners were enjoying themselves as much as we were. Maybe it was fun for them because we were showing an interest in them and had made them part of our project, which must have been better than just cleaning the whole day as normal.

(A)

Then the notorious "juggy incident" is explained in the words of the student involved:

(B), who took trouble to explain about the juggy before I left. You know that we put in water, bread, coffee, protein powder, raw garlic and milk. We make it look as though we put in disgusting things ... there's never been anything really bad like urine in any juggy and none of us have ever been sick – we vomited because it tasted so bad. But we won't put anything horrible into this juggy, I promise you.

I am not sure I understand. You say you had left early to do end-of-year tasks and prepare for the examinations. So how do you know, in such detail, what B told the workers? Was this something you asked B about, or he revealed, after the incident was exposed? I cannot imagine B volunteering this information after the fact unless he had reason to. I also cannot imagine B going to such lengths to explain what was in the juggy when, for example, there is not a hint of such a conversation in the video itself? What is going on here? Is this a lie?

(J)

B said "this juggy won't be awful. Not only because we like you, but if you don't like our juggy you could just tell us we're not going to drink this, and we don't want to be in your video. You can leave anytime you want to, and we know it. We want to scare these first years so that they'll be intimidated about the juggy they have to drink next year."

(A)

While C and I were in class, the other two made the juggy mixture with a mix of chocolate protein shake, milk, water and bread. And afterwards B pretended to urinate into the juggy by squirting some orange Oros from an Energade bottle that he had stuck inside his shorts.

(A)

Once again, the elaborate explanation of the innocence of the concoction and the reassurance that the workers can withdraw at any time does not make sense except as "after-the-fact justification". Still, do you believe that the workers at this point had the power to refuse? And do you accept that the fact that one of you is urinating into the food (mock or otherwise) is precisely what caused the laughter and enjoyment among the white students watching this happen to black people? For whom, in other words, is this funny?

(J)

Then there is a curious set of references to the young white students and much older black workers engaging in the exchange of horrific insults.

D had added a scene where he and F (black woman worker) called each other vulgar names. B and I didn't like this much, but there was no time to take it out because, when we looked at the final version, it was almost time to leave and pick up our dates.

(A)

I asked a Student Council member who was the "mother" of Reitz during 2007 [and she told me] six years later that she'd enjoyed the evening . . . I asked her how she felt about the bit where D and F called each other prostitutes. She shrugged her shoulders slightly: "It was just one of those things and I wasn't so upset that I thought – How could they have dared to do that?" Actually the idea we got was that they were playing. It was just as though they were talking as they always talk . . . We knew about your relationships with one another.

(A)

Think for a moment what you are recording here in the book you gave me. Can you imagine in any culture, and especially in South Africa's conservative black and white family traditions, that a youngster calling an older person a prostitute, seriously or in jest, would ever be tolerated? Now think a white youngster calling an older black person a whore; surely you understand that this is very serious? I mean, how can you even seek affirmation for what you boys did, this racial insult to a black woman, from presumably another white woman (the SRC Council member) who attended the "culture evening"? Simply in going to ask for affirmation you must have known this was so wrong? And in claiming that the black worker returned the insult, are you suggesting some kind of moral equivalence, that in the black person saying the same – in response to the levelled insult – that makes it okay?

(J)

Then to the heart of the matter – why did the students make this video in the first place? Was it really just a desperate last-minute, poorly edited, rushed entry into a residence competition or was there some broader goal behind the production?

[. . .] [W]e needed a theme. If we didn't have a theme the video would have looked like a lot of unconnected incidents that made no sense. C asked, "what about saying it has something to [do] with this integration that everybody's talking about?" "Prof Fourie [the Rector at the time] wants us all to integrate, so we'll be spot on, I said."

(A)

In any case this word integration is the buzz word right now and we really like our squeezas.

(C)

That's true, so shall we say that our theme is integration?

(B)

D agreed and we wrote the word **integration** on a piece of paper and added it to the video.

(A; bold in the original script)

I find it hard to believe, given what happened, that the anti-integration sentiment was an afterthought, and I will tell you why. This is not all that happened. You actually said in the video: "this is what we think about integration." The integration theme was therefore not simply a thematic cover to bring coherence to a series of skits. This was intended to rebuke the management on its integration policies and, in order to deliver this "klap" (smack), you used the workers.

But there is a bigger puzzle here. Why on earth would living in the same residences with black students drive you to such lengths? Did you think you were better than black people? And by your constant references to black students wanting to be separate – do you realise that the only reason was because of the abuse they experienced, as a campus minority at the time, by white students bullying them in their residences? No black student anywhere in this country has ever entered a white university and asked to be separate because of "cultural differences"; so I'm afraid this argument does not work. You have to explain why sharing a residence with other human beings would inspire a video that humiliates older black people in order to carry your message.

I have so many other unresolved questions, A. One of them is your frequent reference to God and his goodness, and how He provided you refuge in these personally difficult times. So here's my question – who exactly is this God? Is it the one who moved seamlessly with whites from apartheid, which he sanctioned, into the post-apartheid period, which apparently horrifies him? Is this a secular God, someone fashioned in our own image of him and us? How could God possibly be drawn in as the silent conspirator in this saga? Surely not?

Finally, I have often asked whites who defended the racist act as "studentepret" (student fun) how they would feel if the workers on their knees in front of you drinking that concoction were white women, your mother's age, and the black students were the one's calling them by the name "hoer". How would you have felt, A, if that was your mother on the floor? I met your mother. She is a wonderful, gracious and kind human being. What, A, if that person were her?

(J)

Interpreting the horror

The play, proportion and perspective argument

To this day, the four students, and their parents, have no idea what the fuss was about. In their view the students knew the workers well, and they participated without any form of coercion. They were adults who could have withdrawn at any time. They even asked for money in exchange for their participation. The workers were simply requested to assist in the preparation of a video for a residence competition, and they did so willingly. They enjoyed the various activities, as is evident from the videos. There was no intention to humiliate anyone; that is a misinterpretation of what happened. About urinating into food? No, that is not what happened. It was *Oros*, a sugary orange squash drink. They were only pretending to urinate into the food to scare future first-years who would have to undergo these initiation rituals; once the new students saw this video, it would convey the intended shock for future students but no, the workers were not given urine in the food.

I spoke to two parents, one on the telephone and the other came to my office. They were heartbroken and told stories of isolation, rebuke and humiliation by former friends and neighbours, and even fellow churchgoers. People spat on them, one said. Others blamed them directly for the kind of boys they produced. But both parents, separately, inquired anxiously: "what did our boy do wrong?" At first I thought this was that kind of instinctive self-defence, or even self-justification, that loving parents tend to cling to even in the face of evidence of wrongdoing by their offspring. But I soon realised there was no planned deception or even an attempt at denial here. They genuinely did not have a clue what could have provoked such intense reaction.

In much of the Afrikaans media with its white, mainly conservative audience, there was also a pervasive sense of the Reitz incident being "blown out of *proportion*", a phrase that would come at me often, even from some colleagues, in reaction to widespread condemnation.

In this view, summarised, boys will be boys; initiation is a time-honoured part of residence tradition. The workers did not complain about the video, or their participation, until the political people became involved and inflamed their emotions. It was simply a prank, get over it. And by the way, why were these workers drinking on the job in the first place? Do they not also share some accountability for their actions? This is simply another one of those nasty black-on-white habits of naming everything racism when it comes to white South Africans. The management of the university did not do enough to protect the boys against the onslaught from outside; instead, they expelled the poor students. Clearly the management was under pressure from the ruling party which was, in fact, responsible for much more dangerous things happening in the country, like farm murders.

Playfulness was part of the justification for the prank. This is what students in their residences did all the time. In fact their parents and grandparents did it before them, and then everybody laughed and had fun. It must be mentioned here that the white defence for hurting black people – "we were just having fun" – lies deep within the very violent history of rural South Africa and the Free State, in particular, as Ivan Evans detailed in his work on racial violence and the legal system.[6] This kind of violence, whether in the countryside or on the campus, was at once personal, petty, playful, punitive and persistent – until it became simply part of the accepted routines of everyday human interaction between white and black.[7]

In the "just having fun" explanation for Reitz, time stood still. The fact that there were now black students and black professors in the former white university community made little difference; the tradition of playful initiation is timeless.

The call for *perspective* would come up often in the defence of racist acts. Why on earth would this video, a storm in a teacup, draw so much attention when there was so much crime and corruption in the country? Is this really more serious than all the car hijackings and farm murders going on? Instead of spending all your time condemning these four innocent boys, how about dealing with the *real* problems out there including death, violence and despair in communities?[8]

The racism argument

For most in the country, and abroad, the matter was quite straightforward. Four white students racially abused five black workers. It was as clear and as simple as that. The white students were racists who learnt this bad behaviour from their parents; the root of the problem lay in their homes and parents should shoulder responsibility for the crime. The poor black workers were victims; in the words of Emeritus Archbishop Desmond Tutu, on visiting the campus subsequently, they were too disempowered to know what was happening to them.[9] The adults were, to put it bluntly, innocent victims in the hands of the racists, oblivious to what was happening to them because of their racial, gender and class status that marked them so differently from the white, middle-class male students.

White liberals took to the media with a typically untroubled sense of self and a gushing ooze of self-righteousness as they condemned the white racists from the Free State on radio, television and in print. I wondered out loud as we watched the performance of the critics on television whether this need of the white liberals to furiously wave the accusatory finger at what they perceived as those rural hicks from the Free State was a means for drawing attention away from their own complicity in apartheid and its aftermath.

Black radicals called for the strongest action, openly blaming the reconciliation politics of Nelson Mandela for such behaviour from unrepentant whites. Ordinary black folk recalled the deep wounds from the past that this racist incident had opened up all over again. Experts hitherto unknown became talking heads in the media on everything from combating racism to trying to explain how something like this could happen more than 15 years after the end of legal apartheid; these boys were children when Nelson Mandela was released from prison.

Print and television would play an important role in memory, as month after month and year after year they would return to the scene of the crime not only because of the horror of the event itself but because of the powerful visual aide – the YouTube video – available for constant replay and recollection in the public mind. To this day hardly a month goes by without some reminder of what happened on the University of the Free State campus in 2008, whether on a celebratory holiday like Freedom Day or the annual Women's Day.

It happened to women, and not any women, black women. Invited by the Premier of my adopted province to explain the Reitz incident, and my handling of it, the head of the province had assembled his Members of the Executive Committee (MECs, as they are called) to hear and question me. A senior woman MEC asked her question with felt pain: "How, professor, could they do this to our mothers?" I felt the deep emotion in that question, and braced as I tried to respond.

This particular dimension of the atrocity was completely lost on the boys. It was not simply a black/white issue, or even a male/female issue; in South African society the students had broken the skin of one of the most sensitive issues in

African culture, the treasured role of the older woman, the nurturing mother, the giver of life. It was, to put it bluntly, a bunch of kids insulting older women. "How could they do this to our mothers?" While age difference might not carry as much weight in Western societies where children, in some places, call parents by their first names, this is a complete cultural taboo among Africans. The authority of the adult is absolute in conservative black communities to the point of being authoritarian. To play initiation games with an adult is unthinkable for a teenager in such contexts; to do this with urination rituals, and that in the case of senior women, is an unimaginable atrocity.

Not a few scholars would make the point that the racism perpetrated was not against anonymous black women. It was against the very people who would have been "the Other mother" to these youngsters as domestic workers on the farm or in the city or in the suburbs. The white boys therefore "knew" the older black women not simply in the immediate sense as workers at the university but as standing in, so to speak, for other black women as domestics in their own upbringing. How, therefore, could they perpetrate such violence against the very nurturers who raised them as co-mothers on the road to adulthood?

Class was not irrelevant in this incident. The four students came from middle-class families, mainly well-established farming communities. This meant they had access to money and food which they would in their long association with the women, in particular, bring to campus as gifts or even as payment for certain favours. It was not a surprise, therefore, that when asked to participate in the making of the video, the workers demanded payment for their time on the project. There was, in other words, a constant reminder of another line separating the working poor from the well-off students – social class.

In the Reitz incident, therefore, race, gender and class came together in a devastating way to act on the bodies and emotions of the five workers. They were black, mainly women, and they were working poor. But those are academic distinctions, for neither the students nor the workers understood Reitz in those refined ways, and that is where the problem of coming to terms with this atrocity really begins.

Problems in the main analyses

The first thing that struck me in some of the more casual responses to Reitz was the claim that the students and the workers were friends, and that the relationship between them was caring and positive. I heard stories of how the students would bring the workers fruit and vegetables from the farms after a weekend at home. And then this, how the boys would oversleep in the morning and the women, who cleaned the Reitz residence, would come in with a whip and wake them for classes. In apartheid South Africa, a black person whipping a white person for whatever reason is unthinkable and would have had catastrophic consequences.

The more I heard these tales, the more I started to doubt the single story of helpless black female victims being coerced into initiation rituals by all-powerful white men lording over vulnerable bodies. The picture of intimacy and control that emerged looked a lot more complicated than the media images and first interpretations would allow.

Then there were the close-up images in the video itself and especially the Afrikaans word-exchange. There is not a single image that suggests physical coercion. Yes, there is encouragement of the workers to drink the alcohol or run the athletics race or dance; but that in and of itself is not coercion. Looking closely, the workers appear to be enjoying themselves and there is laughter in both directions. And then an unpleasant reality – one of the workers in fact returns the compliment and calls the white boy a *"hoer"* (whore). This is a very different picture from the *helpless victim* image told and retold in the media, and surely required closer scrutiny.

The helpless victim narrative had another dangerous downside. It portrayed black people without agency or voice, as simple puppets dancing to the tune of young white puppet masters. This kind of depiction of the black oppressed was untrue at the height of apartheid and it certainly was not valid 15 years into democracy. Nor is that the picture I witnessed first-hand about the relationship between the two parties. I watched the interaction between the workers and the students very closely during the intense hours of the reconciliation process, as well as in the final session where the first, formal public apology was made.

What puzzled me was that the black workers were emotionally in charge of the setting. "Come here and greet my husband," said one of the women with that gentle yet firm voice of a mother instructing her child. The student she addressed responded immediately and came to the other side of the lengthy table to shake hands. It was very clear to me that this was not something new or a sudden injection of confidence now that the racial shoe was on the other foot. No, this was perfectly normal staff–student exchanges between the two groups, and the women were certainly in charge. Suddenly the stories I heard made sense of how one of these women would whip these boys out of bed for being late for classes.

In the *helpless victim* narrative, however, the workers are exonerated from any responsibility for their own actions as if they were innocent children not knowing the difference between right and wrong. Again, while that short-circuiting of moral responsibility on the part of adults might serve immediate political purposes – which is to exaggerate the coercive authority of white racist youth – it is in fact a particularly odious form of racism in itself. The black people in this story are not children; they are adults who made a conscious decision to participate in these games and even made their participation conditional on being paid. They drank alcohol on the job, in the middle of the working day. They abandoned their work stations, willingly. What was on offer was not a pounding burden but a happy diversion from the drudgery of cleaning the same residence spaces day in and day out.

Finally, in this argument there were two main set of actors – white male students and black female workers. In a persistent trend throughout the popular as well as academic literatures on Reitz, the black man, "*Maljan*", was completely edited out of the racism script. Why is he left out, other than, again, to maximise the disgust of man-on-woman racial degradation? But what in fact is the role of the man in this humiliation ritual? Is he simply an onlooker left out of the main event because of diminished capacity as implied in his horrible nickname? Was his emasculation as "*Maljan*" now complete? That is a different story that requires further analysis and I flag it here simply to point to yet another shade of complexity overlooked in the rush for simple explanations of a dangerous liaison.

It should be clear from this particular reading of Reitz that the intimate relationship between the workers and the students cannot be reduced into a simple narrative of bad white racists and innocent black victims. There is a complex entanglement here of white and black that demands another look, for, if we get this wrong, there are very serious consequences in countries where historical enemies live and learn together and where it is assumed that physical proximity through, for example, school or university integration, gradually or naturally "sorts out" human dilemmas. Understanding such complex intimacies is therefore not simply an intellectual exercise but a very practical commitment to enhancing social cohesion and human togetherness in racially divided communities.

And that understanding must at least ponder this astounding statement by one of the Reitz students as he prepares to leave campus on completion of his studies and after the successful staging of the video:

> I packed my things while thinking back on all the amazing memories of the last few years. While I was packing I filled a box with half my clothes, and gave them to F for her son. We said goodbye and I told her that I was giving her the clothes to say thank you for everything she'd done for me. F's eyes had tears and she bent her body making herself small, and said, "Thank you A, go well." I told her, "You stay well F. I'll miss you."
>
> (A)[10]

She bent her body, making herself small.

The problem with deviance

"Where are you from?" I asked the tall white youngster in front of me during one of my walks across campus to meet and greet students. "From the Free State," he said, showing an uncomfortable posture, almost shyness. "Okay, but where in the Free State?" I had by now travelled widely to rural communities and farming families across the vast landscape and would pride myself on knowing a little snippet of information about several small towns and villages, especially those with unusual and even funny names; *Ogies*, *Verkeerde Vlei* and

Vrede were my favourites; *Little Eyes, Wrong Valley* and *Peace*. "Oh, not very far from here," came the response. "Does your hometown have a name?" I followed up, and he must have detected just a little irritation with his evasiveness. He dropped his head and mumbled something. "Say that again, please?" Ah, Reitz.

We could easily remain absorbed in concentrated analyses of these four white students from a now infamous residence. We could ask questions about their families and upbringing, their schools and churches, their friends and the crowd that heaped praise on them during the Reitz Cultural Evening. We could rerun that video over and over again, as I did, to try to locate personal pathologies within the hearts and minds of those four men nearing the end of their studies.

Such personalisation of these violent acts would be unproductive. As should be evident from the constructed dialogue earlier in this chapter, there is an overriding sense of normality governing the entire sequence of events, on the one hand, and a strange affection between workers and students, on the other hand.

It is that normality that must be explained, not the deviance as one study after the next has failed to do in the case of Reitz.[11]

The award must be explained as well as the cheering students at the awards evening; the head of Reitz, who was also the legal representative of the students, should be quizzed; the Student Representative Council (SRC) "mother" of the house who saw nothing wrong needs to be understood; the language of *squeezas* was never questioned; the willing participation of the workers required another look; the entire institutional context that made the video look so normal, even award-winningly good, are among the many other issues that required explanation. The students were simply operating within an institution that made even such an extreme form of racial abuse look like the most normal thing in the world. That is precisely why the students are so genuinely confused: *what did we do wrong*?

"There's a virus in the walls of Reitz," I would often hear from my senior colleagues, a quote whose source I could never quite pin down. "What does that mean?" I would tease with the advantage of a first degree in the biological sciences: "viruses don't survive very long outside the body." It soon became clear that Reitz the residence had been at the centre of institutional storms over decades. One management regime after another had tried to gain some control over the excesses of these male quarters but without success. Reitz had been closed down before, and then reopened, only for the troubles to start all over again.

Reitz, I would come to discover, was the broader institutional culture on steroids. It was the residence into which hardened soldiers, returning from border wars under apartheid's compulsory military service for white men, would be placed. Those men brought their own violent initiation rituals into the residence complete with traumas suffered as young men, straight out of high school, during a year of combat.

This new evidence of traumatised veterans is probably the most significant issue overlooked in the stock of research that proliferated after Reitz. I wish to capture in full the words of the one person with the clearest institutional memory of the university before-and-after Reitz, the acting rector before my arrival, offered with his familiar emotional reserve:

> Another complicating factor in the men's residences was that a considerable percentage of white residents had gone through compulsory military training – with some of them having been deployed at the border in the war between the then South West Africa (Namibia) and Angola. They experienced genuine warfare – chasing the enemy deeper into Angola, blowing up bridges and shooting to kill the black soldiers in the enemy lines. In those years television news bulletins would, on a daily basis, broadcast the names of South African soldiers killed in the border war.
>
> These students had suffered the most terrifying war experiences; some lost their best friends who were shot dead next to them by black soldiers on the other side of the river. And they had never been properly debriefed.
>
> Senior students with war experience would find entertainment in summoning new first year students to the residence quad and then ignite a bomb-cracker un-announced. Students who had been exposed to warfare would instinctively and immediately fall flat on the grass, whilst those who had not experienced warfare would get a fright, but remained standing and looking around for the origin of the noise.[12]

Now in a university residence for the first time, a deadly cocktail of abuse passed off as normal would await first-year students. These initiation rituals, including those violent vomiting episodes, continued for years and spilled over into all kinds of confrontations with the university authorities. As soon as the juniors became seniors they would visit the same rituals on the newcomers. What they had as "stock stories" were the memories of other old boys including fathers, and which, as in the case of the egg story, passes off medical injury with humour and trauma as pleasant recollections long after leaving the university.

I can understand the compulsion to shut down a residence, as was done just before my arrival and after the racist incident. But shutting down Reitz is not the kind of action that renders what is regarded as "normal" to a broad section of the university community as dangerous, demeaning and offensive. That was the main reason why, in my inaugural address as the new rector and vice chancellor in October 2009, I promised to reopen Reitz. Pursuing the logic of my predecessors – and I do understand the pressures they were under at the time – we would have to close down many other residences as well because the assumption of "normality", as I would come to learn over and over again, lies at the root of the difficulties of changing the University of the Free State.

By concentrating both analysis and outrage on the presumed deviance of the four students, the everyday normality of abuse in and around Reitz missed another point – the seamless movement from abusing students to abusing workers; from humiliating white first years to doing the same to adult black workers. Yes, the racist attack on black workers demands our attention but securing racial justice does not even begin to undo human wrongs that have nothing to do with race.

In other words, the courts could resolve the fate of the five black workers and yet the tradition of violent initiations would continue unabated under sanction of institutional normality. The abuse of the black workers was therefore only a momentary diversion of a longstanding tradition of abuse in order, this time, to target blacks, who were conveniently close, as a protest against racial integration.

When your institution is more than a century old, and abusing other campus citizens in the name of violent traditions is the most natural thing in the world, then the change strategy requires much more than shutting down buildings; what you need is to open up eyes – that is, ways of seeing differently the historical enemy near to you. This was the challenge, and would not be possible without an intense focus on the institutional conditions that produced these students.

That approach would, however, also require dealing with unresolved traumas among young white men – the negative and destructive energies unleashed on white students before integration and black workers after the university opened its doors to all citizens, as revealed in this frightening recollection:

> Already in the early eighties, before any black students were staying in the residences, the University continually received complaints from parents about hazing incidents in Reitz, where, usually, senior students who had completed military training were the culprits, and first year students who had not been exposed to military training were the victims. The University's response was to place in Reitz, as from the following year, only first year students who had performed their military service. With the benefit of hindsight, this decision would cost the University dearly.

On the evening of 22 February 1991, first year students from House J.B.M. Hertzog, a men's residence neighbouring Reitz Bungalows, were attacked by Reitz-students for apparently no other reason than they were singing songs while on their way back to their residence after having treated the ladies' residences to a serenade. Four of the first year students had to be admitted to hospital.

The University Council meeting of 25 March 1991 referred to it as "an unpalatable incident" that was investigated "and six residents from Reitz Bungalows have provisionally been denied the privilege of staying in the residence, pending the outcome of the disciplinary hearing".

Sometimes, the parents knew what the violent and disturbing episodes on the part of their children were about, as the acting vice rector recalls:

> In one instance I phoned the mother of a rather aggressive second year student to discuss with her his continuous misconduct. Her reply was: "Professor, the Army stole my child."[13]

And in this peculiar province, the Army did not act alone.

Notes

1. Verschoor, T. 2015. *Mapping Reitz*. Stellenbosch: SUN Media (e-book).
2. Soudien, C.. 2010. Who Takes Responsibility for the 'Reitz Four'?: Puzzling our way through higher education transformation in South Africa. *South African Journal of Science* 106 (9/10), 1–4 (p. 2).
3. Some of the more in-depth analyses of Reitz can be found in the following sources: Boesak, A.A. 2012. Between Reitz, a Rock, and a Hard Place: Reconciliation after the Reitz event. In: Boesak, A.A., De Young, A. and De Young, C.P. *Radical Reconciliation. Beyond political pietism and Christian quietism*. New York: Orbis Books, pp. 93–112; Bryson, D. 2014. *It's a Black White Thing: Forgiveness isn't for sissies*. Cape Town: Tafelberg; Durrheim, K., Mtose, X. and Brown, L. 2011. *Race trouble: Race, identity and inequality in post-Apartheid South Africa*. Scottsville: University of Kwa Zulu-Natal Press; Fricker, M. 2007. *Epistemic Injustice, Power and the Ethics of Knowing*. Oxford, UK: Oxford University Press; Govier, T. and Verwoerd, W. 2002. The promise and pitfalls of apology. *The Journal of Social Philosophy* 33(1), 67–82; Govier, T. and Verwoerd W. 2004. How not to polarize "Victims" and "Perpetrators". *Peace Review* 10(1), pp. 371–7; Haupt, A. 2012. *Static: Race and representation in Post-Apartheid music, media and film*. Cape Town: HSRC Press; Marais, W. and de Wet, J.C. 2009. The Reitz video: Inviting outrage and/or pity? *Communitas* 14(1), 30–41. Bloemfontein: University of the Free State; Naidoo, P. 2010. Three thousand words on race. *South African Review of Sociology* 41(1), 120–6; Soudien, C. 2010. Who takes responsibility for the 'Reitz four'? Puzzling our way through higher education transformation in South Africa. *South African Journal of Science* [online]. Available from: www.sajs.co.za/sites/default/files/publications/pdf/429-2726-6-PB.pdf; Suransky, C. and van der Merwe, J.C. 2015. Transcending Apartheid in Higher Education: Transforming an institutional culture. *Race, Ethnicity and Education*. Available from: www.tandfonline.com/doi/full/10.1080/13613324.2014.946487#tabModule; Taylor, J. 2013. *Facing the Past in Post-Apartheid South Africa: Exploring apology and forgiveness as a response to the University of the Free State "Reitz affair"*. Available from: www.inter-disciplinary.net/probing-the-boundaries/wp-content/uploads/2013/05/taylorforpaper.pdf; Van der Merwe, J.C. 2009. Communicative-philosophical challenges of managing a male residence at the University of the Free State. *Communitas* 14, 43–56; Van Reenen D. 2012. Interfacing metaphors and postures for understanding deep communicative divisions at a tertiary institution. *Communitas* 17, 163–79.
4. The quotations that follow and all the source material are taken from this unpublished manuscript by one of the students involved in the atrocity; the manuscript is titled *The Reitz Video: Innocently racist*.
5. In a middle-class suburb (Waterkloof) on the east side of the city of Pretoria is a well-reputed academic high school called Waterkloof High. It was in this suburb that four white Afrikaans boys, some from this high school, were found guilty of kicking a

homeless black man to death in one of the most notorious racist attacks since the end of legal apartheid.
6 Evans, I. 2009. *Cultures of Violence: Lynching and racial killing in South Africa and the American South.* Manchester and New York: Manchester University Press, p. 229.
7 In language reminiscent of Schultz's personalism in Georgia, Evans distinguishes the racial violence of the state from interpersonal racial violence, the former more common in South Africa and the latter, in the form of public lynching, in the American South. He explains the absence of public lynching in South Africa as a consequence of the bureaucratisation of racial violence in the state. See Evans, I. 2005. Racial violence and the origins of segregation in South Africa. In Elkins, C. and Pedersen, S. (eds) *Settler Colonialism in the Twentieth Century.* New York: Routledge, pp. 183–202.
8 See the content analysis of "Letters to the Editor" in chapter XII.
9 Former Archbishop Desmond Tutu in his speech on receiving an honorary doctorate degree in Theology from the University of the Free State, Thursday 27 January 2011.
10 2014. *The Reitz Video: Innocently racist.* Unpublished manuscript.
11 One piece of recent research is different in that it wrestles not with the four students but with the "'the story stock' within the institutional culture" that made Reitz possible; see Suransky, C. and van der Merwe, J.C. 2015. Transcending Apartheid in Higher Education: Transforming an institutional culture, in *Race, Ethnicity and Education.* Available from: www.tandfonline.com/doi/full/10.1080/13613324.2014.946487#tabModule
12 Verschoor, T. 2015. *The Mapping of Reitz.* Stellenbosch: SUN Media (e-book).
13 Ibid., p. 25.

3 "The misnamed free state"

Introduction

More than 100 years ago it fell to that most distinguished activist of the Cape Colony, one Dr Abdullah Abdurahman, to address the Opening of the 10th Annual Conference of the African People's Organisation (APO) in the booming diamond mining city of Kimberley. In the Chair for that event was the Mayor of Kimberley, Councillor Ernest Oppenheimer, who introduced the charismatic campaigner. The University of Glasgow-trained medical doctor fought segregation in the Cape Colony and found himself elected to the Presidency of the first major Coloured political organisation of that region.[1] As a Cape Muslim activist, Dr Abdurahman had experienced the sting of racist hostility at the hands of his fellow councillors, being also the first black person to be elected to the Cape Town City Council. His fellow councillors initially refused to sit too close to him for his very presence was "an affront to their dignity"[2] as white persons.

It was however in his capacity as President of the African Political Organisation that Dr Abdurahman delivered this memorable address, transcribed in Sol Plaatje's remarkable book, *Native Life in South Africa*, published three years later.[3] After a critical review of progress since the Union of 1910 following the Anglo-Boer War, as it was then called, and the failure of the promises of equality to the Coloured races following this settlement between Boer and Brit, the President concedes that the principle of equal rights was established for all, despite "minor infractions", and with a measure of British reserve notes that "we were not wholly dissatisfied with the white man's rule in the Cape".[4] But it is at this point in the presidential address that he turns to "the misnamed Free State" and makes this stinging remark:

> Cruelty and oppression amounting to serfdom were, and still are, the outstanding features of the Free State. And he would be a bold man who would assert that the native races have progressed at all as a result of contact with the white man in the Free State.[5]

But he is not done, for the doctor trains his attention on Bloemfontein, the capital city, where a youthful University of the Orange Free State was coming into its own identity from its roots in the famous Grey College. The APO

President then compares race relations there to where he was standing, in Kimberley, then part of the Cape Colony and a mere 90 minutes' drive away in today's road travel distance:

> Take for instance a comparison of the condition of the coloured people of this town and that of Bloemfontein, the capital of the Orange Free State. ... In Bloemfontein ... there are practically no educational facilities for children, who, as soon as they reach the age of fifteen, must enter the service of a white man, or be cast in prison. There is no freedom, no liberty, and the result is that the coloured people of the capital of the British Slave State are uneducated, poor, and degraded.[6]

This was a political speech by a fearless speaker, and any hyperbole must have fitted both the occasion and the personality.[7] Yet to this day there is to the north (Johannesburg) and to the south (Cape Town), and everywhere else, an unyielding perception of racial backwardness in the province now simply called the Free State, one of nine established in the new country led by Nelson Mandela under a democratic Constitution since 1994.

To understand how Reitz could have happened in the first place, you have to understand something of the history, geography and economics of this largely rural province in the heart of South Africa and the concentration of its racial anxieties in the "college town" of Bloemfontein housing the University of the Free State. When you zoom in with your lens on the capital you find what geographers call "an ideal apartheid city"[8] kept that way through distancing policies of "disciplining urbanization"[9] so that "in contrast to other cities, inner-city segregation still prevailed in Bloemfontein by 1991".[10]

To understand how Reitz could be resolved – and forecast the future of the country's race relations – you have to start in the same place and, in so doing, you have to understand the lengthy history of settlement, disruption, cooperation, competition, conflict, negotiation, appeasement and shifting alliances in what today is called the Free State.[11]

Long before the British formally established in 1946 the garrison town that would become the capital, or the "*Trekboer*", Johannes Nicolaas Brits settled in the area and named his farm Bloemfontein (fountain of flowers), San hunters, Griquas, Basothos and Zulus occupied the area and confronted each other across the dry stretch of territory called the "*Transoranje*" linking the Orange and Vaal Rivers.[12]

A sense of sadness

As you turn into Bloemfontein off the N1, the National Road that connects the north and south of the country, from Johannesburg to Cape Town, you find yourself on Nelson Mandela Road. But before your car even straightens for the 3-mile run towards the main gate of the University of the Free State, you see a sad and tragic fixture; a Bible House alongside the site of one of the largest concentration camps from the Anglo-Boer War. The plaque is prominent: "Dam of Tears, Source of Remembrance."[13] Legend holds that on this site Boer women and children dug up a dam with tin mugs and whatever they could find to catch rainwater – the only source of water for thousands of prisoners. "Every now and then a British truck would bring water to the camp and dump it into a well," says a source at the site. The Source of Remembrance honours those women and children and stands about 1 km from the dam itself.

There must be few places in the world where the entrance to a city is marked by a place of such intense *sadness*: "a resident inner turmoil", a journalist visiting the area would once observe.[14] And this sadness encases an ethnic identity connected to the Divine (hence the Bible School at the entrance to the camp site) in what Miroslav Volf called "the sacralisation of identity" with its often tragic consequences.[15]

It will not take you long after relocating to the City of Roses, as Bloemfontein is also called, to have a long-timer tell you "you cry twice: when you arrive and when you leave". It is true; the isolation of this rural province from the big cities, the desolation of the endless spread of dry, brown, open veld, the general lack of cosmopolitan entertainment and the rigid conservatism of the place will test your spirit. Even today not too many people would disagree with the wry humour of the settler writer Leonard Fleming from 100 years ago that "You can see more land and less scenery in the Free State than in any other country in the world."[16]

That's the first cry.

And then you meet the people with their warmness of heart, their openness to humanity and their lack of pretence. You become part of the community and begin to embrace the ordinariness, the honesty and the hopefulness of the citizens of Bloemfontein. By the time you leave, as the saying goes, you cry again.

The sadness of the place, however, stays with you. On the other side of the city is another memory of that bitter war with the British, the Boer War Museum, as the locals call it. For years this was the one place that captured the hurtful memories of the Afrikaners, the white descendants of the colonists, mainly of Dutch descent, who came to South Africa from the 1650s onwards, landed in the Cape, trekked north towards Pretoria, and with a sizeable number settling in-between in the Orange Free State – the independent Boer republic formed in 1854.

Here wars were fought with black people, principally the Basotho tribes, but it is the conflict with the British that engulfs contemporary memory, and this Museum captures the angst and the anger, the death and the displacement, of that violent period in South African history.

On the outside of the museum is the Women's Memorial, commemorating the women and children who died in that War. Along the well-paved pathway to the rising memorial there are little plaques neatly embroidered into the cement, each capturing the precise numbers of dead in the various concentration camps spread throughout the Free State and into other provinces. By the time you reach the memorial itself, your heart is burdened by the felt memory of the dead. The graves of prominent people lie at the foot of the massive Women's Memorial, including the Englishwoman Emily Hobhouse who agitated on behalf of the Boer women in her native England. Once a year the young women from the Orange Girls School for Christian and National Education,[17] blissfully unaware of their troubled colonial and apartheid name, make their way to the Women's Memorial to remember the white dead.

Then you enter the museum, passing Afrikaner heroes on larger-than-life horses and the place is dark. Inside the story is told through old, grainy videos of the singular, well-rehearsed narrative – innocent, indigenous Boers slaughtered by vicious imperialists but not without the valiant efforts of the Boer forces that, despite inferior technologies and smaller numbers, took on the mighty British Empire. Fine detail of the various concentration camps is found on the various floors of the museum as well as haunting black-and-white pictures of Boer fighters exiled in camps from Ceylon (now Sri Lanka) to St Helena island. Starving children dying in the arms of mothers grab and hold the attention. Boer heroes are everywhere, together with a long, wooden table giving details of the occupants of the chairs around which peace treaties were signed. Whatever your politics, you leave the Boer War Museum with a deep sense of sadness, even empathy, with the victims of that war between two races, as the Boers and the Brits were then called.

The markers of that terrible period in South African history are everywhere, the hanging sadness coming through in discussions with locals who proudly carry the names of victims of the war from one generation into the next. Outside my office stands the massive statue of the Boer President M.T. Steyn, an immovable reminder when I enter and leave the building where I work that there is a past to look forward to.

Not long after taking up the position of rector, one of his descendants came to see me – a charming woman with remarkably open, even liberal views, who wanted me to know she was a descendant. I proposed around this time in my *Monday Bulletin* to staff, simply as a way of opening campus debates, that we lower the statue and place it in conversation with a black hero from the region, the Basotho peacemaker, King Moshoeshoe.[18] The retribution was quick and sharp; who did I think I was to remove this permanent fixture of Afrikaner identity, memory and history?

Leave the city of Bloemfontein, en route to our campus in the Eastern Free State, and you approach the little town of Bethlehem. On entry there is a neglected cemetery, to the right-hand side of the road, with a difference. Here amid graves overgrown with grass and weed lies another memory, "to the British dead". On trips to our rural campus I regularly stop and walk through the cemetery trying to imagine hearing the young voices of frightened military youth from a faraway country dying in a place they had heard of only on arrival. Here was a connected tragedy nobody talked about, at least not in the Free State. On each grave there is a small, identical tombstone recalling that they died for their King. Over time, a Boer grave slipped in somewhere between these British dead, yet another reminder of our inevitable entanglements.

I made the proposal with successive British High Commissioners to South Africa that the Queen, as she did in Ireland, return to this part of South Africa – the princesses Elizabeth and Margaret accompanied their parents to Bloemfontein in 1947 – and apologise to my people for the horrors of that war a century ago. It would heal an open wound which, as some have argued, contributed to the creation of apartheid by the former victims of the Anglo-Boer War.[19] This lingering sadness continues to mark the Free State landscape to this day.

The sadness of the Boer War presents to Afrikaners a rival memory to what apartheid presents to black South Africans; such complexity makes straightforward narratives of victimhood much more complicated even after the horrors of a more recent, racial tragedy, apartheid.

A sense of separation – by custom, not law

It is, however, not only sadness that marks the province but separation. Here, more than anywhere else, segregation took on additional levels of madness. No other province, for example, had laws preventing South Africans of Indian descent staying overnight. While commercial competition from successful Indian tradesmen threatened white business everywhere, the Free State made particularly harsh discriminatory laws to enforce its bigotry. So, for example, The Statute Law of the Orange River Colony (1901) seamlessly connected Indians and white misfits in its control regimen, as described in the Law to provide against the Influx of Asiatics and for the removal of White criminals entering this state from elsewhere:

> No Arab, Chinaman, coolie, or other Asiatic coloured person may settle in this state, or remain here for longer than two months without first having obtained permission to do so from the State President.[20]

While that kind of language would make any decent person squirm today, and its puzzling ethnic distinctions test the discriminatory instincts of the most committed of race-minded bureaucrats, no one was spared in the implementation. So, for example, Justice Ismail Mohammed, who would become the first chief justice of a democratic South Africa, as well as Deputy President of the Constitutional Court, could represent his clients in Bloemfontein or other parts of the Free State but not overnight in the province; he would have to travel great distances to places like Kimberley to sleep before returning during the day to continue his work. It was a bitter memory that remained with him in later years, as he recalled on taking up the chief justice position at the Supreme Court of Appeals in Bloemfontein: "My return to that province revives fresh wounds and painful memories which I cannot and would not want to obliterate."[21]

The celebrated activist Ahmed Kathrada, close friend and Robben Island prison mate of Nelson Mandela, often tells of his arrest in Bloemfontein. The apologetic white policemen asked where to put him, with the Europeans (as whites were then called) or the Bantus (as blacks were then called), since no provision was made for Indians in the Free State prison system; of course Kathrada insisted on being placed with other blacks in the prison cells.

That period of madness is over, but the separation of the races, now by custom rather than law, continues to thread through every dimension of life in the Free State.

Praying separately

On Sundays, the Afrikaans churches are rigidly separated even within the same denomination. For the Dutch Reformed Church (DRC) it is as if apartheid never ended. The white mother church operates its own branch churches with its own "*dominees*" (ministers), from the concentration of various denominations of Reformed churches in the big city of Bloemfontein to the obligatory single church in the vast "*platteland*" (countryside), whose tall steeple is an early sign that your car is approaching a little "*dorp*" (town).

Attending these churches I find a deep and sincere spiritual earnestness from the pulpit and a general quietness in the pews of this decidedly uncharismatic faith community. I would often be the sole black person in the overwhelming whiteness of the gathering, and nobody comes to greet you before or after the formal service; I would often be the one to make the approach. In the odd case where I found a few black attendees, it would be the result of an open-minded "*dominee*" or the baptism of a white baby to which the minder would be invited. Before and after apartheid, the church once dubbed "The Nationalist Party at prayer" remains solidly white in the Free State without a single law requiring separation.

The African Church, with its nickname the DRC "for Africa", operates separately and is attended by people classified under apartheid as Africans. Here is something very strange. Why would the people who were dispossessed and displaced by their fellow worshipper in the white version of the church bind themselves to such a sister-church arrangement? The black believers are the product of mission and the black church operates separately at a safe distance from where their white brothers and sisters assemble.

I was invited to a ceremony in one of the large DRC churches in Bloemfontein led by a warm and generous "*dominee*" with a vision for the kind of transformations being led on campus. He had become a confidante and family friend, and his son an outstanding example of humanity on a divided campus. So I accepted the invitation "to say a few words" at this special event. The occasion was a tradition strange to my own evangelical upbringing; a few of our theology graduates would be received by the church ahead of their formal ordination as "*dominees*". In that group were a number of younger white students and a few older, black students.

Then, to my horror, the white students were taken through their ceremony, in one set of rituals, and the black students through a separate ceremony with similar traditions. Yes, we were in the same church for the same purpose of recognising these graduates about to become fully fledged "*dominees*". But even in this holy place, under one roof, the ceremonies were segregated. I had more than "a few words" to say.

True to the apartheid script, there was a separate Dutch Reformed Church for Coloureds (mixed-race, in an imperfect description) and even a Reformed Church in Africa for Indians. The DRC for Coloureds carried the undisguised name, the DRC *Mission* Church. It was the church of my mother in her home town of Montagu, a beautiful rural landscape about 200 km north-east from the city of Cape Town. My mother became "born again" to join the evangelical churches in Cape Town where she worked as a nurse, and with that move strained relations with her DRC Mission family. During school holidays we would visit my maternal grandparents in Montagu and on Sundays attend the strikingly beautiful DRC Mission Church for Coloured people in the downtown area – actually, along the smoothly tarred main road running through the town and a few hundred metres from the family home.

The home was flattened for white occupation and the family had to vacate the downtown "mission" church because it was in a white area. To this day the church building still stands because of its monument value; it is now a museum, and inside I find the black-and-white photographs of my family members, the Johnson and the Saunders clans, among others, who led and sang in the church choir before being evicted. The Mission Church, in its new location in the township still operates at a distance from the white church, bound by the same catechism.

And so worship remains segregated in the traditional churches but so does the visible differences in resources; in fact Skip Krige found that "inequality levels measured in terms of access to resources and institutional capacity between traditional black and white churches have increased".[22]

I decided to raise this issue in one of my columns for *Die Burger* newspaper, a Cape Afrikaans publication from which my critical writings are sometimes taken up in the regional newspapers, like the *Volksblad* in Bloemfontein. The letters of condemnation followed swiftly with accusations of "*rasbehepthed*" (Afrikaans, preoccupation with race), but a "*dominee*" from one of the local DRC churches came to pray for me, read from the Bible and to encourage "the prophetic voice" to continue. The separation continues with one exception: the English churches and, in particular, the more charismatic or evangelical churches.

Playing separately

Festivals are separated. The white Afrikaans festival is called the *Vryfees*[23] (Arts Festival) and is held on our campus in Bloemfontein. This monocultural event is almost entirely dominated by white, Afrikaans speakers. Alumni, farmers, ordinary people come mainly from the Free State for a menu of food, music, drama, open-air markets and other festivities. Unlike other regional festivals, this one is attended mainly by locals with little infiltration of other cultures or cosmopolitan intercourses.[24]

I realised that for many alumni the *Vryfees* was a heart-warming link to their old university. Many would not make the annual visit to their campus were it not for music and drama, friends and food, and good business for the vendors. So I walk through the stalls, savour the food and talk to the locals and visitors alike. If you forget who you are, and what you wish your campus and country to become, you can have a really good time. People are friendly and vendors vie for your attention as a prospective client. The rector probably gets more than his fair share of "samples" to taste. And then there is the huge fish restaurant partially under a massive tent in which you sit for hours sampling one fish dish after another with freshly baked bread on ovens outside. My resolve not to eat fish away from the coastal cities is easily broken under the spell of live Afrikaans music and a generally festive spirit.

Then it hits you. Your table is the only one with black (and white) people around it. Suddenly the band strikes up a lively tune of "*Boeremusiek*" (Boer folk music) and a black professor in my company jumps to her feet and dances down the makeshift sandy aisle in the middle of the seated crowd; this is a remarkable woman who researches and teaches forgiveness following her remarkable set of interviews with Eugene de Kock, dubbed *Prime Evil* for leading the murder of black activists on the part of the apartheid government. Her award-winning book, *A Human Being Died that Night*,[25] is a plea for reconciliation. With extraordinary courage and heart, in the middle of the Free State, Pumla Gobodo-Madikizela was inviting others into the dance. Of course nobody responded.

Later in the same year is the black festival called *Macufe* which, while marginally more diverse, is almost entirely dominated by black people. Spread throughout the city, premier acts are brought in from the big cities, mixing with local talent for grand musical events, comedy, drama and much drinking in the city. Fancy cars and rich black men from Johannesburg adorn the landscape as Blue Label whiskey flows and beautiful women are seen everywhere along Second Avenue, Bloemfontein.

At a 2014 performance of the play, *Missing*, by one of South Africa's most accomplished actors, John Kani, I looked around in amazement to confirm that not a single white face was present at this world-class event. "Great to see you here," tweeted one of my students, the President of the Student Representative Council, who was sitting in another section of the theatre as the lights started to dim. "Where are our white brothers and sisters?" I asked. "They're at the *Vryfees*," he joked.

The sporting arrangements are segregated. Blacks play soccer and the Free State stadiums are completely dominated by black people. The Free State Stars in the east of the province and Bloemfontein Celtics in the capital draw large crowds to weekend games. Celtics, or *Siwelele*, its popular name, is associated with the enthusiasm and energy of its partisan crowds. Looking up into the stands, the spectators are black and the players are black. Nobody questions the racial make-up of the all-black soccer team; it is just how it is, a black sport. That same sense of racial resignation does not, however, apply to rugby.

White Free Staters play and support their rugby teams with tremendous passion. Not a day goes by without back-page commentary on the state of the rugby team and it is not at all unusual to have a front-page lead story on the sport ahead of a crucial weekend game. There is a fighting spirit among the fans, a perpetual sense of being disadvantaged by the larger unions who lure top players from the financially limited province to play for wealthier franchises in the big cities. "Where do the Sharks players [a Durban franchise] stay when they play in Bloemfontein?" is a common joke in these parts; "at their mother's homes." Naturally, there is a UFS connection for the schoolboys come into the university and play for its senior rugby team, the *Shimlas*, where they are prepared to be drafted into the provincial team; there is an agreement setting terms for the rugby relationship between the university and the Cheetahs, the name of the province's rugby team.

Thanks to an enforced but hated quota system, top black players over the years made it into the provincial side; it would not have happened otherwise, and several of these players would eventually graduate into the national team as top competitors. Nothing stirs the emotions more, and boosts sales of Afrikaans newspapers, than yet another headline about quotas in rugby. "Merit!" shout the white critics, instantly stigmatising the top black players no matter how well they play. You could swear every white rugby player made the team on merit and every black player as a result of quotas.

I was sitting in the stands at Loftus Versfeld in Pretoria, supporting my team, the Blue Bulls, when two black wingers went on the rampage scoring tries. Those were the early days of "transformation" in rugby when black players were almost invisible in the national and provincial teams. I was also one of a handful of black supporters in the famed Bulls fortress, a place that was off-limits to black people under apartheid. I jumped up in excitement as the wingers destroyed the opposition and, in the joy of the moment, leaned over to a white stranger and said "isn't it great how those two wingers are playing?" He completely deflated me with his less than enthusiastic response: "it's good to see the quota players are at least doing their part." Bryan Habana, one of those black wingers, is now an international star in his position, which he would never have become without forcing the hand of white rugby authorities.

While there might be a handful of black players on the field, it is often the case that a team from England or New Zealand would have more players of colour on their teams than their competitors from an African country. On the field and in the stands there is very little sense of any integration in the Free State, whether it be rugby or soccer. These are the two premier sports of province and country, and whereas black participation in rugby is far ahead in places like Cape Town, in the Free State the race-exclusiveness stands out in those sweeping television camera shots across the audience of spectators and players.

Learning separately

The schools are separated. The vast array of township schools spread throughout the province, and indeed the country, remains black. The elite Afrikaans schools are white, with small numbers of black students in some of them; these are students who speak or are prepared to learn through the medium of Afrikaans. The former white English schools are, like the churches, exceptional for here black students are enrolled, but in manageable numbers, so that most of the schools remain largely white especially as far as the teachers are concerned; where black enrolments reach a tipping point, white students (or rather, their parents) leave in droves turning those schools into black schools. These same patterns are to be found in the rural schools of the Free State where, incidentally, white English schools hardly exist and black numbers are carefully managed so that the Afrikaans schools remain predominantly white in most cases.[26]

In short, there are no white schools in which black students are in the majority and no black schools with any white students. This means that of the students coming into the University of the Free State, only a small number would have come from integrated schools. Put differently, most of our provincial students come from schools which were either mono-racial or in which they were the majority "race"; this has major implications for how incoming students experience and navigate their way through an integrated institution like the UFS.

The racially segregated learning tracks start much earlier, though, in the pre-school years. Despite a nominal commitment from government to provide access to high-quality preschool education for all children, this has not happened and will not happen given the unresolved backlogs in the formal school system. Yet almost every white child in the Free State will have the experience of a high-quality preschool education giving such children – and the children from the few middle-class black families – a significant head start on entering Grade 1. And that is precisely how the racialised inequalities of schooling are made and sustained from the very foundations of learning for preschool children.

The challenge of first-year university studies for most students in South Africa, compounded at an integrating institution like the UFS, therefore presents two serious problems. First, that of vastly different populations of white and black students in terms of academic readiness for higher education; and second, two racial groups that have had, for the majority, little to no experience of learning together. Here then is a toxic mix – strong suspicion, stereotype and disregard among first-year students towards each other fuelled by differential academic performance by race. The white students confirm their prejudices about black people and the black students resent their disadvantage which they have come to understand relationally.

Labouring separately

It is in labouring together that the strict racial divides are still so visible in the Free State, with the smallest population (2.75 m) of the nine provinces spread across the second largest land area (129, 825 square kilometres). What was true in the rest of the country[27] seems amplified in this rural province, which performs below the national average in all major development indicators, and where racial inequalities are sharply manifested in everything from education attainment to employment status.[28] And with 239,000 whites, mainly educated and skilled, and more than 2.5 million blacks, many unskilled and with poor education, the division of labour in every virtually every segment of the provincial economy – except government – would be visibly racialised.[29]

In the predominantly agricultural landscape of the province, race relations have remained largely untransformed. Despite small government-funded programmes for "emerging farmers" (black, in other words), the hard-core relations that define farmer and labourer remain undisturbed. The public debate on farms has largely been restricted to one of ownership and redistribution, generating considerable anxiety without significant progress in this regard. In practice, race relations in farming areas have not changed, which explains the occasional violent responses to incalcitrant officials such as in the Cape wine lands.[30] It is therefore not surprising that the students at the heart of the Reitz scandal came from farming families. Young people from these hard-knuckled environments enter an integrating university to find the transition strange and inflammatory at the same time. Why is this?

A colleague who serves as researcher on the Bloemfontein campus commutes daily to and from her farm and, in the process, discovers a parallel universe:

> The thing is, I work on Campus, but live on a farm . . . The normal social talk in these small-town areas does not even use terms like "black people". They speak of "kaffirs", "boys", "meide", "bobbejaanskinders" [monkey children], "houtkoppe" [wooden heads], "coons", "hotnots" [Hottentots], "coolies", "charras", "wagon burners". The list could go on and on. This is how they talk; this is how their children talk; and this is how they talk to, and about, their workers. I am not talking about a minority, rather the majority, of white people here. It still shocks the hell out of me and I have been living here for 22 years. That is the simple truth. Those of us who did not grow up here and will not allow this kind of talk in our presence are accused of being "raging liberals" who don't care about the problematic state of our country or the appalling farm murders, and so on. This is not true as we are against any kind of harmful speech and behaviour, no matter the race. We are very pro-active in taking care of people in our community. But we will not allow political (or other) failings to determine our interactions with our people. So, there remains work to be done, and I thank you for your support because one can become weary when these setbacks happen.

I have heard this complaint of racist talk far too often from white colleagues living on and around farms, from where they commute to campus, to doubt the veracity of these reflections. These comments reflect a *practice* of racial contempt towards black labourers that is best viewed as a continuum from the past among some (though certainly not all) farmers; as far back as the 1930s, a report on Farm Labour in the Orange Free State reported that: "The use of the word 'jong' or 'boy' or '*skepsel*' (creature), for grown men is significant of the general attitude", as was the tradition to "keep the native in his place".[31] Even earlier, in a moment of frustration with farmer violence, Sol Plaatje once blurted out that: "Anyone thirsting for native blood [ought to] come to the Free State to appease his desires where the law seems to have been slackened to suit the purposes of white murderers."[32]

Around the braai fires, it is voices of racial anger that turn on the University of the Free State with venom for transforming away from segregation and the maintenance of white memories. One of my colleagues kept on his mobile phone after confronting a white vendor about bad practices; he has kept the recording in which the man, who profits from business with the university, calls him by the derogatory term "*Hotnot*" (Hottentot, in place of the more respectful term, *Khoikhoi*).

But these arrangements of master and labourer with their racial patterning are not at all limited to the rural outspans of the Free State province. Hire a plumber or a gardener or a mechanic and the picture replays itself over and over again. The man in charge is white and the labourers, the people actually doing the work, black. Listening to the barking of orders by white men and the quiet taking of orders by black men makes you cringe, but that is the unchanged order of things. Travel along the roads of the city and the contractors are white men holding the surveying maps or the mobile phones while the backbreaking work is done by black labourers. While this is true in much of South Africa more than two decades after apartheid, it is particularly emphatic in the cities and rural outposts of the Free State, a consequence of the severe neglect of black education and training under colonialism and apartheid in this impoverished part of the country.

It is in this cauldron of labour intimacy that racial attitudes are formed on both sides of the divide, and become near-impenetrable to change short of radical intervention. And if you grow up as a South African these patterns of labour relations become taken-for-granted and are only brought to vivid attention by visitors with a critical eye, such as academics, from outside the province and country.

Living separately

The repeal of the Group Areas Act, that hated piece of apartheid legislation that declared "white areas" in the most attractive parts of cities and towns and regulated black entry into and through these towns through pass laws, did not alter the patterns of residential accommodation.

Blacks remain stuck in sprawling shanties and townships around the city of Bloemfontein and far removed into distant areas such as Botshabelo and Thaba Nchu, about an hour's ride by bus, and from which labourers have to travel back and forth daily to work in the old white city. This demographic distribution of residential accommodation has not changed, despite the fact that the new black middle classes have moved into the suburbs of Bloemfontein and other smaller cities of the Free State in small, almost invisible numbers. Most black people come into and leave the suburbs as domestic labourers, gardeners, cleaners and shop workers while remaining at a distance, once dark falls, in the townships. Class now does the work of race.

The other Free State, rightly named

I had hardly been in the job for six months when one of my most treasured pieces of mail was dropped into the letterbox of our home on Whites Road. The handwritten letter was about a retired old couple, white Afrikaans people, for whom the wife spoke with great pain about how they once stood up against apartheid when everybody else was going with the flow, and what the costs were to her husband, especially, and therefore to the entire family in this patriarchal economy.

The moment he raised his voice against segregation, in church and society, the friends dried up. He would not, as a consequence, become part of the Afrikaner Broederbond, that secret society of elite white men which carried great influence in the apartheid state and its network of agencies. Once barred from the *Bond* your life became miserable, since you would not enjoy access to top jobs in any field and your exclusion from community, club and culture would be emphatic. There was the invisible mark of the outcast placed on your forehead and that of your family.

What struck me about this painful letter was that these were ordinary folk. They would not become *causes célèbres* such as Braam Fischer, Beyers Naude, the Schoon family or any number of white Afrikaner struggle heroes whose suffering would, to some extent, be ameliorated by their reception into the warm embrace of the liberation movements and the democratic majority. Vilified and even martyred under the old government – such as Jeanette Schoon and her daughter, blown apart by an apartheid bomb – they became heroes of the new country; everyone knew their names. They would have buildings and memorial lectures named after them, and their families would receive, on their behalf, one of the category awards handed out by the president at the annual National Orders ceremony.

This Free State couple would not make the news, even though the emotional and economic hardship they bore would be carried with them into retirement and the end of days. She just wanted me to know, dropped off the letter, and then disappeared. I have been struggling ever since to find this family and to say "thank you for your service to our country".

There are many such white people still living under the radar in "the misnamed Free State" and whose sacrifices would never be known. This is important to recognise since to portray all white South Africans, especially in this rural province, as uniformly conservative, racially cloistered, ethnic nationalists would be to misrepresent human nature anywhere, even under conditions of oppression. There are always those that resist, in big ways and small. And there are those who make them pay for it, as my dean of students discovered in this handwritten letter that raises the powerful image of the traitor in the survivalist memory of his ethnic group:

Throughout history the Afrikaners have always had the largest percentage of traitors. You are another one of them. Neither the Basothos nor the Afrikaners want to lose their language and culture. You want integration. You are probably messing around with the Basotho girls. What do your offspring look like? What do your bastard children look like?[33]

Tokkie Pretorius is the curator of the War Museum in Bloemfontein. In other words, he is in charge of one of the most sacred sites in Afrikanerdom, the commemoration of that bitter war and its concentration camps. He then did the unthinkable, which was to add to the museum the full range of experiences and participants in the conflict. First there was the addition of the Sol Plaatje Exhibition, dedicated to the prominent black intellectual and activist who made his mark on the South African landscape a century ago.

He added new images representing the 12,000 black "*agterryers*" (riding behind, taking care of the horses), supporters and sometimes combatants on both sides of the conflict. In fact a new book has emerged from the innards of the museum, unthinkable until recently: *An Illustrated History of Black South Africans in the Anglo-Boer War, 1899–1902*. Then, to crown it all, the Union Jack is to be spotted in the museum with a commemoration of the British role in the war; even the British garrison hospital was moved from the city to be sensitively curated in the museum.

For these monumental shifts Tokkie Pretorius would receive merciless criticism from conservative Free Staters. In a moving television debate on *Robinson Regstreeks* with his counterpart in charge of the Voortrekker Monument, the differences could not be clearer – the general in charge of Pretoria's memorial was there to preserve the museum for his people while Tokkie understood his mandate more generously. Still, he has to be careful: "This is the heart of the Afrikaner. We must never forget that. The museum is not being *verswart* (blackened)."[34]

It is unclear to me whether the additive model of curatorship built on a foundationalist memory of whiteness works, but what matters right now is the intention to be generous, inclusive and even conciliatory against the backdrop of a deep and unresolved racial schism in Free State society. I knew the university had to support this courageous man and so all our freshmen were assigned on-site tasks there related to my history lectures in the core curriculum. And in 2014 Tokkie Pretorius would be awarded a medal of distinction for his public duty as curator on a graduation platform of the University of the Free State.

There are so many other examples of ordinary people in the Free State with open hearts and minds who before and after apartheid in quiet, determined ways created the small spaces in which new kinds of intimacies were tried and tested under the threatening dark clouds of an aggressive and intolerant Afrikaner nationalism. The white farmer I met who shared not only his land but also training, equipment and finances with new black farmers. The white teacher who runs after-school classes for black students without any remuneration in her attempts to break the cycles of disadvantage imposed on poor families. There is the white minister who chooses to do his work in the townships, and live there. I know of the white secretary who, from her meagre earnings as a university worker, supports black students to help cover the costs of tuition. And there is the white mother who unofficially adopted black children but kept this a secret from the broader community to avoid being ostracised.

There are hundreds of such stories and, in the cases mentioned, I know these people. What is remarkable is not that these citizens of the Free State's "moral underground"[35] had a sudden burst of conscience when democracy dawned on all of us in 1994. They were doing this when such actions were either illegal or frowned upon. These are the kinds of people I came to know in the other Free State; they are a minority, for sure, but significant enough in terms of presence that they softened the harshest blows of the apartheid system among black South Africans. And in doing so, they laid the grounds for a more public intimacy in human relationships among black and white than would otherwise have been the case.

Coming to university

Students who emerge from such segregated environments as eighteen-year olds entering university not only have a problem of untransformed racial attitudes, they have no language with which to engage and encounter their black peers, those with whom they are now physically close in classrooms, laboratories, libraries and in residences. Some simply go elsewhere, and it is the conservative chime of whites in Bloemfontein that "our children would rather go to Potch", shorthand for the University of the North West whose main campus in the mining town of Potchefstroom remains overwhelmingly white, conservative and Afrikaans.

As the number of black students increased on the Bloemfontein campus of the University of the Free State, that chime would ring regularly in the local Afrikaans press both as warning that desegregation was happening too fast and as a kind of retaliation for whites losing their dominant place in the old institution. Others would flee to Stellenbosch University near Cape Town, the only other historically Afrikaans institution where white, Afrikaans speakers remain overwhelmingly dominant, for now.

Not all white parents think this way and even fewer white students are intent on studying in white-dominant enclaves. Many parents look for high academic standards against the backdrop of a failing school system, something we have made a rallying point in recruitment. Others are attracted by top specialist academic programmes such as Medicine, Architecture and Forensic Science for which entry is very competitive and few spaces available nationally; for example, there are only eight medical schools in the country's universities and they all have limited placements with specific policies favouring black candidates after a long history of racial exclusion.

More than a few parents want their children to gain competence in English, one of the two teaching languages of the university, the other being Afrikaans. And some parents want their children to be prepared "for the real world" by experiencing the multicultural and diverse environment offered in a top academic institution; such parents have read the democratic tea leaves and know their children would struggle to adapt to the new South Africa and in a global economy in which their offspring are likely to travel across cultures, traditions and belief systems. The UFS offers that experience. And then there are others who, despite ideological misgivings, remain attached emotionally to the university as the place where they studied and from which they graduated with pleasant memories.

Those white students from English-medium schools where growing numbers of blacks are enrolled make the transition relatively easily. Others from urban-based white Afrikaans schools also adapt with relative ease to the new university environment. But those students from rural areas, and from homes and cultures where racial separation and racial domination defined their lives, struggle more than others. Placing these white students in physical proximity with black students without any further intervention is, quite frankly, irresponsible.

And yet all first-year students, whether from racially open or closed environments, would still have to negotiate the troubled intimacies created inside this unfamiliar terrain, the University of the Free State.

Notes

1 This book comes as close as any to a contained biography of Dr Abdurahman; Lewis, G. 1987. *Between the Wire and the Wall: A history of South African Coloured politics.* New York: St. Martin's Press.
2 Dr Abdullah Abdurahman. (n.d.). Available from: http://v1.sahistory.org.za/pages/people/bios/abdurahman-a.htm
3 Plaatje, S. 2007. *Native Life in South Africa.* South Africa: Picador Africa.
4 Ibid., p. 133.
5 Ibid., p. 133.
6 Ibid., p. 134.
7 An even cursory survey of "the doctor's" speeches reveals a fiery speaker not easily intimidated by the white authorities in the city of Cape Town, on its council or in the country. See van der Ross, R.E. 1990. *Say it Out Loud: The APO Presidential Addresses and other major political speeches, 1906–40, of Dr Abdullah Abdurahman collected and edited with a biographical introduction by RE van der Ross.* Publication Series B3, Bellville, University of the Western Cape: The Western Cape Institute for Historical Research. Available from: http://v1.sahistory.org.za/pages/people/special%20projects/abdurahman/part01.htm
8 Krige, D.S. 1991. Bloemfontein. In: Lemon, Anthony. (ed.) *Homes Apart: South Africa's segregated cities.* London: Paul Chapman Publishing, pp. 104–19; see also Rex, R. and Visser, G. 2009. Residential Desegregation Dynamics in the South African City of Bloemfontein. *Urban Forum* 20(3), 335–61.
9 Murray, C. 1995. Displaced Urbanization: South Africa's rural slums. In Beinart, W. and Dubow, S. (eds) *Segregation and Apartheid in Twentieth Century South Africa.* London and New York: Routledge.

10 Marais, L. and Visser, G. 2008. *Spatialities of Urban Change: Selected themes from Bloemfontein at the beginning of the 21st century*. Stellenbosch: AFRICAN SUN MeDIA, p. 58.
11 There are very few solid academic works on the early history of the region now called the Free State, but I am grateful to the accomplished Boer War historian, Professor Andre Wessels, for helping to locate the following three important references. Humphreys, A.J.B. 2009. A Riet River Retrospective. *Southern African Humanities* 21, 157–75; Klatzow, S. 2010. Interaction between Hunter-Gatherers and Bantu-speaking Farmers in the Eastern Free State: A case study from De Hoop Cave. *South African Historical Journal* 62, 229–51; Twala, C. 2005. The Batlokoa Kingdom Headquarters at Nkoe and Joalaboholo in the Free State Province – A forgotten history? *South African Journal of Cultural History* 19(1), 119–31.
12 Small and sometimes dramatic, the consequences of those skirmishes last to this day not only in the indelible racial arrangements but in the regional layout of province and countries; see Steinberg, J. 2005. *The Lesotho/Free State Border*. (Occasional paper 113). Pretoria: Institute for Security Studies (ISS). Available from: www.issafrica.org/pubs/papers/113/Paper113.htm
13 It appears in Afrikaans as Dam van Trane, Bron van Herinneringe.
14 Tolsi, N. 2010. Mainlining the rainbow. *Mail & Guardian*, June.
15 Volf, M. 1996. *Exclusion and Embrace: A theological exploration of identity, otherness, and reconciliation*. Nashville, TN: Abingdon Press.
16 Fleming, L. 1916. A Fool on the Veld. Quoted in Murray, C. 1992. *Black Mountain: Land, class and power in the Eastern Orange Free State, 1880s to 1980s*. Edinburgh: Edinburgh University Press, pp. 3–4.
17 Orange of course signifies the Dutch colonial heritage, and "Christian National" was the descriptor for apartheid education.
18 For an excellent analysis of the leadership of Morena Moshoeshoe in and around the Free State region, see Ndebele, N. 2006. *Perspectives on Leadership Challenges in South Africa, Inaugural King Moshoeshoe Memorial Lecture, University of the Free State*. Available from: http://apps.ufs.ac.za/media/dl/userfiles/documents/News/2006-05/Inaugural_Moshoeshoe_Memorial_Lecture_ver_7.pdf
19 The argument for a link between unresolved suffering during the Boer War as a factor explaining victimhood and violence leading to apartheid is powerfully summarised by Smit, D.J. 2007. Shared Stories for the Future? Theological reflections on truth and reconciliation in South Africa. In Smit, D.J. (ed.) *Essays in Public Theology, Essays I, Study Guides in Religion and Theology 12, Publications of the University of the Western Cape*. Stellenbosch: SUN Press, p. 326, but see especially his extended notes in footnote #6.
20 The Statute Law of the Orange River Colony (1901). Chapter XXXIII. Part I. Translated by Botha, C.L. Translation revised by Harber, S.H. and Findlay, J.H.L. Published by the authority of His Excellency the British High Commissioner for South Africa, London: Waterlow & Sons Ltd. p. 199.
21 SAPA (South African Press Association). 2000. Chief Justice Ismail Mahomed dies. *iol*. Available from: www.iol.co.za/news/south-africa/chief-justice-ismail-mahomed-dies-1.40588?ot=inmsa.ArticlePrintPageLayout.ot
22 Krige, S. 2008. Transforming Christian Churches into community-based resource centres, with reference to Bloemfontein. In Marais, L. and Visser, G. (eds) *Spatialities of Urban Change: Selected themes from Bloemfontein at the beginning of the century*. Stellenbosch: AFRICAN SUN MeDIA.
23 The festival was originally known as the Volksblad Arts Festival but changed its name to Vryfees in 2010. More information available from: www.bloemfonteinguide.co.za/vryfees-bloemfontein/

24 Visser, G. 2008. Volksblad Art Festival: Reflections on the product, people and impacts. In Marais, L. and Visser, G. (eds) *Spatialities of Urban Change: Selected themes from Bloemfontein at the beginning of the 21st century.* Stellenbosch: AFRICAN SUN MeDIA, pp. 135–53.
25 Gobodo-Madikizela, P. 2003. *A Human Being Died that Night: A South African story of forgiveness.* New York: Houghton Mifflin.
26 I have traced the various patterns of school desegregation in South Africa in various pieces; see for example Jansen, J.D. 2013. The pursuit of excellence and equity in divided countries. In Malone, H. (ed.) *Leading Educational Change: Global issues, challenges, and lessons on whole-system reform.* New York: Teachers College Press, pp. 73–6; and Jansen, J.D. and Vandeyar, S. 2008. *Diversity High: Colour, Character and Culture in a South African High School.* Washington DC: University Press of America (with Saloshna Vandeyar).
27 See Burger, R. and Jafta, R. n.d. Returns to Race: Labour market discrimination in post-apartheid South Africa. Stellenbosch Economic Working Papers: 04/06. A Working Paper of the Department of Economics and the Bureau for Economic Research at the University of Stellenbosch. Available from: https://www.google.co.za/url?sa=t&rct=j&q=&esrc=s&source=web&cd=1&cad=rja&uact=8&ved=0CB4QFjAA&url=http%3A%2F%2Fwww.ekon.sun.ac.za%2Fwpapers%2F2006%2Fwp042006%2Fwp-04-2006.pdf&ei=yabhVILzM8m8Uae8goAJ&usg=AFQjCNF40dndTMbNAvG58hSYemwRfts1PA&sig2=J2lBIb0ScgoG7A9xxnxj_A&bvm=bv.85970519,d.d24
28 See concise development report and data for the province in Puukka, J., Dubarie, P., Mckiernan, H., Reddy, J. and Wade, P. 2012. *Higher Education in Regional and City Development: The Free State, South Africa 2012.* Paris: OECD. Available from: www.oecd.org/edu/imhe/50008631.pdf
29 I drew the data in this paragraph from: *Census 2011: Census in Brief/Statistics South Africa.* 2012. Pretoria, South Africa: Statistics South Africa. Available from: www.statssa.gov.za/census2011/Products/Census_2011_Census_in_brief.pdf
30 Davis, R. and Stegeman, K. 2012. The day the Cape Winelands burned. *Daily Maverick*, 15 November. Available from: www.dailymaverick.co.za/article/2012-11-15-the-day-the-cape-winelands-burned#.VOGpRvmUc7k
31 SAIRR (South African Institute of Race Relations). 1939. Farm Labour in the Orange Free State: Report of an investigation undertaken under the auspices of the South African Institute of Race Relations. Monograph Series No. 2. Johannesburg: South African Institute of Race Relations.
32 Murray, M. 1989. "The Natives are Always Stealing": White Vigilantes and the Reign of Terror in the OFS, 1918–24. *Journal of African History* 30(10), 112–13.
33 Unsigned letter received 1 April 2014, appears to have been sent on 24 March 2014. I decided against reprinting the worst of the racist abuse in the quotation. The concept of the traitor in an ethnic group that has always seen itself as besieged, whether by Brits or blacks, is a controversial subject not yet fully explored in its contemporary manifestation as an intimidating discipline that demands loyalty and imposes silence on those who step out of line. Albert Grundlingh's work deals with traitorship in the context of the Boer War; see Grundlingh, A.M. 2006. *The Dynamics of Treason Boer collaboration in the South African War of 1899–1902.* Pretoria: Protea Book House.
34 Smith, C. 2013. Hart van die Afrikaner . . . en nou méér. *Beeld*, 1 November. Available from: www.netwerk24.com/stemme/2013-11-01-hart-van-die-afrikaner
35 I borrow the term from Dodson, L. 2009. *The Moral Underground: How ordinary Americans subvert an unfair economy.* New York: The New Press.

4 Intimacy

Introduction

The two bulky white young men sat with their heads dropped on a slab of cement outside the new Chemistry building as they nibbled at their lunch. Their body language communicated "do not disturb". I was visiting the campus a month ahead of taking up my formal appointment as the new university rector. The idea was to move through the university anonymously and get a sense of place, the people and practices on a campus that had just gained worldwide notoriety for the terrible racist incident called "Reitz". Since most campus citizens did not know me, I thought such a casual walkabout could help me understand the task ahead.

I squeezed in between the two men and asked them, in their language, Afrikaans, to share their sandwiches. One of them went red in the face and my long experience as a black man in South Africa taught me that this was a prelude to trouble. So I quickly introduced myself as their new rector and the climate thawed immediately. They were happy to have me as their leader, they said, and offered to share their food.

"What can I do to serve you?" I asked the bewildered young men. "I am not here to give orders but to serve you as leader. I am eager to know what your priorities are, what you expect from your new Rector." Years of working in universities around the world taught me that the menu of action items students were likely to raise was highly predictable – food prices on campus, more parking for students and better lectures in classes. So I was expecting the usual but of course the point was the conversation, the idea that I wanted to communicate early and consistently, and that their leaders were near and accessible.

Then something happened that I will never forget. They spoke as one, as if the response had been choreographed. "Do not force us to integrate," they said with some emphasis. I remember being stunned. Of all the things the two white students could present as demands to the new rector, their mortal fear was living together in the same residence with black students. They wanted to have a choice to live separately, as whites. The timid policy until then of 70:30 of either race in each residence meant, effectively, that there would be 100 per cent black residences since no white student was going to accept minority (30 per cent) status in a place dominated by (70 per cent) black students. Black students had no problem being minorities, and so there were always sufficient numbers of black students in residences dominated by whites. But even this was too much for the two male students with whom I was enjoying lunch – they wanted the choice to be distant and not intimate in their residences.

The conceptual foundations of intimacy

Intimacy has a long, complex and chequered history betrayed in the literature through oxymoronic couplets such as stranger intimacy[1] or intimate aggression,[2] or even deadly intimacy.[3] Intimacy suggests a closeness and familiarity between human beings stretching from the working relations among labourers, living and learning together as students,[4] romantic love or the therapeutic relationship between nurses and patients.[5] What lies inside such intimate relations, whether of work, study or love, is still poorly understood as the massive tome, *Handbook of Closeness and Intimacy*,[6] reveals in its treatment of the subject from across the disciplines.

There is the intimacy of the mother–child relationship and the consequences that follow when that bond is ruptured in the early years. On this subject volumes have been written on "attachment" dilemmas and enduring questions such as the possible link between early detachment and juvenile delinquency.[7]

There is the intimacy that comes from migrant labour crossing geographical borders within countries, into neighbouring states and across the world as part of transnational migration patterns associated with economic globalisation.[8] As men and women become detached from original families and cross borders, other kinds of emotional and romantic attachment are formed away from home. With such movement come the dangerous intimacies that result from the closeness of residential and commercial relations between settled natives and migrant newcomers.[9]

There is the intimacy of romantic partners, which has enjoyed more sustained inquiry than other kinds of close relationships. Of particular interest are the emerging insights about aggression in such relationships. For example, that partner aggression does not mean the souring of a relationship; it is sometimes seen, from the point of view of victims, as an expression of closeness. One violent incident does not represent the couple, said Janay Rice after her once-famous husband, a football running back for the Baltimore Ravens in the USA, was caught on videotape in an elevator knocking his fiancée (now wife) cold and dragging out her semi-covered body with one shoe attached. Unfathomably, she went on to say: "I deeply regret the role I played in the incident." To the outsider, the fact that an abused partner does not simply walk away is puzzling, but not to the insiders, suggesting layers of complexity that require deep understanding rather than easy judgements.[10]

There are the complex intimacies of interracial marriages and the ways in which black and white partners make sense of race within such intensely close and loving relationships.[11] More recently same-sex intimacies and transgender relationships have also become the focus of study.[12] That is, where intimate relations break with custom and challenge local norms for intimacy, there are complexities of a very different kind at play.

There is the intimacy of torture, that intense process of drawing together torturer and tortured in a relationship that tests our very notions of what it means to be human.[13] Whether with the brutal intention to extract information or through the sheer depravity of inflicting suffering, this bond creates depths of trauma, sometimes irreversible, that keeps the perpetrator and the victim in an abiding relationship long after the ordeal is over. This was so powerfully demonstrated in South Africa's Truth and Reconciliation Commission (TRC) hearings where Warrant Officer Jeffrey Benzien demonstrated to his victim, Tony Yengeni, the way in which activists like him were tortured with wet bags around their heads to simulate drowning. What could be more intimate than those moments of excruciating pain, as Yengeni reveals in his TRC questions to his tormentor:

> What kind of man uses a method like this, one of the wet bag, to people, to other human beings, repeatedly, and listening to those moans and cries and groans and taking each of those people very near to their deaths – what kind of man are you – what kind of human being is that, Mr Benzien?[14]

And there is the intimacy promised by technology, that lure of closeness that increasingly leaves users with the feeling of being heard and responded to, of being in touch with invisible strangers.[15] "Technology", avers Sherry Turkel in her gripping new book *Alone Together*, "proposes itself as the architect of our intimacies"[16] – something so convincingly demonstrated in Spike Jonze's movie *her* in which a real man, Theodore, falls in love with Samantha, the voice of his computer's operating system.

Nowhere is this complex subject of intimacy more poorly understood than in research on race, racism and race relationships. Surveying the research on racism, for example, Daniel Tutt makes the relevant point that

> If you look at just three popular academic disciplines and their findings on racism, we find that in the neuroscience of prejudice or in critical race studies and social psychology . . . a number of entry points to the question of racism, but none can answer how the intimacy functions.[17]

This is the complex terrain of intimacy into which this book ventures with the goal of shedding light on, and resolving, the deep fears of physical closeness such as expressed by those two white students on a hard cement block.

Can racism and intimacy coexist?

In 2014, a riveting case of intimate racism captured media attention in the USA for months on end. Donald Sterling, the owner of a successful basketball franchise, the Los Angeles Clippers, was complaining to his black friend, and alleged mistress, V. Stiviano, about a photo she had posted on Instagram the previous year posing with the famous black basketball player, Magic Johnson.

> It bothers me a lot that you want to broadcast that you are associated with black people. You sleep with [them]. You can bring them in, you can do whatever you want [but] the little I ask of you is not to bring them to my games.[18]

He eventually lost his club due to these racist comments, but there was little attention given in the media to the hypocrisy. How is it possible to be so close to a dark-skinned woman and at the same time hold such racist views of "black people"?

Since the logic of racism is physical separation, not intimacy, from this side of the century that ambition often took tragi-comical turns in both the USA and South Africa. It was South Africa's minister of justice, no less, who in 1926 introduced a bill in the House of Assembly that spoke to the mortal fear of racists – interracial sex. The bill proposed that:

> [A]ny European male who has, or attempts to have, illicit carnal intercourse with a native female – shall be guilty of an offence and liable on conviction to imprisonment for a period not exceeding six years and, in addition to such imprisonment, to whipping not exceeding fifteen strokes [*sic*].[19]

The strokes on a white body must have been too much for white sensibility, so that an amended bill was eventually passed "to forbid illicit carnal intercourse between Europeans and natives and other acts in relation thereto".[20]

The point is that "improper intimacy"[21] has always been regulated on both sides of the Atlantic, with the overriding logic being the separation of the races.[22]

But the separating logic of racism was not confined to sexual intimacy. More ambitious than Jim Crow[23] in America, the apartheid government in South Africa invented a much more comprehensive blanket of laws separating black and white citizens from living together (the Group Areas Act and the Black Homeland Citizenship Act), eating or playing or worshipping together (the Separate Amenities Act), learning together (the Bantu Education Act and the Extension of University Education Act) and of course marrying each other (Prohibition of Mixed Marriages Act, the Immorality Act). Every aspect of life, including the free movement of black people (Pass Laws and the Prevention of Illegal Squatting Act), was carefully orchestrated to ensure the complete segregation of black and white citizens, from the hospital you were born in to the cemetery in which you were buried.

Given these elaborate schemes for racial separation, how then does one explain "unwanted intimacy"[24] stretching from colonial times through the height of the apartheid period?

The first reason for undesirable intimacy has to do with economics. Having lived whiteness not only as race but as class privilege,[25] whites became dependent on black labour on the farms and in the home, on factory floors and in family businesses. Somebody had to do the menial labour, in other words. In the same year (1948) that apartheid formally established the Nationalist Party as the ruling party in government, a journal of the Afrikaans Handels Instituut would plead that "[...] a person has to be practical ... the non-white worker already constitutes an integral part of our economic structure ... [so that] ... total segregation is pure wishful thinking".[26]

What government could do, at best, was manage some form of "influx control",[27] but it would be impossible to stamp out physical proximity in its entirety because of the commercial necessity of black labour. Here were the makings of a "fatal intimacy"[28] that entangled black labourers and white bosses in struggles of proximity under conditions of white supremacy.

The second has to do with sexual desire. Men and women had, like human beings across the ages, desired what was beyond their reach, at least in a legal sense. Such desire for intimacy was never limited by borders of any kind, whether race or geography.[29] The migration of peoples within and across borders inevitably generated "intimate labours"[30] across the world, a place in which money and intimacy meet. Whether motivated, however, by coercive or transactional sex, or genuine affection, black and white South Africans had always crossed the colour bar despite state restrictions.

The third reason that racial distancing would never be complete had to do with the civilisational mission of the white churches from abroad as they descended on places like the Orange Free State.[31]

Most South Africans know of the Kliptown People's Congress of 1955, the broad, multiracial alliance of the African National Congress that made the abiding declaration that the country "belongs to all who live in it, black and white". Few know of the imitative Bloemfontein *Volkskongres* of 1956 in which a cross-section of white Afrikaner leaders met to decide on "the future of the Bantu". Without any blush of paternalism, the *Volkskongres* made an emphatic commitment to the ideals of racial segregation, recognised the inevitability of "everyday contact" with black people and decried at length the lack of adequate *sending* (mission) contact with the Bantu.[32]

It is simply not true that the Dutch Reformed Churches were early instigators of racial separation,[33] even if its paternalistic undergarments were constantly hanging out. It was in fact "The Free State Mission Policy" that declared "the native is a human being with similar emotions to ours and that his soul of equal value in the eyes of God", leading to the paternal commitment that "a sacred responsibility rests with us, as a Christian civilised people ... to raise the native out of poverty and misery of barbarism".[34] For this collection of churches, therefore, the racial separation of believers was not a driving ambition but a concession made to accommodate "the weakness of some".[35]

The very establishment of "mission churches" under the Dutch Reformed mother church therefore had as its goal the recruitment of membership through a combination of evangelism and upliftment in Coloured communities. This would explain the openness of white leaders and members to assisting black missions, attending conferences or funerals and weddings "with them", though becoming a member of "my congregation" remains difficult.[36]

For years white men were "called" to serve as "*dominees*" for periods of time in these communities and would relocate with their families to rural outposts; much later men of colour would take to the pulpit. What this meant was that the culture of "*uitreik*" (outreach) would bring white families into especially Coloured communities and, even though the numbers were small, would also contribute to spiritual intimacies, however sporadic and superficial, between black and white worshippers.

The spaces in between

How, then, do black and white live inside these intimate spaces of human entanglement? Or in the earlier words of Tutt, how does intimacy function in such intense human relationships between historical enemies?

Consider, for example, how the affection given or withdrawn by the master impacts not only the subservient target but that person's friends in a constant negotiation of intimacy under conditions of oppression; Andre du Toit captures this dynamism of intimacy in a South African farming community:

> The farm labourers of De Doorns always stand by the "baas". When the baas dislikes you, even your intimate friends turn their backs on you. Not that they hate you, but they do it in a bid to save their poor skins. How else could they escape his wrath? It is one of the norms to save your flesh at the expense of a brother.[37]

In pursuing these questions I am less interested in the horrific elements of intimacy, those singular narratives of slavery as oppression or domestic labour as exploitation. What interests me are intimacies lived in the interstices of oppression. How do black people, for example, make sense of their own lives within these spaces? What kinds of negotiation, or brokering of power, take place that ensure production, cooperation and survival? What powers do the oppressed come to claim, and how is this wielded even under the strictures of oppression? What kinds of intimacies stand out or do not make sense, at first glance, given the nature of racial domination? How, on the other hand, do those in power make those finer distinctions between "proper caresses and prudent distance?"[38]

This complexity is what Martha Hodes brings together in a stunning collection of historical cases in the USA. In relation to sexual intimacy she concludes that: "Any investigation of sex and love across racial boundaries in North America yields a record of violent encounters [and] devout relationships [...]."[39] We know about the violent encounters, but it is worth attending to one of the most comprehensive accounts of intimate relations under slavery, for:

To characterize interracial sex purely in terms of victimization of black women would be a distortion. Not only did black women resist sexual assault successfully, but in addition, sincerely affectionate unions sometimes formed between white men and black women.[40]

And again, "aside from concubinage, more discreet long-term unions between white men and black women involved both economic negotiation and sincere affection."[41] In her path-finding research on the intimate relationship between the American President Thomas Jefferson and his slave Sally Hemings, the historian Annette Gordon-Reed asks the inevitable and uncomfortable question, but "Did they love each other?" Then this:

> The historiography of slavery has long since moved beyond the notion that slave owners were deity-like in their omnipotence and that slaves were actually chattel, like pieces of furniture lacking consciences and will. It is now well-recognized that within this admitted limited sphere, enslaved people helped shape the contours of the master-slave relationship.[42]

This is not to deny the brutality of oppression, whether in the form of slavery in the American South or South African apartheid. It is to suggest, rather, that the discomfort that comes with probing affection and intimacy inside these human existences might rob us of understanding, of hope, and of seeing possibilities for reconciliation that might be lost in the heavy hand of critical dismissal. This is the case I will make from research and reflection on the transformation of the University of the Free State. But there are other cases.

Slavery in the American South

Mark Schultz was not the first to question the notion of the "Solid South", that singular narrative of white supremacy and white solidarity during the period of slavery. He cites van Woodward's memorable words that: "The expression "Solid South" . . . is of little value to the historian" and that "The solidarity of the region has long been exaggerated."[43] On a casual visit to Hancock County, Georgia, the student Schultz finds stories of interracial marriages and black land ownership that "added humanizing texture to the simple generalization" of "frequent lynching, systematic segregation, and universal black poverty and disfranchisement".[44]

In Hancock County, Schultz discovers something interesting – a black majority country in which race relations between poor white and poor black residents were localised, "one marked by personal intimacy"[45] alongside personal violence. Yes, the ideology of white supremacy was in place but, alongside stories of poverty and humiliation, there were stories of personal empowerment on the part of African Americans. Schultz calls this particular expression of race relations "personalism", where race relations were formed in the intensity of face-to-face interactions of black and white rather than through the appeal to formal institutions such as the state for enforcement or the banks for empowerment. The killing of blacks could therefore be personal but at the same time race relations flexible, so that "powerful whites sometimes tolerated a surprising degree of interracial intimacy and black assertiveness".[46] What emerged, in this context, was "a culture marked by intimacy as well as white supremacy".[47]

The tendency to flatten the human experience under oppression is of course not unique to slave histories. The moral outrage of the oppressed and the immorality of the oppressor demanded clear, uncomplicated judgements. But that kind of hyperbole comes at a risk – the risk of overlooking, even denying, other humanities in the cauldron of suffering. The single, uncomplicated story of oppression marginalises white solidarity and underplays black resistance. It reduces blacks to helpless victims rather than as heroic agitators in the face of great odds. It misses ways in which ordinary people calved out for themselves the kinds of existences that made life bearable and the kinds of bargaining that blunted the instruments of power.

The single story of course does not allow for genuine affection. Sexual relations between slaves and slave owners were, per definition, coercive and violent. There was no possibility, in such contexts, of romantic love for the very structures of oppression made such intimacy impossible. Or did it? This is what makes the historical accounts of the relationship between President Jefferson and Sally Hemings so powerful. In her work on the subject, Gordon-Reed constructs a lifetime relationship between president and mistress, slave owner and slave, that throws up an uncomfortable complexity. What if, in fact, this relationship which bore children was not the consequence of coercion or rape, but of affection and devotion? Could such a relationship, which played out on two continents, in fact have been founded on love even under the conditions of institutionalised slavery? The mere fact that the question can be posed in these carefully documented works suggests that intimacy might in fact find a place within, even confound, structures of oppression.

Domestic labour in South Africa

There is no clearer instance of the coexistence of race, racism and intimacy than in the case of domestic labour under apartheid. From Jacklyn Cock's *Maids and Madams* in the 1980s to Shireen Ally's *From Servants to Workers* in the 2000s, the relationship between domestic workers and employers represents a conundrum. In this institution of domestic work, a black women enters and lives within the most intimate of spaces of white existence, the home, and yet at the same time is held at a distance – socially, emotionally and culturally – despite the close proximity. In this space of "intimate inequalities" you find "The irony and contradictions embedded in the tangle of deep intimacy and "positional inequality".[48]

It makes no sense. The white child is reared, almost literally, on the back of the black nanny. For most of the day, especially in the case of working white mothers, the most significant adult in the growing-up years of that white child is the black surrogate mother. It is the black woman who cleans and washes the child's body, takes care of sickness and nurtures the child back to health, prams the baby to the park and follows the young one through the hazards of the playground, sings the infant to sleep and raises it to feed. There could be no closer bond of intimacy between black and white, and this happened through (and beyond) the years of apartheid.

The Apartheid Archive is populated with gut-wrenching stories of white adult memories of this "fraught tenderness" under apartheid.[49] As one recalls, "I was strapped against her solid back to teenage and early adulthood when we mulled over prospective suitors, fashion and haircuts."[50] Gradually these deep emotional bonds of caring and mentorship would, for some, give way to guilt and shame as the young adults started to become conscious of the vexed relationship between master and servant. As the eyes open to what was taken for granted, the beneficiaries of domestic intimacy begin to notice things such as the different utensils set aside for the maid, the careful separation of foods for labourer and employer, the forms of address (maids do not have surnames and their white names are not their first names), reactions to the maid in a crisis, the exaggerated displays of deference and gratitude by the workers, and the entire tapestry of this distant closeness that has come to define domestic labour in South Africa for over a century.[51]

At this point of realisation, the white youth is faced with a choice – to remain true to that founding affection of the black maid, or break rank as in this unforgettable account of a single man's reflections:

> He was a slightly-built, middle-aged white man, probably about fifty-five years old, dressed in a checked shirt and gaudy yellow shorts. The broad Afrikaans accent with which he spoke English was barely audible from behind his hands. He was trying to speak through his sobs, which shook his entire body . . . He was recounting an early memory.

As a little boy on the farm in the Northern Transvaal where he grew up, he had loved his African nanny. He had loved to snuggle his head between her full breasts; he had loved the songs she sang to him in her language; he had loved the food she fed him. But he grew up, his friends had taunted him for his affection for her, as she was "net 'n kaffirmeid" [just a nigger servant girl]. He had learned to deny his love for his first friend in life, and to call her names to prove his indifference. Now he was articulating a deep sense of loss and waste, anger at a social system that had raised him on lies and damaged his humanity.[52]

Sometimes, however, it is in literature such as the novel that the unspeakable can be said about "the tense and intense relations of intimacy and distance in domestic service".[53] Seldom examined in mainstream research, the problem of sexual intimacy between masters and maids is the story everyone knows but nobody talks about. In a review of how domestic workers are depicted in

Afrikaans literature, the dilemma is named as that "secret attraction between baas [master] or son and the servant", yet acknowledging that "this intimacy was always located in an anguished often dangerous and prohibited sphere".[54]

It was Zakes Mda is in his brilliant novel, *The Madonna of Excelsior*, who laid bare the workings of intimacy in a rural town of Excelsior in the Free State, where sexual relations between black women and prominent white Afrikaner men was discovered during the years of apartheid. The fact that there is transactional and coercive sex between white men and black women is in itself uninteresting; what is revealing is the power of the protagonist, the black woman who, humiliated by her employer's wife, responds positively to the husband's sexual interest in part as retaliation against his spouse.

> She was gobbling up Madam Cornelia's husband, with the emphasis on *Madam*. And she had him entirely in her power. Chewing him to pieces (emphasis in the original).[55]

Here sexual intimacy is not neutral but a power play that shifts hands as the action slips from the old South Africa into the new with children – black, white and mixed-race – having to find ways of living together as the products of complex liaisons.

Taking hope and healing from complex intimacies

This review of the intimacies made possible by the institutions of slavery and domestic labour revealed, throughout, a set of binary tensions. Scholars refer to care and violence, tenderness and tenseness, closeness and distance, consent and coercion, intimacy and estrangement, attraction and disgust. Yet the overriding attention of almost all these writings has been extended treatments of the one side of that tension, the oppressive, exploitative and violent character of these institutions.

One of the reasons for the treatment of intimacy as wrongdoing alone has to do with the theoretical lens adopted, especially in earlier writings when Marxian analyses were widely practised as in the Cock research on *Maids and Madams*. Domestic relations, for example, were simply local sites of a much broader "structural" oppression brought on by forces of capitalism, patriarchy and race. Slave or domestic relations could not be understood on their own terms but rather as a simple reflex of something bigger and outside of itself. Human beings were merely actors at the end of historical strings playing out their predetermined roles as dictated by determining structures of race, class and gender. These oppressive relations therefore produced and "reproduced" the kinds of social and economic relations that kept the dominant order in place.[56] Since then many of these authors have moved from crude Marxian explanations of human behaviour to take more seriously the micro-relations of human interaction, though the instinct remains to make the lives of ordinary people a simple metaphor for something bigger.[57] But even such acknowledgement of ordinary lives inside institutions of slavery or domesticity does not proceed without an abiding cynicism.

The second reason for critical dismissal, especially in more recent writings, has to do with the politics of sneer. This is especially the case when enlightened white scholars, after apartheid, write of white grief and shame poured with emotion into the Apartheid Archive.[58] These outpourings are treated with a thinly veiled derision, subjecting the inarticulate woundedness of others to the brutality of clinical, cold-hearted, abstracted theory. Perhaps it is the urge or desire for distancing oneself from fellow whites as a way of dealing with personal guilt, but what is lost is the opportunity for taking these uncomfortable lives and awkward words on their own terms and offering a hand that brings the faltering human back into communion.

For this to happen, one has to take the voice of the actors inside the drama of these institutions seriously. Consider, for example, the data drawn from an interview with Mavis Khubelo, a domestic worker:

> I love the children . . . I can honestly say that I have a deep love for them. Even more than their parents, because I spend more time with them in their home, teaching them, educating them, disciplining them throughout the day. Their parents just come home and play with them, they give them sweets [candy], to make their children like them. That's because they only arrive when all the hard work of parenting is already done (emphasis added).[59]

Love, for the researcher, is merely "what she was required to do, and indeed did [. . .]", thereby dismissing immediately the possibility of genuine intimacy as nothing more than obligation. Of course, that is not what the domestic said; it is imposed on her, this time by researchers, perhaps not unlike the very world in which her labour is managed and given meaning by her employers. "I can honestly say" carries little meaning in the interpretative hand of the researcher.

The masterpiece [*sic*] on which all research into domestic labour in South Africa is based, Cock's *Maids and Madams*, falls into exactly the same trap. It acknowledges true closeness but then avoids the data as if going there would have to come to terms with something far too awkward and embarrassing to handle; or as if those moments of tenderness would undermine the more fluid story of structured oppression. That acknowledgment is brief, and then ignored:

> In other cases, the relationship showed a genuine human feeling on both sides, a mutual trust and caring structured on a daily intimacy.[60]

Rather than probe more deeply this openly expressed love for white children, as in the Ally research, it is theorised away as "ambivalence", an existence in a twilight zone where the domestic is never quite sure whether she is really part of the intimate bonds of family. This cynical treatment of tenderness as some kind of false consciousness threads throughout academic work on domestics in

South Africa, impoverishing our understanding of the full human experience at the heart of our entanglements.

Why, after all, would wealthy slaveholders take their slave mistresses to a resort for open-air vacations? This is what puzzled Dolen Perkins-Valdez as she read about Tawawa House in a biography on the great black American intellectual, W.E.B. du Bois. Wilberforce University, the oldest private black college in Ohio, where du Bois also taught, was part of this famed resort. The questions were obvious – how could this happen under the institution of slavery and why would the slaves not run? The literature of course was sparse, if not concealed, but Adele Logan Alexander, author of *Ambiguous Lives: Free Women of Color in Rural Georgia, 1789–1879*, is not surprised: "nuance in slavery gets painted over all the time."[61]

Like Zakes Mda's *Madonna*, Perkins-Valdez turns to the novel to capture what was real but not spoken in order to tell the story, in *Wench*, of four slave mistresses. One of them, Lizzie, sleeps in the bed with her owner who is also the father of her children. They both think of themselves to be in love with each other. Lizzie sometimes calls him by his first name and tries to negotiate and wants freedom for her own children. The novel "raises questions about complex parts of slavery . . . What kinds of accommodations and negotiations took place between slaves and masters? What passed for love? . . . What history gets privileged and what gets forgotten?"[62] This contribution of mainly women authors of the neo-slave novel "dramatizes not what was *done* to slave women but what they *did* with what was done to them".[63]

Moving between these two institutions, slavery and domestic labour, the picture of race relations therefore becomes a lot more complex, nuanced and even loving inside the overarching framework of oppression. One thing becomes clear, though, and it is that neither slaves nor servants are powerless. As Shireen Ally demonstrates in her research on domestics in South Africa, far from being vulnerable and helpless, the nature of the relationship itself gave them power:

> [they used] this intimacy as a way to independently control their work. They carefully cultivated personal relationships with their employers, recovered the intimacy of the 'like one of the family' myth, used their employers' dependence on them to informally regulate wages and working conditions, informally negotiated the limits of their employers' control over their labor, and strategically engaged in 'emotion work' as a tactic of class combat. In this work culture, they practised power from the most unlikely of sites – the intimacy of their work.[64]

Intimacy, therefore, is never neutral.[65] It is not simply sought after, violated or avoided, it is actively produced for political ends, as Ann Stoler explained in her celebrated work which shows how intimate arrangements were central to the project of empire.[66] Across contexts, therefore, intimacy carries the power to transform the very relationships that produce it, whether in a fish market in Portugal[67] or an interracial marriage in England[68] or in mixed neighbourhoods in the USA.[69]

Intimacy, in any of these contexts, can both hurt and heal but while much has been written of its violence, little is known of its capacity for building bridges across human divides that transform distance into nearness. What then can be learnt from a closer examination of the lives of undergraduate students, "the changing landscapes of intimacies ... [and] its agentic possibilities(?)"[70]

Notes

1 Shah, N. 2012. *Stranger Intimacy: Contesting race, sexuality and the law in the North American West.* Oakland, CA: University of California Press.
2 Lloyd, S.A. and Emery, B.C. 2000. The Context and Dynamics of Intimate Aggression against Women. *Journal of Personal and Social History* 17(4,5), 503–21.
3 Schwab, G. 2010. *Haunting Legacies: Violent histories and transgenerational trauma.* New York, Columbia: University Press, pp. 151–82.
4 Irby, D.J. 2014. Revealing Racial Purity Ideology: Fear of black-white intimacy as a framework for understanding school discipline in post-Brown schools. *Educational Administration Quarterly* 50(5), 783–95.
5 Williams, A. 2001. A Literature Review on the Concept of Intimacy in Nursing. *Journal of Advanced Nursing* 33(5), 660–7.
6 Mashek, D. and Aron, A. (eds) 2008. *Handbook of Closeness and Intimacy.* New Jersey: Lawrence Erlbaum Associates Inc.
7 Cassidy, J. and Shaver, P.R. 2008. *Handbook of Attachment: Theory, research and clinical applications.* 2nd edition. New York: The Guilford Press.
8 Juffer, J. 2013. *Intimacy across Borders: Race, religion, and migration in the US Midwest.* Philadelphia, PA: Temple University Press; see also Boym, S. 2000. On Diasporic Intimacy: Illya Kabakov's installations and immigrant homes. In Berlant, L. (ed.) *Intimacy.* Chicago: University of Chicago Press, pp. 226–52.
9 Griffin, L. 2011. Unravelling Rights: 'Illegal' migrant domestic workers in South Africa. *South African Review of Sociology* 42(2), 83–101.
10 This outstanding piece of thought is one of the best summaries of why women stay; Kantor, J. 2014. Seeing abuse and a pattern too familiar. *New York Times*, 9 September. Available from: www.nytimes.com/2014/09/10/us/seeing-abuse-and-a-pattern-too-familiar.html?_r=0
11 Killian, K.D. 2013. *Interracial Couples, Intimacy, and Therapy: Crossing racial borders.* New York: Columbia University Press.
12 The *Journal of Social and Personal Relationships* runs a steady stream of research reports on same-sex intimacies.
13 Schwab, G. 2010. *Haunting Legacies: Violent histories and transgenerational trauma.* New York: Columbia University Press, pp. 151–82.
14 Quoted in: Herwitz, D. 2003. *Race and Reconciliation: Essays from the new South Africa.* Minneapolis: University of Minnesota Press, p.8.
15 I found this article more refined than most in its reflections on this dilemma. Ross, J., Gallagher, M.S. and Macleod, H. 2013. Making distance visible: Assembling nearness in an online distance learning programme. *The International Review of Research in Open and Distance Learning* 14(4). Available from: www.irrodl.org/index.php/irrodl/issue/view/58
16 Turkel, S. 2011. *Alone Together: Why we expect more from technology and less from each other.* New York: Basic Books, p. 1.
17 Tutt, D. 2012. *A Hatred that Smiles: Kristeva's essay on abjection and intimate racism.* Available from: http://danieltutt.com/2012/06/10/a-hatred-that-smiles-kristevas-essay-on-abjection-and-intimate-racism/

70 *Intimacy*

18 TMZ staff. 2014. L.A. Clippers Owner to GF: Don't Bring Black People to My Games ... Including Magic Johnson. *TMZ*, 25 April. Available from: www.tmz.com/2014/04/26/donald-sterling-clippers-owner-black-people-racist-audio-magic-johnson/
19 Quoted in Martens, J. 2007. Citizenship, "Civilisation" and the Creation of South Africa's Immortality Act, 1927. *South African Historical Journal* 59, 223–41.
20 The Union of South Africa. 1927. Government Gazette Extraordinary, published by authority. (Vol. LXVII, No 1618). p. 2.
21 Furlong, P. 1994. Improper Intimacy: Afrikaans churches, the National Party and the anti-miscegenation laws. *South African Historical Journal* 31 (Nov), 55–79.
22 Novkov, J. 2011. *Racial Union: Law, intimacy, and the white state in Alabama, 1865–1954*. Ann Arbor, MI: University of Michigan Press; and Thompson, D. 2009. Racial Ideas and Gendered Intimacies: The regulation of interracial relationships in North America. *Social & Legal Studies* 18(3), 353–71; see also Bardaglio, P.W. 1999. "Shameful Matches": The regulation of interracial sex and marriage in the South before 1900. In Hodes, M. (ed.) *Sex, Love, Race: Crossing boundaries in North American history*. New York: NYU Press, pp. 112–40.
23 Jim Crow refers to racial segregation laws especially in public facilities of the American South covering roughly the period from the 1870s to 1950s.
24 Dlamini, J. 2014. *Askari: A story of collaboration and betrayal in the anti-apartheid struggle*. Auckland Park: Jacana Media, p. 8.
25 Quoted in Martens J. 2007. Citizenship, "Civilisation" and the Creation of South Africa's Immortality Act, 1927. *South African Historical Journal* 59, 223–41. (p. 224).
26 Quoted in Posel, D. 1995. The Meaning of Apartheid before 1948: Conflicting interests and forces within the Afrikaner Nationalist alliance. In Beinhart, W. and Dubow, S. (eds) *Segregation and Apartheid in Twentieth-Century South Africa*. New York: Routledge, pp. 206–30 (p. 215).
27 Influx control was shorthand for a set of regulatory measures, principally pass laws, that sought to control the flow and presence of black South Africans in designated white areas; the regulating Act was only abolished in 1986.
28 Ndebele, N. 2013. Foreword. In Jones, M. and Dlamini, J. (eds) *Categories of Persons: Rethinking Ourselves and Other*. Johannesburg: Picador Africa.
29 Juffer, J. 2013. *Intimacy across Borders: Race, religion and migration in the US Midwest*. Philadelphia, PA: Temple University Press; the title here is misleading since the text spends considerable space on South Africa and especially the role of the Dutch Reformed Churches, including biographical reflections on the white author's relationship with a black Cape Town man weaved into the account.
30 Boris, E. and Parrenas, R.S. 2010. *Intimate Labours: Culture, technologies, and the politics of care*. Stanford, CA: Stanford University Press.
31 These missionaries seem to come from everywhere; see, among other sources, Schoeman, K. 1985. *Die huis van die armes: die Berlynse Sendinggenootskap in die OVS, 1834–69: 'n Bloemlesing*. Kaapstad: Human and Rosseau; Brady, J.E. 1954. *From Garrison Town to Archbishopric: The story of the Church in Bloemfontein and the OFS, 1850–1954 and of Rev Fr P Hoendervangers O Praem, the first priest*. South Africa: Catholic History Bureau; and Campbell, J. 1993. The social origins of African Methodism in the Orange Free State. *African Studies* 53(1), 147–9. For a fascinating insight into the labours of Andrew Murray in Bloemfontein and elsewhere in setting up the early churches of the Dutch Mission, the letters of his wife Emma provide a mix of cold-hearted assessments of the city and its people, warm-hearted accounts of personal loneliness as her husband travelled constantly, a uniquely English humour and a fair dose of undiluted bigotry towards the Boers – in 1954. Murray, E. and Murray, J. 1954. *Young Mrs Murray goes to Bloemfontein, 1856–60: Letters*. Cape Town: A.A. Balekema.

32 Volkskongress oor Die Toekoms van die Bantoe. 1956: referate en besluite. Volkskongres Bloemfontein. 28–30 Junie. Stellenbosch: Pro Ecclesia; see especially pages (v), (vi) and 136–40 for references to my referenced statements in this book.
33 See Furlong, P. 1994. Improper Intimacy: Afrikaans churches, the National Party and the anti-miscegenation laws. *South African Historical Journal* 31, 55–79; and Saayman, W. 2008. Good Mission Policy is Good State Policy in South Africa: The influence of the Tomlinson Report on racial separation in church and state at the dawn of apartheid. *Studia Historiae Ecclesiasticae* 34(2), 15–39.
34 Evans, I. 2009. *Cultures of Violence: Lynching and racial killing in South Africa and the American South.* Manchester and New York: Manchester University Press, p. 176.
35 This finely argued historical work by Herman Giliomee (2003) must be the best available research yet on the subject of the Dutch Reformed Church and racial segregation; Giliomee, H. 2003. "The Weakness of Some": The Dutch Reformed Church and white supremacy. *Scriptura* 83/2, 212–44.
36 Schoeman, W.J. 2010. The Racial Discourse and the Dutch Reformed Church: Looking through a descriptive-empirical lens towards a normative task. *Acta Theologica* 30(2), 130–51.
37 Du Toit, A. 1993. The Micro-Politics of Paternalism: The discourses of management and resistance on South African fruit and wine farms. *Journal of Southern African Studies* 19(2), 314–36 (p. 314).
38 Dawdy, S.L. 2006. Proper Caresses and Prudent Distance: A how-to manual from colonial Louisiana. In Stoler, A.L. (ed.) *Haunted by Empire: Geographies of intimacy in North American history.* Durham and London: Duke University Press, pp. 140–62.
39 Hodes, M. 1999. Introduction: Interconnecting and diverging narratives. In Hodes, M. (ed.) *Sex, Love, Race: Crossing boundaries in North American history.* New York: NYU Press.
40 D'Emilio, J. and Freedman, E.B. 2012. *Intimate Matters: A history of sexuality in America.* 3rd edition. Chicago: The University of Chicago Press, p. 101.
41 Ibid., p. 103.
42 Gordon-Reid, A. 2008. *The Hemingses of Monticello: An American family.* New York: WW Norton, pp. 353–4.
43 van Woodward, C. 1999. *Origins of the New South, 1877–1913.* Louisiana State University Press (also 1951, 1971 printings).
44 Schultz, M. 2005. *The Rural Face of White Supremacy: Beyond Jim Crow.* Urbana and Chicago: University of Illinois Press. Preface.
45 Ibid., p. 5.
46 Ibid., p. 7.
47 Ibid.
48 Lawrence-Lightfoot, S. 2009. *The Third Chapter: Passion, risk, and adventure in the 25 years after 50.* New York: Farrar, Straus and Giroux, p. 126.
49 Shefer, T. 2012. Fraught Tenderness: narratives on domestic workers in memories of apartheid. *Peace and Conflict: Journal of Peace Psychology* 18(3), 307–17.
50 Ibid., p. 312.
51 Archer, S. 2011. 'Buying the Maid Ricoffy': Domestic workers, employers and food. *South African Review of Sociology* 42(2), 66–82.
52 Steyn, M. 2001. 'Whiteness Just Isn't What it Used to Be': White identity in a changing South Africa. Albany, NY: SUNY Press, pp. i–ii.
53 Jansen, E. 2011. From Thandi the Maid to Thandi the Madam: Domestic workers in the archives of Afrikaans literature and a family photographic album. *South African Review of Sociology* 42(2), 102–21.
54 Ibid., p. 117.
55 Mda, Z. 2002. *The Madonna of Excelsior: A Novel.* USA: Farrar, Straus and Giroux.

56 Cock, J. 1980. *Maids and Madams: A Study in the Politics of Exploitation*. South Africa: Raven Press, p. 9.
57 du Plessis, I. 2011. Nation, Family, Intimacy: The domain of the domestic in the social imaginary. *South African Review of Sociology* 42(2), 45–65.
58 See Derek Hook's treatment of a white man's sincere, troubled and guilt-ridden confessions of his relationship with the domestic worker, Dyson in: Hook, D. 2013. On Animal Mediators and Psychoanalytic Reading Practice. In Stevens, G., Duncan, N. and Hook, D. (eds) *Race, Memory and the Apartheid Archive: Towards a psychosocial praxis*. Johannesburg: Wits University Press, pp. 146–62.
59 Ally, S. 2010. *From Servants to Workers: South African domestic workers and the democratic state*. Scottsville: University of KwaZulu Natal Press, p. 96.
60 Cock, J. 1980. *Maids and Madams: A Study in the Politics of Exploitation*. South Africa: Raven Press, p. 88.
61 Cited in: O'Neal Parker, L. 2011. A tender spot in master-slave relations. *The Washington Post*, 21 January. Available from: www.washingtonpost.com/wp-dyn/content/article/2011/01/21/AR2011012102960.html
62 Ibid.
63 This beautiful summation comes from McDowell, D. 1989. Negotiating between Tenses: Witnessing slavery after freedom – Dessa Rose. In McDowell, D.E. and Rampersad, A. (eds) *Slavery and the Literary Imagination*. Baltimore, MD: Johns Hopkins University Press, p. 146.
64 Ally, S. 2010. *From Servants to Workers: South African domestic workers and the democratic state*. Scottsville: University of KwaZulu Natal Press, pp. 95–6.
65 Welch Cline, R.J. 1989. The Politics of Intimacy: Costs and benefits determining disclosure intimacy in male-female dyads. *Journal of Social and Personal Relationships* 6, 5–20.
66 Stoler, A.L. 2002. *Carnal Knowledge and Imperial Power: Race and the intimate in colonial rule*. Berkeley: University of California Press; and Stoler A.L. 2006. (ed.) *Haunted by Empire: Geographies of intimacy in North American History*. Durham, NC: Duke University Press.
67 Fikes, K. 2005. Ri(gh)tes of Intimacy at Docapesca: Race versus racism at a fish market in Portugal. *Du Bois Review* 2(2), 247–66.
68 Tate, S.A. 2015. Transracial Intimacy and "Race" Performativity: Recognition and destabilizing the nation's Racial Contract. In Bleeker, M., Sherman, J.F. and Nedelkopoulou, E. (eds) *Performance and Phenomenology: Traditions and transformations*. New York: Routledge, pp. 173–85.
69 Gilliam, F.D. Jr, Valentino, N. and Beckmann, M.N. 2002. Where you Live and What you Watch: The impact of racial proximity and local television news on attitudes about race and crime. *Political Research Quarterly* 55(4), 755–80.
70 Frank, A., Clough, P.T. and Siedman, S. *et al.* (eds) 2013 *Intimacies: A new world of relational life*. New York: Routledge, p. 3.

5 The resident swastika

Introduction

I half-expected some level of mischief from the students in one of the oldest male residences named after an outspoken segregationist, the third (1924–39) post-Union Prime Minister, J.B.M. Hertzog. But what was about to confront me was unimaginable even for a veteran observer of right-wing student politics from my time as Dean of Education at a similar institution, the University of Pretoria.

The "*gazellie*", a special room where "house meetings" were held, was uncomfortably quiet as I walked in that evening, slowly, to the front of the venue where I was to take position behind the mandatory lectern. There, in bright paint against the wall, was a large bold painting of a swastika. I adjusted my eyes, just to make sure I was not seeing things but conscious all the time that this was planned and that my reaction to the male students behind me was exactly what this group of white men, with singular black faces dotting the audience, waited to enjoy.

I turned around and with as much restraint as possible ordered the students that I would not be prepared to speak to them until this atrocity was removed from the wall. Someone scrambled for paint and the offensive symbol was covered up quickly. What I was not sure about in that moment was how long it would take to remove the swastikas of the heart. I changed course, and instead of opening the floor to an extended period of questions during this "listening phase" of my new job, I gave a history lesson on the meanings of the swastika. "How do you think a Jewish student in your number would have felt on seeing the swastika?" I asked the students. "Do you understand the meaning of that hated symbol, and the millions of Jews who died simply because of who they were?"

In those moments I was already anguished. How much of this bravado was based on ignorance and how much on deliberate knowledge of what and who was being offended? Did they really understand the depravity that comes with such a display of hatred? Did they not even see the connection between the swastika and J.B.M. Hertzog – a man who had done so much to oppress black people that a distinguished historian records that he "promoted segregation as a white supremacist rather than an Afrikaner"?[1] Or was this also, in the chorus of supporters of the "Reitz four" outside of campus, simply a case of boys having fun? What I did know without a measure of doubt was that my work was cut out for me as a teacher, an activist and a leader. The change would not be easy.

The politics of place

The swastika incident at the University of the Free State (UFS) only makes sense within the political demography of the region. Once outside Bloemfontein the college town, the province quickly becomes rural. Many white residents have lived most of their lives in the province and read the one Afrikaans daily newspaper. Students in the Afrikaans schools are largely isolated from the country and the world around them. Black people are familiar and even close, as labourers, but seldom peers and friends in white-dominant churches, schools and friendship circles. Similarly, most black Free Staters are locked into township life venturing into the smaller cities and larger towns primarily for purposes of work and commerce, before returning home. The spatial geography of apartheid has not shifted appreciably.

In addition to physical isolation there is the cultural isolation of the province. There have never been the kinds of diversities that run through the port cities of Durban, Cape Town and Port Elizabeth, or the bustling metropolis of Johannesburg. There was never a strong liberal party or a communist party, or the various strains of small progressive parties common elsewhere. The Jewish community is small and disappearing, and Muslim and Hindu communities never found a foothold in the Free State because of anti-residential laws keeping Indian South Africans out. The more open-minded English paper, *The Friend* – "an outpost of resistance in what was then exceedingly hostile territory for English-speaking people of liberal or moderate persuasion"[2] – was shut down by the Argus Company in 1985 for financial reasons.

The Afrikaans Daily is openly conservative, publishing whites-only student residence accommodation without repercussion in 2014, and making no secret about the fact that its audience, whether in celebration or tragedy, is white Afrikaans people. Its ample "Letters to the Editor" is engineered to give voice to the most conservative readership and its headlines repeatedly anti-black government (see Chapter 12).

Black students from the province come largely from poor areas and rural township schools completely isolated from interaction with white schools. Their parents are labourers under white authority, whether on farms in the expansive agricultural areas or in towns and cities as domestic workers, gardeners, maintenance workers and semi-skilled labour for small business owners. The small number of middle class black employees fill out jobs in the new black government at provincial level or in the local municipalities; this is a vulnerable group whose class status depends entirely on loyalty to the dominant political party, which exists only because of the numerical majority enjoyed in an African country.

There is a quiet resentment of white people, especially among the black middle classes, and political discourses often tend to carry negative messages about "racist" whites which come into the open in every crisis. The isolation of both poor and middle-class blacks in sports, churches, festivals and everyday life means that separate living remains the norm across classes of black citizens. Even in the few integrated schools and churches, the black numbers are small enough not to make any difference in race relations in the province as a whole.

For a long time, therefore, race relations in the Free State could be reduced to a conflict between two ethnic nationalisms – a white Afrikaner nationalism and a black Basotho nationalism. These two communities were close and distant, forced together through mutual dependence on labour and wages, but living worlds apart in terms of language, religion, education, politics and leisure. As the Boers trekked from the more liberal Cape into central South Africa, skirmishes with the Basotho tribes were eclipsed by the larger conflict of Boer and Brit, though the black–white conflict would continue, and escalate, since Union in 1910 and into the apartheid years since 1948 to the present.

The campus as reflection of racial separateness

It nevertheless still surprised me on arrival in mid-2009 how incredibly separated the Bloemfontein campus was. Racial segregation was a problem on all former white university campuses, but here it seemed complete. There was a white church called *Kovsie Kerk*, a prominent and spacious building on the northern edge of campus where the main services were in the Afrikaans language and, more recently, separate church events in English or Sesotho for black students. Most black students, however, held their services in classrooms spread across campuses in temporary arrangements made with the university management. In effect, black and white students worshipped separately.

The classes were separated into English classes for black students and Afrikaans classes for white students. The university allows for instruction in its historical language, Afrikaans, from a time when only white Afrikaans students could and did attend, and since opening up access, with accelerating black student enrolments in the immediate years leading to democracy, English classes dominated. Whether intended or not as a matter of racial regulation, English classes therefore had mainly black students and Afrikaans classes mostly white students.

The orientation sessions were segregated. The white Dutch Reformed Church organised an orientation session at the beginning of every year in Afrikaans and for students from its church affiliates. A heavy dose of spiritual and cultural immersion ensured that even before they began university studies, the white Afrikaans students already found the umbilical extension from community to campus through this bridging experience. The general university orientation would become the cultural counterpoint to this experience as the university embarked on its own transformation.

The residences of course were segregated. Valiant efforts by previous rectors sought to desegregate the residences but white students resisted, leading to major confrontations with black students and significant physical damage, into millions of Rand, to campus buildings. The violence was intense, culminating in the notorious Reitz incident. Gradually white residents would allow small numbers of black students in, and black students would accept these places despite the constant harassment felt at the hands of white seniors. Black residences simply could not attract white students, especially the men's residences.

The social spaces on campus were segregated. Wherever you looked, white students were gathered together in some spaces and black students in their own spaces. On the "Bridge", the place where the shops and restaurants were located, there were white tables and black tables, in the manner of speaking, and no integrated tables. The same was true at sporting events where audiences were either all-white as at hockey or swimming, or with black and white students in different sections of the stadium as in athletics or rugby.

The political spaces were segregated. The UFS had a deadly arrangement in which student politics was organised on the basis of parliamentary politics. This meant that black students would vote for the African National Congress, the dominant black political party since democracy, and white students for the Freedom Front Plus (FF+), the conservative white political party in parliament. A small number of white and black students belonged to the liberal Democratic Party. But the real conflict would be between the black ANC and the white FF+, and it got ugly. The student parliament would provide opportunities for the black student leaders to routinely insult and demean the white students as "racist". After years in which white students regularly won the elections because of better organisation, the first black President was elected in 2009.

What was fascinating about these arrangements was that as long as the political party system existed, white students – even those who were not conservative or right-wing – would feel the pressure to join the FF+ while black students, though not affiliated to the ANC, would feel compelled by race to join this student body. The few white students who joined the ANC grouping were vilified by conservative students, and black students would, on occasion, express support for some of the pro-student positions of the FF+ but would not dare joining the organisation fearing the charge of being called traitors to their race. Political segregation, therefore, was also complete.

It did not help that the academic staff was largely white and the senior scholars, the professoriate, almost entirely white, male and Afrikaans speaking. As the student body became more and more black, growing to the majority, the untransformed staffing demographic would leave the UFS trailing most of the former white South African universities. The administrative or support staff, in local language, showed a more transformed demographic since the lower skill levels in the more entry-level positions enabled, even required, black employees. In other words, the academic division of labour on campus largely reflected the social and economic division of labour in the broader society.

Singing resistance

I had not even visited the white women's residence, which carries the name of the English heroine who helped Afrikaner women in the Boer War, when Emily Hobhouse "*koshuis*" (residence) decided to make sure everybody knew their position on integration was crystal clear. At the annual Serenade (called by the shortened name *Sêr*), a competitive inter-residence music and drama event, *Emily* decided to sing a song protesting the residence plan "because we are fed-up with the reasoning of the integration generation" (words from song, translated from Afrikaans).

This song, with its curious mix of religious and political appeal, was wildly popular and *Emily* women knew that the mainly white audience attending "*Sêr*" at that stage would find this daring act attractive if not a winner on the night. An almost exclusively white residence at the time, *Emily* had made a name for itself with this song and the hostility towards the university leadership and the integration effort would be felt among the seniors for some time to come.

It was still the first three to six months of my tenure and I dutifully did the rotation rounds through every residence at night, after classes, so that I had as full a house as possible in each of the 23 (at the time) student houses. The reception was chilly in most places, and residence integration was top of the list in the question-and-answer sessions in the white-dominant residences. In the black residences the complaints were against racist whites as lecturers and as students, the questioning of white traditions in which they were compelled to participate – such as the annual inter-varsity with another former white Afrikaans university and the first-year initiations. Black students complained that Afrikaans was even a language of instruction on campus, and the fact that the English classes were held late in the day, when students were tired and had wasted a day on campus, while the Afrikaans classes, for whites, were held during daylight hours. What the black students did not complain about was the racial integration of the residences; if anything, they would come to complain about the fact that despite their efforts to comply with institutional policies, they could not get white students to enrol in their mainly black residences.

During these residence visits I would come across a strange but persistent refrain – "*gedwonge integrasie*" (forced integration). The white students had picked up this language from outside of the campus where right-wing parties, conservative parents and voices in the local Afrikaans newspaper had couched their complaint against residence integration in the language of rights. It was, except for some, not necessary to say straightforwardly that they did not want their white offspring sharing campus residences with black people, which was in fact the underlying racism. A more noble cause could be pursued towards the same ends, and that was one that insisted on free association; after all, the new democratic constitution allowed for citizens to choose with whom they wished to associate.

I came down hard on this polite racism by insisting, even before the listening campaign was over, that such reasoning was not only flawed, it was offensive.

Universities across the world set goals for their residences, such as the number of international students or whether the residences will be single-sex or "co-ed" and whether the residences would serve undergraduate or postgraduate students, single or married students. In none of those contexts would "forced integration" be charged and therefore having diversity as a goal is a perfectly reasonable position for an institution to take. Clearly, the issue here was racism, I argued.

Alibi arguments citing freedom of choice would sometimes yield to blunt bigotry, as in the stream of correspondence to the local Afrikaans press which served as a public depository for white anxiety. One reader, a Dr J.A.L Theron, put his *Letter* this way:

> The rector should rather take an interest in academic excellence than be involved in experiments in racial integration ... Successful academic progress of black and white students who are forced to become roommates without their permission is highly dubious given the following scenario. In one corner of the room you find a black student studying Political Science, an adherent of Karl Marx's Communist Manifesto, who regularly plays "bring me my machine gun"[3] on his laser player. In another corner of the room you find a white student studying Theology and reading from the Gospel according to Mark with further explanations from the Heidelberg Catechism while his laser player plays Psalm 130.[4]

The reader warns of "catastrophe" that comes with racial integration and the "spiritual violence" imposed on the rights of young students whose primary interest in coming to university is their academic advancement.[5]

At least the letter was honest. Here was the worst apartheid stereotype of the godless, violent black communist and the civilised, peaceful white Christian living in catastrophic closeness to each other. Black students, preoccupied with violence, did not read the Bible and white students were heavenly minded angels. Anyone who had even a casual acquaintance with residence life at any university, including the UFS, would of course have found these stereotypes quite funny. In fact, the primary objection of white male students at the time of writing was the closure of the alcohol-serving bars in residences where senior students routinely got drunk.

Still, the clamour against integration of the residences continued fiercely outside the campus and primarily through the more than willing newspaper publisher of any Letters to the Editor condemning "forced association".[6] But the anger against integration also simmered among white students on campus, as in this memorable event with prospective student leaders.

There was an obligatory orientation session for students who were contemplating leadership roles in the following academic year, and I was asked to address them. The auditorium in the medical school was packed with students, mainly white in clearly identifiable clusters and black in separate rows. I shared my vision for a diverse campus in which respect and cooperation was based on character and not colour, and that the university lagged behind the country when it came to normalising race relations among students in and outside of the residences.

Then something happened that will remain with me for a very long time. A young white woman stood up and lambasted me in front of the assembled audience for daring to come in, as an outsider, and trying to change things that were settled very nicely since the days when her parents and grandparents were students on this campus. Who did I think I was coming in here and trying to change everything? Her language was sharp and unflattering, and I could sense in the student body a mix of feelings from shock to delight, even anticipation at what would happen next.

Eventually the young woman sat down, and I thanked her for the contribution. I knew that in another time at this kind of university she would not dare launch out like that to someone in authority and, if she did, it would be her last day on campus. It was not difficult to understand why she thought she could do this to the new rector. I thanked her for her contribution, conscious that the audience for my response was the rest of the student leaders; what I said next, and how I said it, could permanently mark my tenure at the University of the Free State.

I spoke slowly but firmly. The country had changed; the campus will change. The residences will be integrated on a 50:50 basis, black and white. The time for racial segregation is past and we will, like universities around the world, set goals for our residences including greater diversity within the resident community. Any other questions?

The next morning I was in my office very early and by this time students realised they could use the "open door" policy to see their new leader on any matter of concern. Then, to my horror, in walked the same student who had given me a tongue-lashing the night before. "Do you still remember me, professor?," she asked in Afrikaans and with a barely audible voice. "Yes I do," I mumbled, "and I'm scared." She walked right up to me and, with a tear in the eye, said: "I am really sorry about what happened last night, professor, and I would like to apologise." That was the easy part, and I held back on my own emotions and wondered at her genuine grace and contrition. What she said next came out as a question, and completely floored me: "Please make me part of the solution?" As she left, I closed the office door to deal with the flood of emotion. In that moment I knew for sure; it is possible, after all, to change these students.

The mathematics of integration

Of course the 50:50 plan was in itself never going to work in practice. It was merely a start to break the calcified, stalemate situation in which black and white residences remained largely unmoved in their racial demographic. In reality, with the slow but steady increase in black undergraduate enrolments, there would always be more black students demanding residence spaces than white students.

Nor would it be possible to manage and maintain residence integration on this basis in the black men's residences; male students, for reasons that require further research, simply do not integrate in any significant ways because white men do not want to be in a minority. By contrast, white female students move quite quickly so that both the black and white women's residences soon reached their integration goals.[7]

Still, the goal was not mathematical integration but an integration of humanity. Whether this meant 70:30 or 80:20 in any direction was not important, in the final analysis, but simply that students found some way of living and learning together, and not harming each other. This has been achieved, but with interesting results.

Patterns of integration

Welwitschia, the name of a hardy xerophyte plant that survives in the Namibian desert on minimal condensation, was an all-black, angry women's residence when I first visited there in late 2009. I could not believe the levels of disaffection and despair among the women students. They hung over their chairs or laid back in them, completely disinterested in the new rector who was about to address them. Unlike any other residence, they continued talking to each other as I got started and walked in and out during the speech. One slept, another read a book. Many of them were completely unkempt and their questions were lists of complaints. Something was horribly wrong.

I would come to understand a crucial error in university admissions policy during those early days. In its understandable need to swing open the doors of learning to black students following the demise of apartheid, the university maintained very low standards of entry. Black students from the poorest schools, hopelessly underprepared for higher learning and through no fault of their own, came through the gates and failed miserably. The UFS in fact had one of the lowest pass rates of the public universities in South Africa.

The students sitting in front of me at *Welwitschia* were frustrated because not only were they unwelcome in the broader institutional culture, they were failing like flies. One of the bitter consequences of openness, coupled with the institutional need to raise student numbers for purposes of financial survival, was that weak students entered and dropped out of the system. The result was unbearable hardship on families who made great sacrifices to bring their children to university, and now they were saddled with unemployed youth without degrees and a huge debt burden. This, I argued with my colleagues, was a more devastating form of racism.

But the growing numbers of weak academic students, mainly black, meant that the performance of these students reinforced the very racism that sought to keep disadvantaged students out in the first place. Here stereotype found happy confirmation in struggling black students whom, through no fault of their own and severely disadvantaged by apartheid schooling, now had to compete with privileged white students many of whom did not want them there in the first place. Three things needed to be done – recruit more and more top black students from around the country and the region, raise the academic standard of admission for all students, and create alternate pathways for disadvantaged students to eventually enter and succeed in tertiary education. As long as poor, underprepared black student was pitted against privileged, well-schooled white student, the chances of combatting incipient racism were going to be very slim.

This we did, raise the academic standard and recruit top black and white students from all nine provinces and beyond to break, in part, the old lines of association and conflict between white Afrikaner and black Basotho. It worked. Then the task was to prepare the residence heads, staff members, to buy into the new vision and here *Welwitschia* was blessed to have an open-minded white woman who called parents and students personally in order to invite them to take residence in *Wel-Wel*, the abbreviation by which the residence was affectionately called. In very little time white women students flooded the residence and the 50:50 goal was achieved, even exceeded, but the problems of integration dissipated very quickly.

Emily Hobhouse, the former white women's residence that welcomed the new rector with an anti-integration song, would take a little longer but did eventually achieve integration. In successive visits to the residence, however, the original seniors would sit towards the back of the "*gazellie*" looking angry and uninterested. These were the young women who were part of the resistance. I was not sure whether it was shame or disappointment that their residence was no longer lily-white, and so I reached out to them, without much success. What was clear was that the new student leadership, optimistic and integrated, was completely in rhythm with the new changes.

In *Emily*, and elsewhere, we had to introduce another level of integration, and that was the residence heads and the house committees (called HKs after the Afrikaans "*Huis Komitees*"). Without setting initial targets, HKs would be all white or all black since the dominant demographic of the house would vote in people like themselves. Until we became "normal" and voted competence and not colour, this was another one of those temporary measures to ensure some degree of leadership integration. This modelling of integration was of course important at all levels of leadership and, especially, in residence leadership. New first-year students coming in would recognise, immediately, the new value system and adjust accordingly.

What *Emily* was able to achieve was to appoint a very smart and impressive black woman student as their "prime", the woman student head of residence. She was, also, the first black woman head prefect at her school, a traditional and conservative Afrikaans institution close to the university. And her Afrikaans was fluent, enabling her to build bridges between black students and white students in ways that few others could. This emotional security of language and the familiarity of racial face, for black students, and cultural face, for white students, helped the prime to build a strong, united and integrated residence through exemplary leadership.

Tswelopele (progress, in Sesotho) is a black men's residence. On every visit the young men, immaculately dressed in their dark blazers, shirts and ties, would quiz me. What more could we do to attract white students to our residence? It was a question my students once asked the President of Spelman College, a black women's college in the USA, about why they did not have white students at her distinguished school. Her response on a visit to the UFS was "white consciousness", meaning that the doors were open but that white students would not come because of racial preferences if not, also, racism. *Tswelopele* was in every sense a model residence with strong academic standing, inclusive cultural symbols and practices, and a well-managed house. It then did something I thought was impossible: the residents elected to head their residence one of the few white male students in the house. They trusted him, loved him and asked him to lead. Here the goal was achieved in that intimacy did not require numbers for the transformation of minds and hearts, among the black students, and was being achieved.

It required a common language of understanding that went much deeper than epidermal affiliation.

Notes

1 Dubow, S. 1995. The Elaboration of Segregationist Ideology. In Beinhart, W. and Dubow, S. (eds) *Segregation and Apartheid in Twentieth-Century South Africa*. New York: Routledge, pp. 145–75 (p. 147).
2 See Chapter 7, "The Friend": Green, M. 2004. *Around and About: Memoirs of a South African newspaperman*. Claremont, Cape Town: David Philip Publishers, p. 67 (quotation).
3 The reference here is to a controversial song from the anti-apartheid struggle era which the then Deputy President, Jacob Zuma, used to sing in front of large audiences especially during the period of his firing from office while charges against him were being investigated. He would later be reinstated as president after his party, the ANC, relieved his accuser, President Mbeki, from his position.
4 Translated directly from Afrikaans.
5 Theron, J.A.L. 2009. Vraagtekens oor Jansen. (Letter to the editor). *Volksblad*, 8 September. Available from http://152.111.11.6/argief/berigte/volksblad/2009/09/09/VB/6/aakkorterbrifffuv.html
6 Another example is van Zyl, A. 2014, March 24. UV se verpligte assosiasie. (Letter to the editor). *Volksblad*, 24 March. Available from: www.netwerk24.com/stemme/2014-03-23-sanral-ontgroening-en-tuie
7 On the role of gender in intimacy, the explanation might well reside in the observation that "women tend to focus on interpersonal connections to a greater extent than do men" and also "experience greater intimacy related behaviors and feelings than do men [. . .]". Laurenceau, J., Rivera, L.M., Schaffer, A.R. and Pietromonaco, P.R. 2007. Intimacy as an Interpersonal Process: Current status and future directions. In Mashek, D.J. and Aron, A. (eds) *Handbook of Closeness and Intimacy*. Mahwah, NJ: Lawrence Erlabaum Associates Publishers, pp. 61–78 (p. 71).

6 Intimacy demands a common language

Introduction

It used to happen often. A white student would stand up in a public campus meeting and address the audience in his mother tongue, Afrikaans. There would be murmurings of discontent around the room. He would continue for a while and then, just to make a point, a black student would rise and speak in Sesotho or isiZulu. There would be muffled laughter and light applause from his friends. What was going on here was a lightning rod for conflict which, at a first glance, appears to be about mutually incomprehensible languages but was in fact about culture, history, politics and place. Without intervention, such situations would deteriorate very quickly.

The original Afrikaans universities – Stellenbosch, Pretoria, Free State and Potchefstroom – were created more than a century ago when their founding languages were Dutch and the professors taught in English. There was no well-developed Afrikaans language at the time nor were there sufficient numbers of locals as professors to start those small institutions. As Afrikaner nationalism gained momentum after the Boer War and Afrikaans was developed as a scientific language, it was this proud language which would become the foundations of resilient, white nationalist institutions closely tied to the project of the apartheid state. Afrikaans, in other words, was not simply a language of classroom instruction or scientific inquiry in places like the University of the Orange Free State, as it was then called; it was a symbol of identity, culture and self-realisation for Afrikaners. English would be displaced and Afrikaans became the sole language of these institutions, including the more recent ones like the University of Port Elizabeth (now Nelson Mandela Metropolitan University) and the Rand Afrikaans University (now part of a merged University of Johannesburg).

As the Afrikaans universities gradually opened up to black students in the immediate years leading to the demise of apartheid, English would again appear on campus as a joint language of instruction alongside Afrikaans. Some universities dealt with the two-language dilemma primarily through either parallel-medium instruction (UFS, separate classes in Afrikaans and English) or dual-medium strategies (University of the North West, both languages in one class using interpreters).

Dwell in white Afrikaans communities and you would hear this expression often: "I speak Afrikaans and I only speak English in self-defence." It is only partly a joke for in that political humour is a more serious reference to Afrikaans as the enemy opposite of English, the language of grievance that has its roots in the Boer War and the humiliation of ancestors who were forced to speak English in schools. Without understanding Afrikaans as a cultural belonging and political asset, and not merely a medium of communication, it is impossible to grasp the perpetual anxiety in the white Afrikaans community and its universities about the status of the language inside these changing institutions.

Black students on the other hand have a completely different conception of Afrikaans which, for most of them, is nothing more than the language of the oppressor. In their inherited knowledge it was Afrikaans that provoked the Soweto Uprisings of 1976 when the hated language was extended into additional school subjects in one of the most misguided policies of the Bantu Education administration of apartheid.[1] Afrikaans, in their experiences as students, was a language of exclusion. Students would complain often that in the parallel medium policy of the UFS, white students in the Afrikaans classes were better taught and given advantage in their language than when the same lecturers switched to English in the black classes. Such discrimination was difficult to prove, but for black students this was simply another example of how Afrikaans wielded power and privilege at the expense of the disadvantaged. Not a visit would go by during those early days of addressing the residences when black students would not challenge me to make the UFS an English-medium university and in this way level the instructional playing fields.

The reasoning of the black students was pragmatic and reflected a broader problem not evident in the English universities. "We also gave up our own languages so they – the white Afrikaans-speaking students – can give up theirs for the sake of the conversation." For black students, English was the language of compromise since their home languages were Sesotho or isiZulu or isiXhosa, etc., and common ground could easily be reached if the Afrikaans-speaking white students also gave up their language for the sake of communication in one, commonly understood language.

There were two problems for Afrikaans-speaking students. Many of them, especially those from rural areas, had very little fluency in English and speaking in the language would embarrass them in a public forum. Where students had very little exposure to English in their day-to-day lives, the grammar-oriented English subject in school did little in terms of fluency of communication. But the barrier was not simply linguistic: it was also the colonial language and that made it even more difficult to speak English without inherited memories of a self-defence posture.

Black students switched from mother tongue instruction to English from as early as the third grade and, even though the education of black youth was of a poor quality, at least there was an exposure to the language that came much earlier in terms of formal instruction. Black students entering the first year of classes at university were therefore much more fluent in English than their white

Afrikaans counterparts from especially rural Afrikaans-medium schools. To insist on English as common language would, therefore, disadvantage the white Afrikaans rural student especially in that critical first year of transition to university.

Such problems of communication would be easy to overcome, however, if the problem was only the language of instruction and interaction. The heavy weight of history hung over Afrikaans in this former white nationalist institution, and any move even mildly suggesting a change of language policy would be vehemently opposed outside the gates of the campus. The language stood for something else and its demise as an institutional co-language would be experienced, especially among conservative whites, not only as an emotional and political loss, but as personal and ethnic defeat as well.

I tried to explain to black students not the political dilemmas of going English, so to speak, but that there was a broader narrative of Afrikaans that they were unaware of. Afrikaans was not simply the language of white Afrikaners; it was in fact built also from other languages including Malay in the Cape, where former slaves helped shape the language into what it is today.[2] These facts of history were largely unknown to black students who grew up in the north of the country. They had little exposure to the great black Afrikaans novelists, poets, writers and intellectuals who inhabited a completely different Afrikaans world to that of white Afrikaans speakers. They knew only of the oppressive tradition in Afrikaans, not of its critical traditions which led to the banning of works by prominent white writers in the language. Afrikaans, I insisted, was a South African language that speaks to our diversity and enriches our campus cultures. The residence students listened respectfully but I knew that on the hard edges of black student politics this message was not getting through.

The problem remained: intimacy needed a common language. Being physically close, as in the integration policy of the residences, would become quite dangerous in the absence of a connecting language. Normally this would not be troublesome; after all, love does not require that the lovers use the same spoken language. But it does where the language substitutes for history, memory, identity and power.

The remarkable shift to accommodation and inclusion

In the course of the first year of multiple visits to the white residences, the pattern of communication described earlier remained unchanged. A white student leader, with assistance from a friend, would open the meeting, pray and read from the Bible, and plough through the agenda in Afrikaans. The black students, particularly those from outside the Free State, had absolutely no idea what was being said but sometimes just sat quietly, as the minority, complaining later but not daring to do so in the house meeting. It was clear that two impulses were at play – a hardened resolve not to yield to black students, the insurgents into white residences, and a fear of embarrassment if they were to speak in English.

Gradually, and without fanfare, the hard attitudes changed and all the residences conducted their meetings in English only. Of course this did not happen automatically, as the next chapter will show, but was the result of intensive training, education and reorientation led by the dean of students and his remarkable team. This shift towards a common language that enabled all students to communicate with each other was the single most important variable in the integration of the residences and would build goodwill in ways that no other strategy could.

What was important about this shift towards language inclusion was that it did not, of course, mean the end of Afrikaans. Students still spoke Afrikaans to each other, to their friends, to their lecturers and to me as their rector even though it is not my home language. There were still Afrikaans festivals and speakers, musical events and debates, visiting professors and public communication, in Afrikaans. The external charge of "*verengelsing*" (Afrikaans for anglicisation) as if to mean a complete disappearance of Afrikaans in the day to day lives of campus dwellers was, of course, cheap fearmongering. What these shifts on the part of residential students did allow was for a very practical accommodation to include all students, thereby making Afrikaans itself more attractive to non-speakers as another language option they could pursue.

Soon the shift towards an English language practice would also be seen in the management meetings of the university. With more and more black and white staff without any background or competence in Afrikaans, the solution presented in recent times was to deploy translators in these meetings. But this became cumbersome, expensive and practically silly. Why in a meeting of 15 people have two interpreters when in fact everybody in the room, and certainly as far as senior people were concerned, was highly competent in English? There was no political point scoring necessary for most Afrikaans-speaking staff, only a hardnosed pragmatism – let's get on with the meeting and enjoy speaking Afrikaans in contexts that did not exclude.

Slowly the pressure came from some of the faculties, especially in the sciences, to teach only in English rather than duplicate lectures in both languages. This too was becoming cumbersome given the high costs of duplication and, for the lecturers themselves, repetitive and uninspiring. The technical and professional worlds in which graduates would work demanded, with few exceptions, English language competence so that the UFS commitment to teaching in Afrikaans was in fact disadvantaging white students.

The science texts were almost all in English as well, so that teaching in Afrikaans while learning from English texts was making the parallel-medium policy a real strain on scholars. And then there was the problem of research. The more time spent duplicating lectures the less time there was available for research. And less research in a national climate and institutional context that demanded higher levels of productivity from academics in order to optimise the subsidy income from the state meant that teaching in both languages was decidedly unattractive. Lastly, the chances of individual promotion were also compromised by teaching in Afrikaans given the doubled time of teaching – for which there was little institutional reward – and the fact that there was now less time to do research and writing for publication.

I was cautious about abandoning Afrikaans as a medium of instruction for a number of reasons. It would, to begin with, lose faith with the broader community around and beyond the university who saw Afrikaans as a deeply emotive issue connecting them to the university. It was important, I felt, to retain those emotional ties of alumni and Afrikaans speakers in general to the historical university; many of my colleagues, especially Afrikaans speakers, felt differently. In addition, I felt that our cultural diversity was an important part of the rich intellectual and social histories of the UFS; a new, inclusive, progressive Afrikaans would greatly enhance the institutional climate and demonstrate, further, a leadership position that was not narrow and mean in its understanding of majoritarian democracy. And then there was the simple fact that a small but significant number of students do prefer to receive their instruction in Afrikaans for ease of access and for recognition of identity. For the UFS to continue to build on its public reputation as inclusive and embracing of all our differences meant retaining, in fact expanding, the number of Afrikaans speakers on all three campuses. It is therefore a position that I will continue to defend, but I cannot be certain that into the future of the UFS my successors will be able to continue the practice of language inclusion with Afrikaans in mind.

Where demographic shifts happen at pace, such as the University of the Free State, Afrikaans would maintain neither its dominance in teaching nor its currency in administration inside a changing institution. In universities where non-Afrikaans-speaking blacks remain a small minority, the Afrikaans question is defended with all the zealotry of conservative voices bringing unbearable pressure on the rectors there. In that context, Afrikaans is a handy instrument for keeping out black Africans, whether intended or not.

At the University of the North West the problem of non-integration is resolved in a different way. By keeping an almost exclusively white campus (Potchefstroom) in one part of the province and a black campus (Mafikeng) more than 100 miles away, the argument could be made that the former serves Afrikaans-speaking students. This argument would of course not be sustainable as local black Africans eventually demand access to the campus on their doorsteps; racial exclusion would simply not be possible any longer.

The University of Pretoria, situated as it is in a large urban metropolis surrounded by government departments, embassies and sprawling townships on all sides would, like the University of the Free State, experience the kinds of demographic pressures that demand racial inclusion and, with it, the expansion of English usage on campus. The preservationist politics that imagines Afrikaans dominance in any of these former white universities is, quite simply, misguided. This realisation is what lies behind conservative speculation, and initial planning, around a private Afrikaans university; its racial intentions could not be clearer.

Language as invitation

"Language itself both murders and welcomes," writes Donna Orange in a meditation on Nelson Mandela which appears as Foreword to a book on human dramas in post-conflict societies.[3] Indeed language remains one of the most powerful instigators and mediators of conflict between enemies. Nelson Mandela knew this as he practised his Afrikaans in prison so that by uttering words in the language he immediately gained access to hearts and minds in ways that made attentive listening possible, whether it was with his prison guards on Robben Island or when he invited the white Afrikaans-speaking woman from the secretary pool, Zelda la Grange, to work as his personal assistant.[4] The language has the potential to melt bitterness and build bridges across deep divides.

It is, perhaps paradoxically, the accommodation of Afrikaans to other languages that secures its future within the former white Afrikaans universities. This *"toeganglike"* (accessible, friendly) Afrikaans is what draws non-speakers to want to learn the language and communicate with friends on the other side of the racial divide. I saw this over and over again with undergraduate students when the language was no longer imposed as a barrier to communication. Black students wanted to learn the language, to memorise choice phrases, to show off to their friends in residence that they could, in fact, also communicate in Afrikaans. That shift from "take away Afrikaans" to "teach me to speak Afrikaans" is one of those remarkable transformations that would only be possible if intimacy, or physical proximity, was first established through the drive for desegregation of the university.

There is another reason for this relaxation of the demands for ideological Afrikaans, though, and that is the opening up of the world for students who wish to work and study in other parts of the world. Many white students plan to leave South Africa either temporarily in order to travel and experience the world, as au pairs for example, or to find work as professionals overseas if not eventually to emigrate to safer shores. For this to happen, facility in English becomes more and more important. This is what lies behind the shifts in language demographics not only in top English-speaking public schools where more and more Afrikaans-speaking parents send their children, but also in the university where the English classes now have Afrikaans-speaking students in attendance, making language planning on the basis of home language all the more difficult.

The problem for now is generational. Older academics, particularly in the humanities disciplines, are strident in their defence of the home language of the institution. They sense deep loss, even disrespect for the founding language of the university. They would write to and in the Afrikaans newspapers and email aggressive complaints to senior leaders who share their mother tongue. There would be complaints to governors of the university and an insistence, despite the laborious and costly exercise, that governing council documents be duplicated in English and Afrikaans. The individuals, and they are few, would insist on speaking Afrikaans in large gatherings, not simply to keep the policy of a parallel-medium institution alive, but to make a point even as many other colleagues begin to recognise the practicality of the situation where more and more academics now hired simply do not understand the language. Younger academics, and in particular young students, do not share this obligation for both reasons of pragmatism and economics, but express a commitment to include in a common campus language.

Such an achievement does not happen by osmosis. It required a comprehensive strategy that sets the conditions for accommodation, a labour of intimacy by a broad leadership collective.

Notes

1   The Bantu Education Act of 1954 came in the wake of the first Nationalist Party government edging to power for the first time in 1948 on the political platform of *apartheid*. Since then, Bantu Education has become the shorthand reference for black education under apartheid and, in particular, the education of black Africans.
2   See for example Willemse, H. and Dangor, S.E. 2012. *The Afrikaans of the Cape Muslims*. South Africa: Achmat Davids, Protea Boekhuis.
3   Orange, D. 2015. Reconciliation without Magic: Preface honouring Nelson Mandela. In Gobodo-Madikizela, P. (ed.) *Breaking Cycles of Repetition: A global dialogue on historical trauma and memory*. Germany: Budrich Academic Press, p. vii.
4   A warm-hearted bestseller written by Zelda le Grange gives unusual insight into the enjoined lives of the white woman assistant and the black President; le Grange, Z. 2014. *Good Morning Mr Mandela: A memoir*. New York: Penguin Publishing Group.

7 The labour of intimacy

Introduction

"Kill the Rector" would not be the last time a death threat would come my way, but this certainly was the first to appear on lamp posts around the country, visible to my children as they drove to school in late 2009. The black Ayatollah was a young leader of the African National Congress (ANC) in the Free State, Thabo Meeko, who got carried away in the excitement in front of the courts in Bloemfontein where the initial hearings for the "Reitz 4" were underway. Inciting the small, angry crowd, the youth leader made it clear that the new head of the UFS should be "shot and killed like a criminal". I remember thinking that there were some terrible leaders of universities, especially during the apartheid days, and none of them would have been issued with a political fatwa from a person belonging to the ruling party.

It helps enormously during such times to have been raised on the Cape Flats, that expansive, flat, colourless working-class area that runs across much of the otherwise beautiful city of Cape Town and where many people racially classified as "Coloured" were dumped during the years of forced removals under apartheid. The Flats is also home to the country's most notorious gangsters and, as young church leaders, we would frequently have to run, outrun and sometimes confront these mobsters as we tried to make our way from church to home without having to sacrifice a watch or money and, in some cases with fellow brethren, a life. Kevin, a dear friend and fellow youth leader, was merely walking two of the young church "sisters" to the train station for their ride home when one of those gangs plunged a screwdriver into his body. He expired in the car as we rushed him to Victoria Hospital in the Cape Town suburb of Wynberg.

You learn on that turf to be tough and to distinguish exaggeration from real threats. As much as these murderous words shocked many at the time, including my children who were born in another country, I knew these were the spontaneous, unthinking words of a populist caught up in one of those opportunistic South African moments where your radicalism – and therefore popularity – was measured by the extent to which you could sound completely outrageous. Still, the words stuck in short-term memory.

Now, several weeks later, Thabo Meeko was part of a delegation led by the national leader of the ANC Youth League to "sort me out" in my office – at least that is how the meeting was billed in some of the press. Outside the building a noisy crowd had gathered, baying for blood of the rector who had "forgiven" the white Reitz students. The media was there before everyone else with cameras set up and ready to flash as soon as the big men of the youth movement emerged from our meeting to announce their quarry dead. The meeting ended peacefully and without incident and, in words that would make me cringe, the youth leader announced to the deeply disappointed crowd: "He is one of us."

But the real drama happened immediately after the formal meeting when I asked the men around the table which one of them was Thabo Meeko, as if I did not already know from the televised shots of the "Kill the Rector" moments. A short, well-set man raised his hand tentatively and I asked him to follow me through the adjoining door into my office. I stood on one side of the room and Thabo on the other side, looking scared. "Come closer," I asked him, and as he made the hesitant steps forward I stretched out my arms to embrace him. No words needed to be spoken. I wanted him to feel close no matter what had happened. "I am sorry," he said in apology.

The grounds for change

Change cannot happen without trust, and in a deeply divided country and on a deeply divided campus, symbolic actions mattered as much as practical steps to undo the wrongs of apartheid. Reitz offered a unique moment to demonstrate compassion, a drawing closer to those who held power for so long and now, suddenly, were lost in the numbers of majority rule. The overriding logic of majoritarian rule could isolate, marginalise and drum home the defeat of white minority rule; or it could offer a stake in a very different kind of politics based not on the force of numbers but on a shared humanity.

The immediate task, however, was very practical. My white colleagues told me over and over again that the four white boys were really just a small group of bad apples. In other words, "*ons is nie almal so nie*" (Afrikaans, "we are not all like that"), a refrain I would hear often beyond that incident.

But I had seen enough during my listening and observing campaign across the campus to realise that there was something deeply wrong in the very ways in which the university constituted itself. In its architecture, paintings, rituals, ceremonies, initiations, hierarchies, messaging and organisation the institution had itself created the very conditions for young racists like this to emerge. They had, after all, won an award for their anti-integration video. Their head of residence, a lawyer no less, would not only have known about the horrific incident, he would defend them when discovered. In other words, until the video leaked on YouTube it was a non-issue in institutional terms.

It was clear to me that while the criminal courts (the workers represented by the director of public prosecutions) would have their say on the matter, as well as the civil court (the workers represented by the South African Human

Rights Commission), the institution stood blameless in the whole saga. This was simply not right, and so as the new head of the university and on the occasion of my inauguration in October 2009, I apologised to the workers as well as to decent black and white South Africans, and announced that the UFS would *as an institutional matter* allow the students back to complete their studies (two had already graduated at the time) with the purpose, of course, of dealing with them should they bother to show up. Something told me the suspended students would not take up the offer, given the potential for violence against them. But the symbolism was important.

It was this announcement that led to the "Kill the Rector" pronouncement and a flood of angry attacks from around the country and carried by every major news outlet at home and abroad. The Cabinet, for the first time in history, condemned a university rector from its chambers. It was a feeding frenzy as one politician after another tried to get in on the attack. Of course there were many expressions of support, especially from religious communities across the board, and from politicians, claiming that the country was born in the spirit of conciliation and that this action was consistent with what was done before by greater men and women. It was, however, the public letter of support issued by former Archbishop Desmond Tutu that turned the tide of criticism with his memorable words that "forgiveness is not for sissies" and his commendation of the decision. This action, together with the endorsement of Julius Malema, the firebrand leader of the ANC Youth League after his visit to my office, effectively ended the harshest criticism.

Then the hard work of reconciliation began as workers and students slowly found ways of coming together outside of the legal system in order to reset intimate relationships which had broken apart in the process of producing the humiliating video. In a dramatic evening inside the offices of the main building, the talking began with nobody present but the workers and the students. It was quiet for a long time and then, suddenly, a burst of laughter. We knew, then, that a breakthrough had been achieved and this was confirmed as white students and black workers came through the door. "The act of humiliation was public," I told the group; "the quest for forgiveness would have to be public too." This was done in a smaller ceremony that also involved the families of the workers (the families of the students did not show up) and then in a larger public ceremony as well. The grounds were now laid for the broader transformation of the University of the Free State. What should we do next?

Immersion abroad

It was clear that to change the university we would have to begin with the first-year students. The seniors were far too compromised by the deadweight of race socialisation at the UFS and any investment in those who were a few months away from graduation would have little impact on deep transformation. In theory, the first years would be immersed in a range of activities to prepare them for a new campus and country and, over time, these students would become the seniors and senior leaders of the university over the three–five-year period of their undergraduate degrees. By the fifth year, we expected to see positive outcomes since the seniors would then dictate the new institutional culture and climate, and set the pace for social cohesion. In other words, there would be no short-term turnaround because the debilitating practices associated with racism, authoritarianism, initiation and the other humiliation rituals were so deeply embedded in the experiences of seniors that there was little we could do – apart from imposing external discipline – that might change that scenario. One example would make this point.

After repeated visits to one men's residence, we were beginning to feel a sense of deep frustration. Despite the ban on liquor, the seniors found ways of bringing in the offending bottles and hiding them in the residence. Our position was not against students' drinking; that was their prerogative having reached the legal age for alcohol consumption as senior students. The problem was the very strong correlation between drunk students and racist, sexist and other violent behaviour on the campus. The university needed some respite from what was becoming a very serious problem in some of the men's residences. We pleaded and warned. We opened our offices for victims to come and talk, and put the seniors on notice. But the stories kept coming in of abuse of juniors late at night when the doors to the residences closed. The juniors were scared witless and would not tell of some of these abuses. "What happens in the House stays in the House" was the familiar mantra.

And then it happened. A few black boys were ejected from their rooms and the drunk white seniors decided to urinate on their bedding. I was over there with my senior team in a flash. The hasty investigation confirmed what had happened, and the leader of the pack confessed to the dastardly act. I told him to leave immediately and not come back pending the formal investigation. That would be the end of his studies. Since that day the house returned to normal and there would be no incidents of that kind ever again. The student pleaded, citing the earlier reconciliation initiatives of the leadership. Our response was clear – "You understood the rules of the new game and, despite repeated warnings you decided to abuse students anyway. That is it; you're out of here."

I am still convinced that anything short of clear, decisive action would have kept that residence, and all male residences, in a continued tailspin of racist abuse and humiliation of first-years, black and white, for years to come. But what was also clear was that many of the seniors were beyond redemption given the little time we still had with them inside the institution, and given their own brutalisation at the hands of seniors when they were juniors. Here was an eerie reproduction at play: even though junior students hated the initiation at the time, and all the silly rituals that go with it, when they became seniors they, too, wanted to have those privileges and scare the living daylights out of the new juniors. And that is how the culture of abuse sustained itself. What was equally disconcerting was that black students were beginning to claim the privilege of handing down abuse as they moved towards senior status.

The problem for students, and for much of the surrounding community, is that stuck within the immediate world known to you, you begin to think that that is the only reality and the only possibility, in this case, for student life and learning. We then designed the Study Abroad programme called the F1 Leadership for Change initiative. More than one hundred of the most talented first-year students, diverse by race and class, would be selected to spend a short time studying abroad. The students were carefully chosen for future leadership potential and the groups of six to eight students were intentionally diverse so that their long travels abroad would require close interaction in buses, planes, residences abroad and classes in another country.

Initially the students were all placed in US universities simply because we had regular contacts with colleagues from that side of the world. The US Embassy, in response to the crisis of Reitz, had generously allowed Fulbright scholars and language specialists to be placed at the UFS to assist, and to learn. This, together with my own networks of academic friends from Cornell University in the east to Stanford University in the west, enabled us to quickly create placement opportunities for our undergraduate students. Other institutions included Cleveland State University, New York University, the University of Minnesota, Clark University, Appalachian State University and others.

We did not overprescribe content, but for the two to three weeks of immersion students typically were exposed to critical conversations, workshops and classes on citizenship, race, identity and multiculturalism. Each university, within the broad directive to expose the students to the range of diversities in US institutions, composed their own programme emphases, with great success. It must be said that the degree of care and the diligence of planning on the part of the US universities were really outstanding.

Our students worked with diverse groups of US students and came to understand common struggles for racial justice, but also other kinds of identity politics including lesbian gay, bisexual, transgender (LGBT), gender and disability discrimination. For many students from conservative Free State, this was at least initially an experience of significant disorientation as they tried to learn new languages even as they recognised that their own experiences were not exceptional. They would struggle, as expected, to find each other never previously having, in many cases, been so close in either travel or learning to white or black youth. And they would struggle with the new content to which they were now being exposed.

The results were stupendous. Out of this group of students came the senior student leadership in almost every segment of university life, from residence heads to Student Representative Council (SRC) leaders to heads of student associations, and more. They became, without exception, men and women of great character and over time they would model in their very behaviour the kinds of racial intimacy and maturity that we had worked towards. You would begin to recognise the F1 graduates simply from their optimism and energy. One such student was almost breathless as he told what happened on his return. "Prof, I ran home and I told my parents 'not all white people are bad'."

Reorientation at home

Our dean of students came into the UFS from his position as a consultant of a small company doing diversity training for the university in the wake of the Reitz scandal. A young man active in citizen politics from the more conservative, white University of Stellenbosch, he had a fine understanding of the fears and hopes of young white Afrikaans-speaking students. A theologian by training in the Afrikaans churches, he was nevertheless ecumenical in his understandings of faith, hope, healing and the transformation of South African youth.

Across the campuses the dean led workshops amounting to more than one hundred hours per year, targeting all students from first-years to seniors, from residence students to commuting students, and from local students to students from all over the country, and other parts of the world. The core of this training was a simple but very effective curriculum in stereotype reduction. Students generated from within themselves, and then analysed, their own preconceptions of black and white people, for example, and then discussed the nature and consequences of stereotyping among themselves.

There were many workshops on leadership development and how to lead within divided communities. Speakers from inside and outside campus populated the lives of students. Throughout, an emphasis was placed on bringing in facilitators who themselves came and spoke from very diverse life experiences such as white or black, gay and lesbian, able-bodied and disabled. Training took place before campus opening at the beginning of the South African academic year (January) and after campus closed (December) for the Christmas holidays. No summer or winter vacation would come and go without training workshops for students on, around and at some distance from campus. Some of these workshops were led by university staff but, in the course of time, they would be led by students themselves. Some were run by church groups and non-governmental organisations and others by departments within Student Affairs, as the dean's office was called. In short, the campus was saturated with training workshops from early in the morning to late at night. And the core message was remarkably stable – we care about the human project and about the academic project.

Laying the foundations of change

We needed a compelling message that would capture the imagination of staff and students in their everyday lives on campus. The communication system contained two simple, consistent messages – the human and the academic projects. Nothing else.

The *human project* stressed, in everything we did, our common humanity. We held countless workshops about race as a social construction, and therefore open to change, and yet race as real in the experiences of students. Our goal, we reminded students at every turn, was to transform these categories so that, over time, we would begin to approach each other not through our apartheid nicknames but through the lens of our common humanity. This would prove to be difficult not only because of the emotional attachments to the racial identities being challenged, but because of the everyday common sense by which South African students, and the citizenry at large, came to believe that there were four fixed, insoluble, unchanging "racial groups" – African, Coloured, Indian and white.

There was, moreover, real material benefit in giving new life to these apartheid identities; for whereas before they yielded privilege to whites, this side of apartheid these labels would once again yield real material benefit for Africans, in particular, given new government policies of affirmative action. Needless to say, Africans wanted race back to claim benefit while whites, with a sudden affliction of amnesia, complained bitterly against racial distinction in the awarding of everything from jobs to tenders to promotions to university places. The cause of racial nationalism had merely changed hands.

The human project was, moreover, not a racial project and this would have to be seen in our public actions. So, for example, by far the most public of our human commitments, apart from reconciliation, was the No Student Hungry Campaign – a major investment in feeding top academic students who had no money to feed themselves. What made this campaign so successful in the public mind was its emotive power – the linking of a university's sense of duty to the very real hunger pangs experienced by young students. The problem was counter-intuitive: universities pretend that this is not a problem and the public assumes that students who manage to access higher education naturally also have access to food. Yet our research showed that around 60 per cent of our students experienced food insecurity. The public face of this campaign was not, however black. It was, throughout, a demonstration of need among both the white and black poor, and that in this most basic of human needs the UFS would respond to a human problem rather than a racial one.

No other university in the world has the human project as part of its bold mission statement, and we were proud of that distinction. Few things mattered more given our divided and clamorous past than to elevate our common humanity to centre stage in the life of a public university. With every racial incident that occurred on campus, our first instinct was to see whether the parties were prepared to talk and resolve the problem through dialogue. Sometimes this worked but at other times the victim, or the parents of the victim, wanted nothing less than justice in the courts. The case of two special young people would, however, surprise me beyond my own expectations.

Two black women students claimed that they were crossing one of the many roads criss-connecting the sprawling main campus when four men in a car approached the pedestrian crossing. They barely stopped but missed the women students. Hanging out of the car, one of the white male students made a derogatory remark to the young women whereupon his friends laughed loudly and the car drove off. I remember being deeply saddened as the soft-spoken women took me through their ordeal without a hint of anger. They had taken the licence plate number of the car and so it was easy tracking down the culprits.

Within an hour, security had found the driver of the car and he made his way to my office.

After some discussion, the driver confirmed what had happened and I called in the women students. I was quite frankly tired by now, two years into my tenure, by the constant stream of micro-aggressions of the kind reported by black students and gay and lesbian students, the two main complainant groups. As the young women sat across from me in the lounge area I promised firm disciplinary action. And then this: "No, no professor, we do not want to hurt them. Don't do anything to them. That was not our intention. We simply want them to acknowledge what they did and say they are sorry. That would be the end of it." The male student driver, and his companions, did just that. I hugged them and sent them on their way. I told one of the women students, "I think you understand the human project better than I do."

Leadership action was required to constantly demonstrate the human project in action on and off campus. Here the university would respond quickly to stories in the press about very real human dilemmas, and act swiftly – like the white student who was refused entry into a Cape Town medical school. Despite her near-perfect academic marks in all her subjects, the racial quota system of that institution kept her out. We called the young woman and gave her a place in our medical school. Or the black student from Durban who achieved straight distinctions in all her subjects despite living in a shack and studying by candlelight. We flew her to Bloemfontein and paid for her studies towards becoming a chartered accountant. Or the poor white student from a fishing village in the rural Western Cape who was so poor she was forced to enrol in a black school where she made close friends and excelled in her academic work. We brought her to campus. All three enrolled and the public nature of their dilemmas, and the resolution, symbolised the human project more than any words in a mission statement could ever accomplish. The fact that these human interventions were always pursued without regard to race also communicated a more powerful message about inclusion and embrace.

The *academic project* would become an equally important symbolic statement about what the UFS stood for. It was common cause throughout the country that the standards of school education were very low and that this held dire consequences for the production of talent through our universities, the provision of skilled labour for our economy, and the morale of young people graduating from schools. On paper they appeared to pass, with 30 per cent and 40 per cent the minimal pass marks in various subjects, but in reality the students did not have the competence and skills for jobs or higher education. They knew that and the high dropout rates in the 23 universities would confirm this lamentable state of the public school system.

There could be no more powerful signal to the public, but also to the students themselves, that the academic bar would be lifted. Of course this was counter-intuitive. For decades the white universities had claimed to have superior standards and the racist argument would be made with varying degrees of politeness that admitting black students, and hiring black staff, would somehow drop the standards. That trope had a taken-for-granted, common sense meaning in the white community no matter the facts. The truth was that the academic standards in South African universities, white or black, were always low by international comparison, made worse by the fact that our institutions of higher learning were ill-equipped to teach effectively and compassionately to students from more and more diverse social, economic and political backgrounds.

The idea therefore that the UFS would raise its academic standards was interpreted in some quarters as a handy way of keeping out black students. Conservatives responded with glee since they thought this would ensure the university retained its dominant white student demographic. Black activists responded with dismay because they reasoned that black students were deliberately being excluded, again. Of course this did not happen, since the recruitment net was now national and regional as we pursued the best students from every demographic in South Africa and outside its borders. Suddenly English-speaking white students, black private school students and white Afrikaans-speaking students from the top schools in the northern and southern provinces would grow their numbers on campus, especially as the reputation of the university for academic standards and human togetherness took hold around the country.

On campus the students were not happy at all. The entrance scores for first-time students were higher. Class attendance was compulsory, with electronic fingerprint technologies in place to monitor attendance. Entrance to examinations now required a predicate (i.e. a mark of at least 40 per cent in various subjects) simply to qualify to write the finals; gone were the days of wasting time throughout the semesters and then hoping for a miracle in the final examination. Then, as time passed, the students started to experience success and hailed the same measures they had complained about. Slowly the UFS moved from having one of the lowest pass rates in the country to something more respectable.

But the real bitterness would come on the side of academics. The standards were especially low for the professoriate. The criteria for excellent scholarship were not demanding enough and this reflected, also, in the low prestige of scholars as measured by the ratings of individual researchers by the National Research Foundation. At the time we had no A-rated scholars, for example. There was understandable angst from academics who were coming up for promotion based on the old criteria. "The goalposts were shifting," they said, having played by the familiar rules. "I do not know of another way of raising our academic status," I responded. But it was tough and there were threats of legal action, and one or two left the university to institutions where they would more readily be promoted. In time the research performance of the university would also grow exponentially, and top-rated scientists and scholars would come through the ranks.

As a comparativist, there was a much bigger risk at play in the post-apartheid university, and that was the demise evident in so many post-colonial institutions where democracy somehow came to be defined by the lowering of standards, by rampant state intervention and by the reduction of resources for scholarship. Standards, I argued, were not a white thing but a postcolonial dilemma and, despite the troubled history of the word in relation to exclusion of black and poor people in South Africa, we needed to bring white and black students, and faculty, of top quality into the same institutional spaces if racism was to be effectively countered.

The academic standard, in other words, could overcome prejudice.

Changing symbols

There was a deep need within the University, as in the country, for symbolic reparation. In the country it happened unevenly from one province to the next, with the wholesale changes of names and street buildings from Pretoria to Durban and, more slowly, to Cape Town. Few countries built more museums following regime change. The national icon, Nelson Mandela, must have been embarrassed by the number of streets named after him and the number of busts planted in his honour. But the former white universities changed their symbols very slowly, if at all. Rhodes University is still called by the name of the imperialist Cecil John Rhodes and whose symbols still adorn prominent parts of the University of Cape Town. The University of Stellenbosch buried its first black rector out of the D.F. Malan Memorial Centre. Black universities, without a conservative white alumni base to attend to, would quickly name every building after a black nationalist leader, especially if that person was from the ruling party.

Black students made it clear through various institutional surveys at the University of the Free State, and through a project called Sense of Belonging, that they felt estranged from the place. Something had to be done, and our approach was to do this sensitively but firmly, and without the heavy hand of the black universities where "everything had to change". The UFS position was that the very naming and renaming process should, in itself, reflect the spirit of conciliation. Obviously offensive names had to make way and, at all costs, we would avoid naming buildings after politicians, especially living ones.

The first set of changes did not require a policy but simply a change of practice. The opening of meetings with Christian prayers and Bible readings stopped. It was simply untenable that as we hired Muslim, Jewish and also non-believers, such exclusionary practices were, as I tried to convince my colleagues, in fact unchristian. Elevating those kinds of changes to a policy change would have raised considerable political noise on the outside, especially from the watchdog of white conservatism, the local Afrikaans newspaper. But colleagues, to my surprise, were quite happy to allow this practice to simply slip away. "We are a public university," I insisted on inquiry, "not a parochial institution" and therefore open to all believers, including unbelievers.

The next change, which did require policy approval by the highest authority of a South African university – the council – was the emblems of the university. This was going to be difficult. I remember how the former vice-chancellor of the University of Pretoria, where I was dean, tried to change the emblem of that institution, marked by the Afrikaner ox wagons, and replace it with the Mapungubwe rhinoceros, and the heavy resistance that otherwise inclusive move encountered. The ox wagons, a racially exclusive symbol, remain to this day.

On this proposed change we wanted to be as consultative as possible and opened the door for comment from both the campus community and outsiders. But first we had to put something on the table. Working with a consulting firm, and conscious of the mandate for change and continuity, the team created a beautiful logo that captured the wheat fields of the rural province, the light of the intellect and the union of our people. Gone were the Boer War insignia of the trumpets. But what really caused an uproar from white conservatives was the changing of the motto which read, "*In deo sapientiae lux*" (In God the light of wisdom). We wanted to keep the transcendent meanings of the motto but in ways that opened spirituality to a broader community of interpretation. And so, after much discussion and debate, the Council settled on "*In veritate sapientiae lux*" (In truth the light of wisdom).

"They removed God from the motto," was the outcry. Strong language, including violent expletives, was signed onto the blank canvases put out for the campus community for comment on the new logo and motto. I wondered in those moments how such violent language could come to defend a God of peace. Of course in matters of religion emotions take over and the chance for reason, dialogue and exchange takes a back seat. This certainly was the case with the transformation of the institutional emblem.

Throughout this process, and in part as a result of the nature of the conservative backlash, I became aware of how secular God had become for this segment of our people. It was not the God of the Bible but an ethnic, violent, sectarian god who not too long before that had sanctioned apartheid, all its laws and its military violence against the people of the country. It was that narrow, Afrikaner, Calvinist god of the mind that appeared on the motto, not the God of "whomsoever believeth" but a racist construction of the divine. In my heart as a leader I was at peace; this was the right thing to do.

Much easier was the introduction of new artistic symbols throughout the campus. Fortunately a generous donation from the Lotto and a progressive young Portuguese South African artist came together at the same time at the UFS. Angela de Jesus designed a set of African art symbols, from a thinking stone to wooden sculptured animals and open-air seats, that immediately provided a genuinely indigenous art form to which students could relate. Some of the wire sculptures were deliberately provocative, such as the man on an ox-like creature being led by another, suggesting an interpretation of master and servant, and yet wonderfully ambiguous about the identities of the two men.

Perhaps the best appointment in the university was a progressive Afrikaans cultural activist appointed to Student Affairs who would transform all public events involving students but within the spirit of conciliation. The standard musical events – the "*Klein Sêr*" (Small Serenade), involving first-year student residence competitions, and "*Sêr*" (the all-student competition) would be carefully composed to ensure diverse participants for the first time – previously, reflecting also the white- and black-dominated residences, these events were mainly segregated. The criteria required a diverse repertoire, including traditional African songs and in different languages; previously, Afrikaans songs and popular English songs dominated. Then there was a spectacular, annual musical event open to the public, The Extravaganza, in which the visiting musical acts were always black and white, catering to the range of musical and cultural tastes. So too the large concert after the Rag competition, in which students raised funds for welfare organisations, would create at least two big "acts" from Afrikaans (white) and non-Afrikaans (black) artists. In other words, great care was taken in the range of artistic performances to make sure that all students felt included throughout the academic year. This was expensive but necessary to build, from the ground up, a very different kind of institutional culture, welcoming and inclusive.

Changing who teaches and who leads

You cannot change a century-old university without transforming its teaching staff. What government pressed for was "employment equity", meaning equal access to job opportunities in line with "the demographics of the country", as its most ardent advocates would advance. For purposes of social justice this relentless if sometimes clumsy push for job equity by the Department of Labour made perfect sense given the long history of race-based job reservation and the banishment of especially Africans into unproductive rural economies. In a university such a simple equation cannot be easily transplanted from factories into lecture halls.

The problem is especially marked in the social sciences and humanities where the disciplines were soaked in the ideologies of apartheid even as some colleagues would deny, or fail to see, its social and epistemological dilemmas. This was not a white thing: it was a problem for both black and white graduates from these disciplines who now taught the received canons from the past disconnected from the tumultuous changes in politics and society since apartheid. Whether it was *"volkekunde"* in anthropology or *fundamental pedagogics* in teacher education or *race-essentialist medicine* in psychiatry, you cannot simply charge people with new knowledge. Academic teachers need to be trained differently, obtain their doctorates outside the country, immerse themselves in unfamiliar literatures and be prepared to emotionally and intellectually disconnect from what is intimate and secure knowledge on which their careers were built. For many South African colleagues who obtained all their degrees from the same university, or the same subset of universities, the task of transforming knowledge was near impossible. This is a problem for all South African universities whether in the English, Afrikaans or historically black institutions.

For this purpose we invested heavily in new scholars and especially young post-doctoral academics through the Prestige Scholars Programme. One of the key strategies behind this initiative was to place these young scholars in the international academy alongside leading researchers in their fields for periods of one year or less. The other strategy was to hire "from outside" both the province and the usual network of universities but also outside of the country. One key appointment, especially as head of department, would yield immediate curriculum impact in the direction of more critical and diverse literatures, methodologies and perspectives on traditional disciplines; and the students would notice.

Given low turnover among academics, conservative labour relations regimes and pressure from government to extend retirement ages (a strange orientation for a presumably radical Ministry of Higher Education and Training led by the Communist Party secretary-general), it would be difficult to alter the face and perspectives of those who teach – quite apart from *what* they teach.

No transformation within universities is possible, however, without changing the knowledge base for learning. Both social and institutional knowledge are artefacts of colonial and apartheid histories, and yet South African universities have not had any fundamental renewal of the core knowledge that constituted the disciplines over decades.[1] Knowledge is, however, the most difficult thing to change for its encapsulation in curriculum is expressed as values, interests and power which are emotional, unequal, partisan and entrenched. That was the next task.

Note

1 The point is made at length in my book: Jansen, J.D. 2009. *Knowledge in the Blood: Confronting race and the apartheid past.* Stanford, CA: Stanford University Press.

8 Intimate knowledges

Introduction

This would not be the only case in the history of universities where a curriculum would generate heated controversy.[1] The anger was palpable. White students were angry that they had to discuss and debate the apartheid past. White male students, in particular, stuck together in the long rows of seats in the massive auditorium, and in the mandatory tutorial sessions where smaller groups would assemble to deal with the more difficult questions presented in the large lecture hall. The body language, part aggressive and part disinterested, told the whole story. The well-trained facilitators had their hands full in the tutorial sessions, especially where conservative students were present in visible numbers.

But the newly arrived high school graduates had to be there for no student would graduate without completing UFS 101, as we called the compulsory core curriculum for every first-year student. Black students, by and large, went along with this controversial module though few among the 5000 students had much interest in learning about the past, let alone how to deal with it. What created this consternation among entry-level students into the University of the Free State was the subject of *intimate knowledges* that they had never before been required to grapple with at close quarters, black and white students together at the same table, around a common offering.

The knowledge of good and evil

The transformation of what we know, and how we come to know, about ourselves and others has not been part of the change at South African universities since the advent of democracy in 1994. For the most part, all public universities continued to teach the same chemistry or architecture or anthropology or medicine that they did under apartheid. Where there were changes, these were incremental and predictable, the kind of evolutionary changes that good scholars bring to the discipline not because of upheavals in science and society but as part of the normal updating and revisioning that accompany curriculum change everywhere.

In the almost two decades from Knowledge and Power (1991)[2] to Knowledge in the Blood (2009),[3] the core of what we call curriculum knowledge has remained largely undisturbed over the period of regime change in South Africa. This in itself is an indictment of the superficiality of change in a country whose history, culture, economics and polity remains trapped inside the twin legacies of colonialism and apartheid.[4] This does not mean that nothing has been done inside institutions of higher learning.[5] Under the authority of the South African Qualifications Authority (SAQA) and its demand for statutory compliance, university modules and programmes have been formatted into qualifications organised into neatly manageable teaching and learning "chunks" with credit hours, assessment criteria and exit-level outcomes.[6] But knowledge itself lies undisturbed, its troubled origins and purposes remaining largely unquestioned.[7]

This is partly what motivated the introduction of the first ever undergraduate core curriculum in South Africa on an institution-wide scale and required of every first-year student at the University of the Free State. The idea was to add value to the technical and disciplinary knowledge that every student would receive over 3–5 years of study. In South Africa there is no concept of a liberal arts curriculum. Students start to study for careers from the moment they first set foot on campuses to become engineers or teachers or accountants or lawyers. There is little exposure of science students to the humanities or nursing students to the arts. From day one, a future doctor learns anatomy and a future journalist media studies. The result is a narrow professional or technical training that makes students largely inarticulate in the broader realms of knowledge about, say, global economics and finance or the origins of human cultures.

More seriously, students never have to grapple with the foundations of the old and new South Africa, how we came to be and why we are the way we are. It would be like German students after the war never having been taught about the Holocaust, or Rwandan students after the genocide never having to dialogue about the ethnic massacres even though thousands of sanitised skulls were visible in any number of public displays. This powerful *null curriculum*, as Elliot Eisner once called it,[8] with its potentially dangerous consequences – ignorance is not a void – was what led to "the history question" as part of the UFS 101 curriculum.

The design of 101

The core curriculum is organised around universal, enduring questions from across the disciplines. In its first iteration, the core questions were the following:[9]

1. How should we deal with the violent past? (history)
2. Are we here alone? (astronomy)
3. How small is small? (nanotechnology)
4. Why is the financial crisis described as "global"? (economics)
5. What does it mean to be fair? (law)
6. Did God really say? (theology)
7. How do we become citizens? (sociology)

The questions and disciplines involved would change from year to year but our goals were the same, as advertised: "UFS101 exposes students to challenging questions aimed at disrupting existing knowledge and ways of thinking, by engaging them in current issues across different disciplines."

It is very difficult to introduce a core curriculum into any university, anywhere. Professors are reluctant to give up disciplinary time when they already feel there are not enough contact hours with students. Students, especially in countries without a liberal arts curriculum tradition, feel strongly that they came to university for a specific technical or professional training, not a broader education. Parents feel they pay for that degree with vocational purposes and, in conservative communities, there is a strong reaction to "liberal" ideas in general but especially on controversial subjects such as apartheid or slavery.

We were very much aware of these difficulties. Our strategy was to involve senior professors from different disciplines in the very design and teaching of the core; to lay emphasis on the secondary benefits which everybody agreed were lacking – academic literacy, critical thinking, basic writing competences and online computer skills; to absorb the financial outlay in the central administration even though the educational benefits would accrue to all faculties; to pilot the core with a smaller number of students; and to make successful completion of the curriculum a condition for application to study abroad programmes. It did help that the core was championed and, initially, driven from the rector's office.

The problem was that the students still had to engage the curriculum and I was very conscious of the brooding negativity in their ranks, tempered somewhat by first-year curiosity that the rector would be teaching the first unit: "How should we deal with our violent past?" I knew I would have to model the teaching for subsequent units, and that the entire curriculum could stand or fall by whether its content and pedagogy were intellectually engaging and technologically cutting-edge in ways that the students might not experience in all their formal degree courses.

Teaching 2000 or more students at one time was something none of us had ever done. As I looked out across the huge auditorium, my heart raced with excitement. I had taught large classes before, as a schoolteacher and a university professor; the only difference was scale. I tried to persuade sceptical academics that this could be done by showing Michael Sandel's videos teaching large classes at Harvard using interactive questioning in the application of political philosophy to everyday problems.[10]

The violent past, Unit I

I split the module into two units. In Unit I, I drew attention to two heroes in their respective communities. The one, JP v der Merwe, was a teenager who fought on the side of the Boers in the Anglo-Boer War (1899–1902). He was caught by the British and, despite his youth, executed. I presented the case for "JP" from the point of view of the ill-armed Boers, long settled in their country, fighting the mighty British imperialist forces coming south for no reason other than to exploit the new-founded minerals, gold and diamonds, and extend their colonial powers. What else could the Boers do than to resist colonial occupation, and draw on the few men available, young and old, to fight? There seemed to be general sympathy for the young soldier so far, from both black and white students in the auditorium.

I then presented the case of Solomon Mahlangu, the very young anti-apartheid struggle hero who went into exile and then sneaked back into the country as an armed combatant and who was caught by the apartheid police, imprisoned, and hanged in Pretoria. I presented his case. The ANC had tried peaceful protests and official deputations to petition for democracy and the right to vote, without any progress over decades since its founding in 1912. Eventually, and reluctantly, in the 1960s Mandela and others decided to embark on armed struggle, careful not to harm people but to sabotage apartheid installations. Solomon Mahlangu, despite his youth, was executed like JP for the right to be free. Again, the students went along with the argument and there seemed to be sympathy towards Solomon and his cause as well.

Then it got interesting. I opened the floor to the main question: which of the two should be remembered as heroes in history textbooks today? "Both", said most of the students, though I depicted some murmuring in the audience. At this point I turned the tables on both proposed "heroes" through routines of Socratic questioning.

"But JP was fighting not for black people but for one group of whites to rule instead of another invading group," I queried. "The last thing on his mind was liberating black people," I pushed. "Surely JP also represented an outsider group that settled in the Cape from Europe and violently opposed and suppressed native majorities?"

This set of questions started to divide opinion and I had to constantly remind the students that this was a "devil's advocate" position and that I was less interested in the "correct" answer than in their ability to reason and provide justifications for whatever answer they were prepared to put on the table. This cold, clinical reasoning sometimes went over the heads of the passions now driving the response. For the most part, however, I was able to contain the responses from both sides. What was a complete surprise, though, was the number of black students granting native status to JP, and defending his standing as hero.

I did the same with Solomon. "Surely this man was a terrorist?" I argued. "He went into a shopping centre heavily armed and, despite the ANC's promises, real people, non-combatants, were also killed in the armed struggle." Then I insisted that while anyone had the right to take up arms for their cause, that person has to foresee and accept the consequences of their violent actions. Once again, passion surpassed clinical arguments and, surprisingly, there were white students defending his courage in the face of the mighty apartheid state.

"What about the argument that they were both simply used and abused by older people in recruitment for adult causes? Is that not how many young people die today in wars dreamed up by older people?" The argument for a pacifist position was lost on the crowd as a broad, not complete, consensus emerged supporting recognition of both young men as heroes. I concluded with brief summary notes on the dangers of moral relativism and the fact that despite our best efforts, the past remains with us and affects our choices today, even though these events happened many decades before. We fool ourselves, I concluded, that we are unaffected by the passions and decisions of war from long ago. The question is not how we forget the past and move on, as many argue today, but how we deal with its consequences in the present so that we can, in fact, move beyond its shadows and not repeat the horrors of history.

There was a polite recognition of the point being made, but nothing could prepare me for the explosive reactions to Unit II. The gloves would come off and any soft consensus shattered, though not along completely along the lines I expected.

The present past, Unit II

This unit hit close to home in that the case up for discussion involved medical school admissions, a sore point for many top academic students who had failed to obtain placement. South Africa has only eight medical schools with limited, government-funded places. The University of the Free State has 140 funded seats but more than 3000 applicants per annum, most of them from the top academic students in the country and from the southern African region. In part because of pressure from the government's Department of Health, which funds medical school places, there is a requirement that more black students be admitted especially at the former white universities. Needless to say, when white students are not admitted, even when their exclusion is because of other top white candidates, there develops a rage from some parents and applicants against what they see as "affirmative action".

The UFS does not have a specific affirmative action policy since it recruits students, at the time of writing, primarily on academic marks and choice of English or Afrikaans instruction, based on the parallel-medium position of the institution. This means that most white students find themselves in the Afrikaans classes and most black and white English-speaking students in the English section. Needless to say, the system is far from perfect, in part because white English-speaking students from privileged schools tend to displace black students with less impressive academic scores, and because of Afrikaans-speaking white students indicating that their instructional language is English simply to secure a place in medical school. And then there are the demanding academic entrance scores, which effectively means that the long history of disadvantaged black schools continues to deliver students without the basic science, mathematics and language competences of middle-class white students with the social and educational privileges carried over generations. From the point of view of the medical school professors, they need students with strong academic records to ensure that those students actually complete the five-year medical degree, especially once they enter the clinical training component of the qualification in the third year. From the point of view of the university's senior leadership, there must be a mechanism, through recruitment and academic development, that ensures the success of all students and in particular those from disadvantaged backgrounds.

Nothing, however, brings home the fact of a "present past" more powerfully than the medical school case study. A white student Gertruida comes from a middle-class home but has to work very hard for her academic results. She is certainly not the typical white South African student, given that she volunteers her time working with dyslexic children in the black townships. Her marks are exceptional, with six distinctions in the final grade of high school.

Nthabiseng, the black student applying alongside Gertruida for the one remaining place in the medical school, has good results – three distinctions – despite studying in a shack without electricity and coming from a lousy township school. Which one of the two should be awarded the one remaining place in medical school?

At this point the 2000 students are jumping out of their seats, even before I descended from the teaching platform to walk among them and solicit their reasoned choices as to who should be admitted to medical school.

Then something strange happens. Black students start to make the case for Gertruida on the basis of academic merit. Of course most of the more conservative white students do so too, with a visible anger sometimes on their faces as if to say: "this is precisely what we're up against as whites in this country and as applicants to the medical school; blacks who are inferior are chosen for their skin. This is reverse racism." Some in fact put it as bluntly as that.

At this point, my own biography as a black South African and my intimate knowledge of racial exclusion and accommodation in medical schools must be managed. I cannot allow the students to sense my own emotions, even irritation, with some of the unintended but clearly racist arguments being made in defence of the not-so-mythical Gertruida. Jenna Min Shim, in one of the very few academic reflections on this dilemma, discusses the emotional and psychic toll of "doing" what she calls multicultural education when your own biography is implicated in the story.[11]

The surprise, though, was that black students were making the case for merit. Gertruida worked hard, they argued, and deserved to be recognised for her efforts. As I listened I wondered how black students supporting the white student, the first generation to benefit from a free society, made sense of the past. Did this history already pass them by? But I was fascinated by their voices; were they perhaps more enlightened than those of my generation who still insisted on reparation almost two decades since apartheid ended?

Of course many black students were vehemently opposed to Gertruida getting the vacant seat in medical school. Their arguments were more familiar: if Nthabiseng could do so well despite material and educational disadvantage, just imagine how we would fare in medical school once the playing fields were level?

With every argument made by the students I argued for the other side. "But what about Gertruida?" I asked some of the hyperventilating black students. She did not choose to be white. She did not benefit from apartheid. She was not even born when Nelson Mandela was released from prison, so why must she be held to ransom for the sins of the fathers? Was this not the kind of student you want in medical school – the kind that sacrifices from her position of privilege, her own time and resources to make a difference among black township children with autism? And what about our country, founded on the ideal of reconciliation? What message are we sending white youth who want to be part of our democracy – that no matter how hard they work, they still will come second best to black students? The mainly black students fumed even as they wondered whether these were my own ideas on the subject. Still, they understood these where the kind of questions they would need to work through with logic rather than anger, the mind rather than muscle.

Just as they were settling in, even enjoying these instructor-led questions, I then turned to the conservative white students who were taking emotive standpoints in favour of Gertruida. How could you claim she would make the better doctor? Can you really decide on the quality of a physician on the basis of high school marks? And then to the heart of the "present past" argument – is Nthabiseng responsible for her own miserable conditions of living quarters and schooling? Surely she should be rewarded for doing so well despite disadvantage? Since she was born she was behind, trying to catch up with Gertruida whose parents and grandparents could give her social, educational and financial advantage because of white affirmative action over more than a century.

The very word *apartheid* is like a red flag to a bull for conservative white South Africans, the students included. It is dead and buried. There were elections. Blacks have had almost 20 years in charge to sort things out. Why must white youth now suffer? "Reverse apartheid" once again. Let's just leave the past behind and move on.

It was time to conclude the heated lesson. I thanked the students for being honest about their feelings and thoughts on the matter. I emphasised that this module was less about who was right than whether they could reason their way out of controversy. I reminded them that this was a violent country and that one mark of the miseducation of South Africans, especially men, was the quick resort to physical confrontation in a difficult situation. A university, at the very least, has to privilege reason over rage, and that is why this module forms part of their broader education.

I tried to persuade the students that here was evidence of William Faulkner's well-known epithet: "the past is not dead; it is not even past."[12] What we were debating was not simply admissions to medical school but how the candidates came to be where they were – in terms of housing, education and opportunity – and how that long history continues to allocate life chances, and future physicians, even though we would like to imagine that we all start as equals with no lingering shadows from the past.

I suspect most of the students "got it", intellectually speaking, but in their own lives where these kinds of decisions to include or exclude were very real and immediate dramas, it might take some time, I pondered, for the history lesson to sink in. But their real emotions on the subject would come not from the teaching in the large auditorium but from the online exchanges in which they would engage me – I tried to respond to every question or challenge – and the small group tutorials, as well as the formal module evaluations that followed.

So what do students really feel about the knowledge of the past?

What follows is a sample of some of the more negative student responses, unedited except for grammar, and is noteworthy not only for the content but also the tone.

> I find UFS 101 a waste of time to those students who know what they want to study. It is an unnecessary subject to have and the fact that we should pay to listen to racism is just absurd! Gosh, they are bringing up apartheid up again.
>
> (Student 01)

> JUST stop with the racism! It is frustrating to dwell into the past of South-Africa. It is good to learn something and not be forced to listen to one person's opinion of white/black people . . . I would love to go to UFS 101 if I knew I would find it relevant to my life.
>
> (Student 02)

> The fact that they bring up the apartheid and racial discrimination often and it gets uncomfortable to sit there and be reminded of the past, most of us were too young to understand then. It is pushing for a racial argument that can intensify.
>
> (Student 03)

> Just cancel the subject . . . we are in varsity because we already know how to think critically . . . have you ever tried to apply for varsity?? It's not like the diploma just falls into your hands . . . we don't need to hear any more about the apartheid . . . it's over.
>
> (Student 04)

> STOP HAMMERING ON APARTHEID!!! WE WERE NOT APART OF IT!!! [sic]
>
> (Student 05; note that the upper-case emphasis comes from the student)

The history component is played out; I don't think people like discussing this anymore.

(Student 06)

Everything, it's discriminating towards white students and portrays them as horrible people, we live in the 21st [*sic*].

(Student 07)

I would like to know from you why things ALWAYS have to do with race? Don't you get tired of always having to make a fuss about race? It DESTROYS the little student life remaining on campus! It tires me, personally! It actually exhausts you this persistent thing about racism and discrimination. Can we all just become peaceful? We are STUDENTS!

(Student 08)

How should these sharply negative comments on the history core, in particular, be interpreted?

The first thing to note is that most South African students do not do the subject History in school. It is not a compulsory subject in the final three grades of high school, where students choose subjects in alignment with their vocational ambitions at the time. There has, in fact, been a sharp decline in the number of students taking History at school since the coming of formal democracy in 1994. In the minds of students, black and white, History is irrelevant to their present lives and disconnected from their future careers.

The argument, therefore, of overexposure to the past does not refer to formal education but rather to public conversation in general. There is, in the public sphere, often in relation to politicians a regular back-and-forth in the media about the legacy of apartheid, by black activists, and the need to move beyond it, by conservative white activists. When a prominent black person says "we can no longer only blame apartheid", such an utterance carries enthusiastic coverage in the Afrikaans press.

The second observation is the extreme sensitivity to even the mention of the word apartheid. This comes across, as in these selections of evaluative quotes, as aggressive and dismissive of any discussion on apartheid. As I indicated in *Knowledge in the Blood*,[13] the roots of this prickly reaction among white South Africans lie in shame and guilt, the constant embarrassment that comes with the reminder of the evil of apartheid perpetrated by whites and from which whites benefitted. The students merely reflect the angst and sometimes the very words of their parents when *apartheid* is even mentioned, and perceived to be used as a never-ending whipping to shame whites into silence. As one student (03) admits: "it gets uncomfortable to sit there and be reminded of the past."

The third important observation is the claim of innocence and ignorance in several of the responses. "We were not there." This is difficult to teach, the idea that not being physically "there" does not mean you were not a beneficiary of a system that carries unearned benefits over to you, as whites, and imposed impoverishment, as blacks. Here again is an understandable anxiety to start fresh, to wipe out handed-down memory and to imagine, however far-fetched, that inherited privilege has nothing to do with the apartheid past but with the industry and good fortune of hard-working parents; the corollary therefore has to be true as well, that blacks owe their disadvantaged position to personal and cultural group defects such as laziness and dumbness.

The fourth observation of relevance is that the mere discussion of apartheid is itself equated with "racism" in the minds of white students (students 01 and 02). There is no discussion on racism at all in these lectures, only on the legacies of apartheid in the present. The charge can be the result of poor understandings of *racism* as a concept, but it is more likely the result of the prior experience of apartheid in public discourse as an ever-present charge sheet against whites. The course itself, for obvious reasons, takes great care to present the case for JP (Unit I) and Gertruida (Unit II), the real and not-so-imagined white actors, as part of the intellectual engagement on the subject of History. But even this is not enough in a learned reaction from outside of class where the word *apartheid* carries, even for the second generation of white South Africans, considerable reactive hostility. Such volatile white reaction to the violent past, and the anxious need "to just move on" is not, of course, unique to South Africa as Nicholas Kristof wrote of Americans in a New York Times Editorial, *When whites just don't get it* (part 4).[14]

It should be said that the negative comments come mainly from white students and, in particular, from white Afrikaans-speaking students. Such collective criticism bound white strangers together in a very different kind of intimacy, one "formed around threats of the image of the world it seeks to sustain".[15]

Those resistant views certainly do not present the more general feeling about the history core among all students, black and white, including other white Afrikaans-speaking students. This became clear from the comments by students on my post-class blog:

> I would like to say that I have learned a lot from UFS101 to such an extent that I feel that UFS101 time it is very much limited, the issues that we have dealt with I think that we need to go deeper, for example the issues of how do we deal with the past. I felt that there is more that as youth we can achieve in healing our country because UFS101 it is the only module that give us the platform to discuss such issues.
>
> (Student 09)

> We now can talk about our history so freely with other races and not feel offended about the past.
>
> (Student 10)

> I think the content was relevant, however, from my observation what is said in class is forgotten when students get home. There is some stigma

on certain topics that make students feel uncomfortable. An example was the one on unit 4, How do we deal with our violent past? Before the lecture started a friend of mine said: It must be discomforting for many people, Black, White, Indians Coloureds, Asian for the topic to be brought up, as much as we would like to not repeat the same mistakes. When we get home we cannot openly discuss some of the topics as questions of who to blame pop up.

(Student 11)

The issue of Gertrude and Nthabiseng is one that made me think deeper before I give my final judgement.

(Student 12)

I did not find UFS 101 to make much sense either, but I have come to see what despicable and twisted things our forefathers have done ... For me it feels like people that were put in positions that should never have been allowed in civilisation in the first place.

(Student 13)

Coming into UFS 101 I was optimistic but I leave this classroom with absolute hatred in my heart because Afrikaans people have NO CLUE what black people went through and what black people continue to go through.

(Student 14)

I certainly learnt more about myself and my country. We grew up with parents that were open-minded and I am thankful for that.

(Student 15)

I think we should really learn more about our country, the mistakes of the past because there is no future without the past and we cannot come up with solutions without knowing the history behind the problem.

(Student 16)

The lecture ... made me realize that as long as we do not take affirmative action seriously we will always face problems of imbalances.

(Student 17)

The first thing I learnt was that the past should be a reminder of where we come from and that it should not determine where we are going.

(Student 18)

After today's lecture I realised how many more aspects one has to take into consideration before making complex decisions.

(Student 19)

If we as a nation can make peace with what our history entails [then] we can move forward. We can learn from it and apply our knowledge to become better citizens, if not leaders, for the future.

(Student 20)

I do want to say that this year's UFS 101 has changed my mind about so many things and I had become more open-minded about so many topics.

(Student 21)

The Lecture today really upset me mainly because I grew up in a "history museum" and was taught the Afrikaner history from an early age but never the South African history.

(Student 22)

I have a tendency to become uncomfortable when apartheid matters are being talked about . . . but I was very challenged in the Lecture when you brought up the powerful quotations that the past is not gone, in fact it's not even past.

(Student 23)

Clearly there were students who appreciated the historical insights, the commitment to logic and reason, and the opportunity for self-reflection. The selection above captures both white and black student experiences that go beyond "I liked" or "did not like" the course, and merit further reflection.

From the various student inputs it becomes clear that the subject of the past and especially the trigger word, *apartheid*, are uncomfortable for all students, black and white, conservative and more open-minded. For black students it is about not making their friends and peers feel uncomfortable. For white students it is the feeling about being in the dock, again. This hypersensitivity poses a difficult challenge for progressive pedagogy and that is why so many teachers and academics try to avoid the subject altogether – for the sake of the peace, as it were. And yet race, racism and its historical antecedents is the elephant in the classroom in a society, and on campuses, still so unequal and, at times, at war with itself.

There is also in these comments a sense of the broader problem, of what is allowable in the home when it comes to talking confidently about controversial matters such as the past (student 11). As indicated earlier, students come into university with learned sensitivities from their parents; for conservative white students it is the transferred anger and anxiety on everything from quotas in rugby to affirmative action in the job market. These measures are conveyed as remedies for the past, and the students learn to hate it.

It is not, therefore, a case of ignorance, that students simply do not know the South African past; it is that such knowledge is partial, incomplete and dangerous (student 22). Notice the anger on the part of this student as he comes to realise that he was not told the bigger story in a white nationalist home where history was in fact taught. And so whether or not students are taught formal history in the schools, they do learn about history, in a particular way, from other sources – the home being one of them.

Nor do the student's reactions simply project the absence of *factual knowledge* about apartheid history; what is on display in their response is *felt knowledge* about a past they would rather forget. The feeling of knowing substitutes easily for evidence, and it is this emotional conviction of being right that again shows up the curriculum reform fallacy that merely by teaching "the right history" students will change their minds about the past.[16]

Still, some black students are clearly agitated at the lack of understanding and the misplaced anger on the part of white students (student 14). While some black students clearly felt empathy with their white counterparts, others were inflamed by the insensitivity – the fact that white students do not "get it". The emotional impact of UFS 101 therefore splits both ways in what I elsewhere called, in referencing Eva Hoffman, "a clash of martyrological memories",[17] where both sides conceive of themselves as victims of a distant past and a still-unresolved present.

On the positive side there is a hint in several student comments, such as one above (student 15), that the home could be the place of a more open, tolerant and receptive context for learning about the past. This is also true for students who went to more liberal schools, particularly the old English schools, where deliberation and reflection on the past was encouraged and acknowledgment of historical harms publically stated. In such cases, students, black or white, would come into university with less of the harsh, emotional and aggressive responses to stories about the past.

What makes UFS 101 such a boiling pot for historical conversation is precisely because it is rare, something that does not happen in universities except for those students, a minority, who might find themselves in classes on southern African history or African literature and, even in such contexts, the texts and contexts might be deprived of a critical encounter with the colonial or apartheid past. But are white, and black, students really ignorant of their pasts, or is there something deeper lurking behind the sometimes aggressive responses to teachings about our violent history?

The power of ignorance

In 2014, two South African universities were rocked by very public racist scandals in what became known as the *Blackface* incidents. At the University of Pretoria two white women students dressed up as domestic servants, their chosen target for racial humour among friends.[18]

> All the tropes are lovingly – or should I say, hatefully – sculpted into shape: the *doeks* [headscarves] wrapped around heads; the wide unthinking grins; the shelf-like buttocks tilted prominently toward the lens. Thick gobs of black polish have been slathered on white skin: Project Dumb-Ass is complete.[18]

They are seen smiling brightly for a photograph at a student's birthday party that would be published on social media. The students were suspended from their residences, the university condemned the incident and after "mediation" by the South African Human Rights Commission the two offenders were to be allowed back into residence – they never lost class time – in 2015.

At the University of Stellenbosch, not long afterwards, two white male students painted their faces black, donned black and blonde wigs and held a tennis racket in their hands as they smiled at the cameras for another photograph that would be posted on social media. As in the Pretoria case, the two white men were targeting a specific group of black people, in this case the US sisters Venus and Serena Williams. The university made some mild statement that distanced themselves from the two students, declared the incident "unacceptable" and advised that there would be no action taken against them as they continued their studies uninterrupted.

The published images of white students poking fun at familiar black faces primed the public sentiment with a vengeance that saw the usual accusatory fingers pointed at individuals and institutions alike: universities were "not doing enough" and "how could these young people born in a democracy commit such racist acts?" From the other side, white friends of mine were instantly defensive, including liberal colleagues from other universities: "I know those girls, and I can honestly tell you they're definitely not racists." As in the Reitz case, denouncement and defence played see-saw at opposite ends of the racial playground.

Throughout the Blackface sagas few paid attention to what the students themselves were saying – that they *did not know* that they were offending anyone, followed by a hasty "sorry". In the case of the Pretoria girls, of white Afrikaans origin, their statement of apology read that "they had become more aware of" the need to act sensitively towards diverse cultures. "We now know," said the Stellenbosch boys, of white English origin, after the exposure, "that [blackfacing] is a disparaging practice used to portray offensive racial stereotypes and we cannot stress enough that this was not our intent." In short, they did not know then that their actions were offensive but now they knew, or were starting to know, what they did wrong.

The question I have put consistently to those defending these acts of "ignorance" is, why black people? Of all the stereotypes to make fun of within their own cultures – Afrikaans in the case of Pretoria and English in the case of Stellenbosch – why choose the most vulnerable citizens (black working-class women as domestics) or the most successful sporting stars (tennis)? Why not choose some other group other than, in both cases, black women – as in the Reitz case where the single man was not the original invitee to the initiation games? Then, of all the women tennis players in the world, why *these* two?

These are uncomfortable questions but, unless other possibilities are posed, it is difficult not to read the choices of these students as *racial* rather than *random*. Why would these students not choose their mothers or aunts or any other relatives? Of course it sounds absurd because these are not images of fun;

nobody in their white circles at the birthday party would find that humorous at all. You do not examine yourself in the mirror and have a hearty laugh.

That these could have been innocent cases of gross ignorance stretches credulity. Must we really believe that these white youth smearing dark polish or paint on their faces were completely unconscious of the horrors of apartheid where a black face meant discrimination, exploitation and worse? Should we further accept that young white youth, raised by domestic "servants", were not at all conscious of how they might hurt the very same people who reared them with love and care since birth?

I have come to understand that ignorance on the part of South Africans is not the absence of knowledge. Ignorance is, rather, a carefully cultivated position that relieves the culpable from any responsibility for the past. The excuse that censorship shielded whites from knowing how the system of apartheid operated, and with what effects, is a weak one. As former Minister of Police Leon Wessels eloquently put it, many did not want to know about the worst atrocities surrounding white citizens and in which many participated and all benefitted.

This is a point made incisively by the philosopher Charles Mills when he speaks about "an epistemology of ignorance". Ignorance for him is not an intellectual vacuum but a particular way of knowing the past that helps make the present appear innocent.[19] In this frame of mind whites are therefore able to:

> nominally decry racism but downplay the impact of the racist past on the present configuration of wealth and opportunities. So remedial measures of racial justice are not necessary, and white privilege from illicit structural advantage, historic and on-going, can remain intact and unthreatened.

In 2015, an entire *Handbook of Ignorance Studies* was published, a first in the social sciences, and one dedicated to examining the content, purposes and effects of ignorance across disciplines; it was also the book that would give the study of ignorance a name, *Agnotology*.[20]

"I do not know" in fact means "I do not want to be reminded that I know", for the burden of such knowledge is, in emotional terms, unbearable and in material terms a real risk to clinging privileges. The children of adults have learnt to shadow-box around these same issues from their parents. They have learnt hardness and sensitivities to a fixed set of South African tropes. Here the work of historian of science Robert Neel Proctor helps us understand the intergenerational transmission of the problem when he observes that "ignorance and uncertainty can be manufactured, maintained, and disseminated".[21] His finding would explain why 18-year olds, especially white men who had not lived through apartheid, would react with such fury in a non-accusatory class lecture that draws out discussion on the legacy effects of apartheid.

These are the kinds of question taken up by South African scholar Melissa Steyn, who examines deposits of white and black citizens into the *Apartheid Archive* as she tries to understand the making of ignorance in the upbringing of white children under apartheid. She finds an active ignorance among white South Africans and how families reared their children so that "learning what not to know, what not to notice, was integral to being socialized"[22] into and given safe passage through apartheid society. And in learning ignorance, "intimate relationships [played a pivotal role] in securing the racial order".[23]

Ignorance is calculated bliss. The standard policy response in reaction to a racist crisis in the schools – children need to be taught "our" history – is a necessary but hopelessly inadequate response in an ignorance analysis of knowledge. They already know the past and the assumption that some corrective knowledge in the formal curriculum will alter minds, much as an injection into the bloodstream deals with viral load, is naive. As one of my doctoral students found, even when using the same state-sanctioned history curricula in which the teaching units were the Sharpeville Massacre (1960) and the Soweto Uprising (1976), white schools taught completely different content than black township schools in the same academic term.[24] That is because curricular knowledge is mediated in powerful ways through the institutional culture of the school and the ideological orientation of the teacher. Simply "putting in" new knowledge to dispel ignorance is not the answer. Something much deeper and more intimate has to be attained for change to take place.

Notes

1 In the USA, it was the so-called "Western Civilization" requirement at some universities that remained the landmark case for curriculum controversies at North American universities; see Lindenberger, H. 1990. On the Sacrality of Reading Lists: The Western Culture debate at Stanford University. In Lindenberger, H. *The History in Literature: On value, genre, institutions.* New York: Columbia University Press. In South Africa, the most memorable of such curriculum controversies took place at the University of Cape Town; see Mamdani, M. 1998. Is African Studies to be turned into a new home for Bantu Education at UCT? *Social Dynamics* 24(2), 63–75.
2 Jansen, J.D. (ed.) 1991. *Knowledge and Power: Critical perspectives across the disciplines.* Johannesburg: Skotaville Publishers, was an edited collection of papers on how apartheid had constituted a range of disciplines from dentistry to sociology, and from education to urban planning.
3 Jansen, J.D. 2009. *Knowledge in the Blood: Confronting race and the apartheid past.* Stanford, CA: Stanford University Press, was my account of the circuitry of trans-generational knowledge as it flowed through the agencies of socialisation of young white youth and into an uninterrupted formal curriculum of a historically white Afrikaans university.
4 Nobody has made this point more graphically than Mahmood Mamdani in various talks and papers during his time at the University of Cape Town.
5 It could be argued that the more exciting revisioning of the curriculum has happened in the public sphere, though the rush to memorialise everything that used to move, and often the same events and people (like Mandela), itself requires critical examination; see Coombes, A. 2003. *History after Apartheid: Visual culture and public memory in a democratic South Africa.* Durham, NC: Duke University Press.
6 See Chapter 6 in Jansen, J.D. 2009. *Knowledge in the Blood: Confronting race and the apartheid past.* Stanford, CA: Stanford University Press.

7 Some of these issues are taken up in Lange, L. 2014. Rethinking Transformation and its Knowledges: The case of South African higher education. *Critical Studies in Teaching & Learning* (CriSTaL) 2(1), 1–24; and Jacklin, H. and Vale, P. (eds) *Re-Imagining the Social in South Africa: Critique, theory and post-apartheid society*. Durban: University of KwaZulu Natal Press.
8 Eisner, E. 1985. *The Educational Imagination: On the design and evaluation of school programs*. 2nd edition. New York: Macmillan Publishing Co.
9 The idea for some of these questions comes from the sizeable text by Muller, G.H. 2006. *Seton Hall Edition of The McGraw-Hill Reader: Issues across the disciplines*. 9th edition. New York: McGraw-Hill.
10 See Sandel, M. 2009. *Justice: What's the right thing to do?* New York: Farrar, Straus and Giroux.
11 Shim, J.M. 2014. Multicultural education as an emotional situation: practice encountering the unexpected in teacher education. *Journal of Curriculum Studies* 46(1), 116–37.
12 Faulkner, W. 1950. *Requiem for a Nun*. Act I, Scene III. London: Vintage Books.
13 Jansen, J.D. 2009. *Knowledge in the Blood: Confronting race and the apartheid past*. Stanford, CA: Stanford University Press.
14 Kristof, N. 2014. When Whites Just Don't Get It, Part 4. *The New York Times*, 15 November. Available from: www.nytimes.com/2014/11/16/opinion/sunday/when-whites-just-dont-get-it-part-4.html?hp&action=click&pgtype=Homepage&module=c-column-top-span-region&region=c-column-top-span-region&WT.nav=c-column-top-span-region&_r=1
15 Berlant, L. 2000. Intimacy: A Special Issue. In Berlant, L. (ed.) *Intimacy*. Chicago, IL: University of Chicago Press, p. 7.
16 The *feeling of knowing* is crisply explained by the neurologist Robert A. Burton in his book: Burton, R.A. 2009. *On Being Certain: Believing you are right even when you're not*. New York: St Martin's Griffin; the implications of felt knowledge for curriculum theory represent fertile ground for future inquiry.
17 From Hoffman, E. 2004. *After Such Knowledge: Memory, history and the legacy of the Holocaust*. Cambridge, MA: Public Affairs, Perseus Group, p. 140, quoted in Jansen, J.D. 2009. *Knowledge in the Blood: Confronting race and the apartheid past*. Stanford, CA: Stanford University Press.
18 Poplak, R. 2014. White folks + shoe polish = The edge of South African discourse. *Daily Maverick*, 7 August. Available from: www.dailymaverick.co.za/article/2014-08-07-white-folks-shoe-polish-the-edge-of-south-african-discourse/#.VIyPj1_aOM8
19 Yancy, G. and Mills, C. 2014. Lost in Rawlsland. [Opinion Pages, The Stone]. *The New York Times*, 16 November. Available from: http://opinionator.blogs.nytimes.com/2014/11/16/lost-in-rawlsland/
20 Proctor, R.N. and Schieburger, L. (eds) 2008. *Agnotology: The making and unmaking of ignorance*. Palo Alto, CA: Stanford University Press.
21 Proctor, R.N. 1995. *Cancer Wars: How politics shapes what we know and don't know about cancer*. New York: Basic Books, p. 8.
22 Steyn, M. 2012. The Ignorance Contract: recollections of apartheid childhoods and the construction of epistemologies of ignorance. *Identities: Global studies in culture and power* 19(1), 8–25 (p. 13).
23 Ibid.
24 Gamede, T. 2005. The Biography of "Access" as an Expression of Human Rights in South African Education Policies. Doctoral dissertation: Pretoria: Faculty of Education, University of Pretoria.

9 Portraits of intimacy

Introduction

One of the senior members of council drew me closer after my interview for the job of rector. He had a smile on his face suggesting playfulness, but his grip on my arm also suggested there was something more serious at play. By this time I had a sense that the university might offer me the job but I was not sure as yet, so what he wanted to say certainly piqued my interest. I was expecting something very serious in relation to the post-Reitz reconstruction, the incident which had caused so much damage to the university and eventually led to the resignation, if not removal, of my predecessor. Still, I could not be sure. "Listen, let me give you some advice," he said in Afrikaans. "You can lose all our rugby matches but you dare not lose against Potch." We both laughed, the way one does to relieve pressure.

"Potch" was the short-hand name for the auld enemy, the university once called the Potchefstroom University for Christian Higher Education. Now it had merged with a former black university, the North West University (itself formerly the University of Bophuthatswana) in Mafikeng, to be called the University of the North West. But for the old-timers, it was still Potch, the campus nickname derived from the old mining town of Potchefstroom where the white campus had stood since 1869.

The old Afrikaans universities all had a twin competitor with which they staged annual rugby matches and, sometimes, full inter-varsity competitions. The University of Pretoria, for example, alternated home and away rugby clashes every year with its auld enemy, the University of Stellenbosch. For the University of the Free State, it was Potch.

Nearness as courage

I had no choice therefore but to make it to Shimla Park, named after the senior rugby team of the UFS, the Shimlas, for the match against Potch. There were more than a thousand people in the small stadium that evening, mainly white, and the match was a tense affair. I remember the awkwardness of that evening. Reitz was still fresh in the mind of campus citizens and here two virtually all-white teams were replaying old Afrikaner rivalries in front of a home crowd with very few black students and hardly any black staff in attendance.

124 *Portraits of intimacy*

And then the unthinkable happened. In the dying minutes of the game one of the Shimla forwards took the ball from an intense tight-play situation and ran, unhindered, towards the try line of Potch to score the winning points. The home crowd was in a frenzy. What I did not see, until the coach showed it to me afterwards, was the picture in Figure 9.1.

There is something powerful about the photograph. A black woman student runs, unselfconsciously, onto a rugby field in full view of the mainly white audience to give a congratulatory embrace to the white man on his knees. This takes an enormous amount of courage, especially on a racially wounded campus. In the long run from the stadium to the middle of the field, the black student has to overcome her own memory of racial fear and rejection as she works her way towards the white male student. He might ignore her or worse. She might be ushered off the field as a non-player; after all, the match was not over as yet since in rugby a try is followed by a kick, the conversion, even if the official playing time is then over. As a woman the rugby field was not her place. As a black woman this testosterone-fuelled game was definitely not her place.

After the photograph was given to me I called the woman student to come and see me, in part out of curiosity to know what on earth was going through her mind when she ran onto the active field, and in part to thank her for breaking the racial ice on campus through this wonderfully courageous deed. She was smaller than I thought, gentle in spirit and slightly apprehensive about being called to the rector's office; after all, being called to the office, for staff and students alike, presaged trouble. "I want to tell you how much I admire you,"

Figure 9.1 Celebrating victory

I started as I pushed the photograph to her side of the table. "Now what on earth were you thinking?"

She looked puzzled, then laughed. "No professor, I do not have a problem. He is a Shimla, our player, so I wanted to congratulate him and tell him we are proud of him." I was choking up and shifted the subject to her life growing up in the rural parts of the Eastern Cape and how it was that she would come to Kovsies for her studies.

There are, I would discover over and over again, many young people with the capacity for overcoming their own biographies and, against the political grain of society, reach across great distances to heal a broken campus and rebuild a broken country. I could imagine that this young woman had much she could dwell on, such as the severe disadvantage she experienced because of apartheid growing up in the rural Eastern Cape; she could lay out her grudges against the past for marginalising her family into economic desperation where they now had to scramble to find the resources to simply bring her to Bloemfontein for a degree. The difficulty of studying under constant financial uncertainty could have produced a hardness against white students, academics and administrators whom she saw every day and who were so obviously better off than her. And she could have turned her back on that most muscular of demonstrations of white nationalist power and pleasure, the game of rugby, and stayed away. Instead, not only does she attend, she rushes onto the field in gleeful celebration.

Nearness as trust

None of the changes at the university would have been possible without black and white student leaders who were prepared to make that shift on their own and in response to the leadership cue for change. It all started, I suspect, on a Friday afternoon a few months after I arrived, with the two young student leaders in the picture in Figure 9.2.

The transformation of residences was proceeding very slowly at first. While the messaging was clear, consistent and persistent inside and outside the campus to counter the drone of "forced integration", there was resistance all along the road. Some administrators, long schooled in the use of computer-based placement systems to ensure racial separation, would carefully manipulate the numbers to maintain the status quo. Parents would call in and make deals with administrators to place their child in a particular residence where they knew a majority of white students was to be found. Students would cut deals with some of the heads of residences to ensure that they, and siblings, would end up in their residence of choice. There would be emotional appeals through my office in writing, often citing parents and grandparents who lived in the same residence, to keep offspring in the same "*koshuis*" (residence).

It was not desirable, on the one hand, to come down with a heavy hand on the placement of students given the sometimes real need of students to want to stay in a residence because of a family member's attachment to that "res",

Figure 9.2 Former student leaders of the UFS

sharing a room with a sibling or other practical considerations such as better disability access to nearby classes. At the same time, nothing would change if the 50:50 policy depended only on the choices of the students and their parents. Yet what would changing the mathematical distribution of placement mean if the students were still unchanged in their ideological commitments to separateness – that is, without the "desegregated heart"?[1] They could be physically integrated, in other words, and still live worlds apart.

These were the kinds of question I raised with the student heads of residences in a meeting scheduled in a large room down the passage from my office on a late Friday afternoon. It was a difficult meeting. The students claimed they too wanted change, but that it should not be rushed otherwise their residences would lose top students or good rugby players or money – at that stage the residences were losing money because of under-enrolment.

And then something happened that would turn the tide of transformation irreversibly. One of the student leaders, a white woman, spoke up and said the following: "We know what you want, but you do not know how to do it. Leave the transformation of the residences to us. Let us do it." My instinctive response, in my head, was "no ways". How could I leave the single most important arena of transformation struggles to a 19-year old? Immediately afterwards her friend also joined the request. "We can do it." I sat stunned, for this was the last thing I expected from the assembly of student leaders. This,

I knew, was a huge risk. All my life, as a good South African man, I believed that managers should manage and drive change processes. I was confident in my ability as a leader to get this right, not to give up my authority to a bunch of students. But the change was not happening, and I knew why; it was too far removed from the locus of student control.

Silence around the table and I was aware of the fact that all eyes were now on me. They must have been thinking, "How would he respond"? I could collapse my entire tenure as rector with this one decision. The student who spoke remembers that moment and the emotion in my croaking response: "Okay then, go and do it." I stood up, left the room and the meeting was over. That day I learn that counter-intuitive lesson that your strength as a leader lies in your weakness, the acknowledgment of your vulnerability and the recognition of the limits of your own authority.

Nida Jooste, the white woman who spoke first, moved into Akasia residence, an uninspiring black women's residence at the time. There she led the transformation that allowed for a slow but steady admission of other white women students. Soon Akasia would become a model residence as she lived the life of a role model among black students, with a caring and compassionate style of leadership that overcame the fear and alienation of her housemates.

Soon after that I was rushed by a white woman in a small rural Free State town called Welkom. I had just spoken to high school students from around Welkom, inspiring them to raise their academic game and to overcome their racial fears. At that time I was persona non grata in the local Afrikaans press for "forced integration" and as this white woman came rushing towards me I was convinced she was going to attack me. She came right into my face and said, "I am conservative; my generation finds it difficult to change, but thank you for what you are doing for my daughter." Surprised, I asked: "and who is your daughter?" "Nida," she said, "Nida Jooste."

Her friend, Mody Motholo, a black woman student leader, decided to take responsibility for a white men's residence, JBM Hertzog. She would become the mentor and leader to the young men in this old residence. I thought it was a mistake, but she went in and over time became deeply respected by "the boys" of JBM. There could be no doubt that the softening attitudes of the house with the swastika was in no small part a consequence of her soft, firm and directive leadership inside JBM. As in the case of Nida and Akasia, counter-intuitive choices by remarkable student leaders led the change, not the senior leaders in the main building.

Mody would go on to become the leader of all the students of the UFS and Nida, her deputy.

Nearness beyond physical proximity

With three campuses and 30,000 students it is impossible to come to know every student and be close to them. Yet it was clear that in this tactile society, where the demonstration of emotions mattered, it would be important to find other ways of connecting with students in real time. It would be through technology.

I could not sleep in the early hours of a visit to Japan on university business. Suddenly the inbox on my Twitter account lit up. "Prof, we have not had water in our residence for three hours. Please help." This was not an unusual request in the Twittersphere or on Facebook. Students inquired about funding for their studies, more parking spaces on campus, access to the books I had written, announcements of birthdays or illness, and more. "Give me minute," I asked the student, and fired off a "help residence X get its water supply back on" to a colleague in Maintenance. Within 30 minutes, water was restored to the house. "I can't believe how close you are to the problem, Prof; thank you." The student had no idea I was on the other side of the planet.

When students discovered that the rector was on Twitter, it became for some a wonderful diversion, a way of conducting informal conversation such as "So, how are you today Prof?" or "My mother says hello." But for many Twitter followers it was a handy way of fixing problems quickly since in a hierarchical institution, staff respond quickly to an instruction from above and slowly to an appeal from below. For now I needed to respond at "the speed of trust"[2] until we could develop within the institutional culture a deep-rooted sense of students as central to the life of the university and deserving of the same rapidity of response as any senior person.

Quickly the number of "followers" grew from 5,000 to 15,000 to 66,000, many of these being my own students. For me, doing Twitter messaging remains easy to manage. I use the time waiting in airports or in cars being driven by colleagues or in the gaps between meetings to fire off rapid-response messages. For those who abuse the facility or, in the case of hostilities from the outside, the blocking function works very well; over time that message of possible exclusion also gets across and the people who access you via Twitter remain respectful and not overbearing. There is also the forwarding facility in which more incoming messages are rerouted via my secretary for a scheduled meeting or referral.

The social media platforms in large organisations such as the UFS allow for an efficient system of communication as well as a sense of closeness in real time which would not be possible in a busy life. Linked smartly to our Office for Strategic Communications, the everyday messaging would also be picked up by my colleagues upstairs to warn of a crisis or alert us to abuse or to capture affirmations which we post to the "What they say about us" on the main university website. Most of all it gives students a sense of connectedness and an unwarranted perception of the rector as being "cool", since he makes the time to communicate via a youthful technology platform.

On divided campuses, social media have another inventive use – it can allow for messaging that not only reaches the students, but also the broader public wondering about the transformation of a university it continued to hold under suspicion because of Reitz. Here we cultivated a messaging system that communicated our values on a daily basis – from the affirming words of

Desmond Tutu or Oprah Winfrey on visiting the campus, quotations of gratitude from students for being part of a reconciling campus, and posted images of interracial intimacy.

In a tactile culture, however, physical touch is important. The ability to shake a hand is so fundamental, especially to rural communities. The handshake itself confirms something personal, accompanied by the direct look into the eye. Its firmness seals a pact, an understanding, trust or even friendship. It cannot be substituted by social media. And so the open-door policy was announced especially for first-year students. The parents liked this for it conveyed a sense of connectedness to leaders after coming from small schools where everybody knew each other to being lost inside the campuses of a very large university.

We not only used the office, situated centrally on the main campus, but also regular sessions under trees or umbrellas where the students would come to talk. These "Talk to me" sessions remain very popular and I seldom get through the long lines of waiting students.

Initially, the students came with complaints. Common concerns included the price of food on campus, the lack of finances for studies, the cost of textbooks and the shortage of after-hour transport for those who had to navigate the sometimes dangerous roads to private residences off-campus. Gradually, the tone and the content of the visits changed.

Jenny (not her real name) stood in the long line and, as I looked up, I remembered this courageous young woman who had travelled 1000 kilometres by herself from Cape Town to Bloemfontein hoping to find a place to study. Her grades from school were unexceptional and she was very poor. In fact few students finished high school, let alone graduated from a university, if they came from Vrygrond, a largely informal settlement camp outside beautiful Cape Town where violence and substance abuse were common experiences among black youth. I had no choice but to offer her a place and find funding for her studies since I knew Vrygrond, which was literally across the road from where I grew up in Retreat (aptly named). If she went back, I reasoned, she would fall pregnant and find herself in cycles of unemployment and a joyless life for the rest of her time on earth. The odds were heavily stacked against Jenny, and the fact that she could travel this far showed toughness and determination. We made a plan.

Eventually it was her turn in the line to see me. Quiet and reserved, she started slowly. "Do you remember me, Prof?" I smiled, "but of course I do; you're from Vrygrond." She said she had nothing to complain about but wanted to show off her test marks and how well she had done in the first year of study. I was astounded by her solid grades despite social and economic hardship and a shaky school experience. But she caught me completely off guard with her next question, which also abruptly ended the "talk to me" session. "So tell me, Prof, are you proud of me?"

Maybe it was the soft but searching manner in which she posed the question, but I immediately felt the lump in the throat. I knew what great distance, physical and emotional, she had covered to get to this point. I knew Vrygrond. She waited in that hot sun for no other reason than for this moment. I knew that in her hardscrabble life there were few opportunities for affirmation; she and her mother lived simply in a quest for survival from one day to the next. The question rang in my ear and at first I turned my face from her so that she could not see the tears forming. Then I faced her and said firmly: "My child, I am more proud of you than you can ever know." I left soon afterwards as I drove from her South Campus to my office on main campus overcome with emotion.

Nearness as communion

The Free Staters love their food. The braai (barbeque) is much more than meat grilled outside for the purposes of a meal. It is a place of conversation around the fire, a rite of passage for a young man doing the braai for, by some remarkable division of labour, the women are inside making the salads. The braai is a metaphor for "*geselligheid*" (easy, entertaining conversation) though the sinking of teeth into a good cut of beef is not to be taken lightly. There is a manliness to the whole thing; it is here where I heard some macho types telling me that "here we eat meat, and if we want salads, we slaughter a pig". But to "*kuier*" has a wonderful Afrikaans meaning; to visit friends and relatives as a fun outing for individuals or friends and whole families. All of this happens around food.

I proposed therefore that we arrange regular breakfasts with students, an opportunity to eat and enjoy each other's company; to "*kuier*", in other words, and in this way to get a sense of the heartbeat of the campus. The students loved this. The typical pattern would be to issue open invitations on the university website and the first dozen or so students who signed up would come for an early breakfast at my office. From time to time I would decide whom to invite, often because I wanted to honour a particular group of students such as the national championship team in netball or a section of international students and so forth. Depending on my sense of the group, I would invite one of them to say a prayer of thanks for the food while we held hands around the table. Several students would volunteer for this task. After introductions, I would ask a single question: "What can we improve in our service as leaders"?

In all breakfasts, the invitees are diverse. One such group was chosen because there were individual students who had made such an impression and I felt needed to be recognised. One student collects stray cats on campus and sterilises them before putting them back onto the grounds to control the rodent population. Nobody told her to commit this public service and nobody would have known about it had she not run out of cash. The student in the wheelchair, a delightful young woman, leads the university wheelchair rugby team consisting mainly of white men. But she came to make the case, a black woman for "my boys" as she put it, to be given the same management attention – such as facilities – for wheelchair rugby as was the case with the able-bodied rugby teams.

The male student in the group runs a major community radio station in the region; a postgraduate student, he has done much to create opportunities for journalism students to learn their craft on the air as a young entrepreneur himself.

One of the students was accosted by men walking home after late classes but fought her way to freedom, determined not to be assaulted by the thugs. We walked the road to recovery with her and what really struck me was her singular determination that nobody could take away her dignity that terrible evening; she survived without any physical harm. And so around the table there were these remarkable young people who needed to be seen, to be heard and to be loved from close by, and what better way than to break bread together.

Our homes therefore became places for students to visit over weekends, especially those who lived in residence and far away from home. The obligatory braai with games and lots of discussion brought the students into close communion with our families, especially in the home of the dean of students across the street from our home in, yes, Whites Road. I remember long nights of conversation in our home as student leaders talked openly about the struggles for transformation in their own lives and on campus; there was a remarkable openness to talking about their own experiences and extraordinary capacity for critical self-reflection, something that would not be as readily achieved in formal workshops on campus. It was from these close encounters that deep friendships were made between and among students, and with our families, which remained after they graduated.

It was because of the centrality of food in reconciliation that we brought to campus Anna Trapido, author of *Hunger for Freedom: The story of food in the life of Nelson Mandela*. Anna's brilliance was to be able to sense the campus and our ambitions for human togetherness, and draw from the life of Mandela the ways in which our foods can bridge social and cultural divides as well as satisfy that most human of hungers for connection and conciliation.

It was also food, or the lack thereof, that first brought to my attention the power of nearness that goes far beyond physical proximity.

Notes

1   Boyle, S.P. 2001. *The Desegregated Heart: A Virginian's stand in time of transition*. Charlottesville and London: University of Virginia Press. Originally published 1962 by William Morrow & Company.
2   I borrow the term "speed of trust" from Stephen Covey's book by the same name; Covey, S., with Merril, R.R. 2008. *The Speed of Trust: The one thing that changes everything*. New York: Free Press.

10 From intimacy to nearness

Introduction

The young woman student came in first, unannounced. She was smiling broadly and took up one of the two visitor seats on the other side of my desk. "Prof, I just wanted to tell you something," she said in Afrikaans, still smiling. In this polite culture of middle South Africa and in the very hierarchical structure of society and universities, I tried in vain to have the title "Prof" abandoned as a form of personal address.

"Thank you, first of all, for putting me on the No Student Hungry programme; it really made a difference in my life and my academic marks are also very good." I sensed this was not the real reason for the meeting since she was still smiling in a way that suggested there was better news to come. So I waited.

Melanie was one of those students you liked immediately – always pleasant, always positive and easy to talk to. She was one of the small number of white students on the No Student Hungry (NSH) programme. Her life story was striking, of the "Homeless to Harvard" variety. She grew up in the small city of Welkom in the rural Free State where she distinguished herself as a top academic student. Then her parents died in quick succession and the young Melanie was left to fend for herself on the streets. She fell in love with a white, unemployed youth and, unplanned, had a baby she could hardly afford. Her academic plans nosedived and she was left stranded to care for a baby and an out-of-job partner. Without parents things looked very bleak.

By some miracle Melanie made it back to university but without money to feed herself or her family. Her marks were still good so she qualified as an NSH student where for R25 (South African rand) she could at least purchase a meal every day. Students receive an academic bursary loaded onto their student cards so that they can buy meals without the potential stigma of being on food support from the university. They also have to pay back in the form of community service of some kind, and maintain good academic scores. Like so many other students, Melanie flourished on NSH and this was the minor reason she came to express gratitude.

"I met a friend in class," she said smilingly "and I noticed that he too studied without food. While I was eating he did not, and I discovered we had the same problem. So I shared my NSH food with him. We have become best friends." I choked up, realising that in order for Melanie to use her meagre food bursary to support another student, there would be less available for her child and partner. "I am so proud of you," Melanie, I offered. She kept smiling.

Suddenly a young black man whizzed into the office. I was a bit confused that my secretary let him through given that I was in the meeting with Melanie. "This is my friend," said Melanie, "his name is George."

Beyond intimacy

I want to make a distinction here between intimacy, as physical proximity, and nearness as something much deeper, more personal and surpassing everyday human contact. Intimacy represents physical proximity; nearness, spiritual closeness. Intimacy offers tolerance; nearness, embrace. Intimacy resolves an immediate problem; nearness seeks long-term relationships. Intimacy is tactical, a head calculation; nearness is binding, a heart commitment. Intimacy is transactional; nearness is unconditional. Intimacy sets spatial limits to relationships; nearness has no boundaries.

I draw a transcendent notion of nearness from the book by C.S. Lewis called *The Four Loves*, in which he distinguishes brotherly love, erotic love and divine love, and those three from what he calls *friendship* which expresses itself as "nearness by resemblance" to the divine.[1]

My intention is not to delve into the religious realm from which Lewis speaks but to point to something important offered in his understanding of nearness – the spiritual dimension of human relationships which is transformative and goes much deeper and further than simply a superficial, physical relationship. The spiritual is uncomfortable territory for the social sciences,[2] but what I found in the transformation of student relationships on campus were clearly distinct forms of togetherness – *strategic* (a physical relationship, intimacy) and *transformative* (a spiritual relationship, nearness). It is something deeper, even transcendent, that binds Melanie and George in their human relationship, and that transforms both of them; this is what I call nearness.

Strategic closeness

For many students, white and black, the integration requirement in the residences was at first experienced as something to be tolerated. White students, in particular, made one of two choices – to leave for private accommodation or to accommodate black students through various kinds of tolerance measures. One was to arrange the floors of a residence by race so that even though the house as a whole was integrated, there were clearly segregated rows of accommodation on different levels of the building. This was especially the case for seniors and in the men's residences. Another tolerance measure was to limit the black numbers through criteria which combined academic and sports or other considerations; one of the semi-private residences was particularly adept at such internal management despite the overall policy of a 50:50 requirement.

As indicated earlier, initially there was another level of micro-politics at play where the residence heads would negotiate with a kindred spirit at the administrative office to channel white students or rugby players or family members or old school friends to a particular residence; this has largely been stopped but points, again, to ways of allowing for physical proximity but on terms of a managed distance.

The most common strategy, and one in which we did not interfere as senior managers, was of course segregated rooms. Most rooms in a residence allow for two or more tenants and this is where the real segregation played itself out; once again, student leaders could claim to have an integrated residence but in fact operate segregated rooms.

These kinds of strategic relations are always bound by time and space. The students become friends out of necessity and by virtue of sharing the same physical space of the residence. But it is limited in scope. Being friends in the residence does not mean being friends outside of it. Playing together on the rugby team does not mean going to the same bars afterwards or the same church on Sundays, or the friends' farm over the weekend for a hunt. Those intense moments of togetherness in the residence or on the rugby field start and end in the activity itself; the friendship is momentary and convenient, strategic, in other words. None of these relationships survive the degree so that when the students graduate they go their own separate ways, seldom becoming life-long friends.

The question that could of course be posed at this point is why the senior leadership of the university did not immediately intervene and change these micro-arrangements for managed intimacies. The reason was simple. We did not wish to put too much pressure on integration from the top. The first goal was integrating the residences as a whole, and the next task was to work on changing "hearts and minds" inside the residences which in turn, we reasoned, would more gradually change the various circumventions within a house. Knowing the balance between broad policy requirement from the centre and self-driven change "on the ground" is one of the most important management wisdoms that apply in sensitive situations where too much stress on the system, at the same time, could in fact backfire and cause long-term harm. Genuine integration, or what here is called nearness, cannot be compelled but it can and must be pursued through small, deliberate steps.

This is where the arguments of critical theorists cannot be taken lightly – the inherited "structural arrangements" that give racial separation an ordinariness of meaning and an internal logic to justify segregation do not simply dissolve at the point where formal democracy is obtained and where policy intention is declared. This is as true in the macro-politics of a nation as it is the case in the daily operations of a university campus after apartheid.

Take something as simple as class times. For years the UFS had most of its classes for white, Afrikaans-speaking students during the day since these were middle-class students, in the main, whose parents could afford full-time studies. As the university opened its doors to black students, in English classes the calendar allowed for many of the lectures to be held in the late afternoon and early evening. This not only meant that lecturers were free after day teaching to give the additional classes, it also meant that black students who had no choice but to work to pay for their families and studies now could attend classes after a day on the job.

In a perfect world, where the dividing line was socio-economic class alone, these arrangements would to a large extent have passed without much notice. But in a racially divided community this would become a point of agitation for black students and politicians. White students could study during normal hours and be "fresh" for learning while black students would come with tired bodies, from work, and have to be alert to evening instruction. Worse, blacks who were on campus as full-time students wasted an entire day waiting to attend evening classes in some of their subjects.

The same arguments were heard over and over again, at the UFS and at the University of Pretoria (UP), that the reason the white choir had no black singers is because "they" did not have transportation back to the townships after evening practice sessions and therefore could not attend the mandatory training and preparation classes at night. The white students had cars and parents who could collect them.

The point is simply this – that for those desiring segregation in classes or choirs, this was largely achieved without having to make racially inspired arguments since the structural arrangements inherited from the past played perfectly into continued segregationist practices such as the ones described.

Unsurprisingly, insisting on the unity of the choir or the end of evening classes brought protests from black students. They wanted to sing "their own songs" and they needed money and so terminating evening classes, as we tried to do, meant that the working students could not afford to come to university. Integration was never going to be easy, and these challenges suited the strategic circumventors of the project.

Spiritual closeness

How and when that transition from strategic reckoning to transformative reasoning happens will vary in place and time on a large campus, but I bore witness to those moments over and over again.

Early on, it happened with the evening of the inauguration of the new rector. Things were still difficult at the time, and I had insisted that we could not have two university choirs – a black choir singing African traditional songs and a white choir singing European classics; that was exactly how the division of cultural labour was played out at the UFS for some time, and at the University of Pretoria during my time there as dean of education. Here once again was a perfect rationale for racial separation – the celebration of the *multicultural* as cover for organised racism. You could escape the burdensome argument of racial separation simply by pointing to the very different repertoires that black and white choirs "enjoy" singing.

I would have none of that. What made sense to me was a choir of black and white students singing common songs from our many traditions – English, Afrikaans, Dutch, Malay and many others – as well as international traditions such as African American struggle songs and, of course, European music. We needed through the musical arrangements also to break through the lazy monotony of two rigid nationalisms, Afrikaner and Basotho, from the misnamed Free State's past. Here was a wonderful opportunity for white students to learn "black songs" and the other way round, until they all came to recognise the range of African/South African music as their own.

The choirmasters of the two choirs agreed, and the arrangement was that they would exchange the baton for the songs they were familiar with but the choir was one. Long before the inauguration got underway the nervous joint choir stood outside Centenary Hall, the main building for the evening's events. Then something remarkable happened – a white student from the choir voluntarily called the members together for prayer. They all held hands and in an emotional prayer he asked for them to be blessed in their efforts on the night. Remarkably, he prayed in halting English at a time when the most ordinary thing in the world to do was pray in his mother tongue, Afrikaans. Here was a courageous young man wanting to make that transition from simply black and white bodies joined at the hip to a single choral body joined at the heart. I had never seen the white conductor so moved as he told this story. Their singing together was moving: "Make me an instrument of your peace", in more than one language.

That moment of transcendence had been reached in the relationship between Melanie and George. As a poor white student she had the most to lose from the new country where a black government, in the conservative white view, cared only about their left-behind black constituencies. Melanie could claim to be aggrieved as poor under both regimes, white and black, and as a young white person born after apartheid, deserved to be recognised for special treatment on grounds of poverty. For these kinds of reasons, working-class whites are often the recruitment terrain for right-wing, racist movements. She could have been strategic in her approach, holding back on the little she had and saving it for her family, while tolerating the hungry black classmate from Kimberley; that would be reasonable and acceptable to even the most prejudiced observer of this dramatic encounter. But Melanie goes the other way.

Perhaps Melanie's generosity comes from the fact that she was welcomed into the NSH community as a poor student, not as a white student. It could be her sense of a changing campus around her in which overt racial hostilities had begun to subside. What she recognised in a critical encounter with George, however, was not a black man but another hungry student. That capacity to see beyond the epidermis on this kind of campus and in this kind of country is nothing short of remarkable.

Nor is this a private tryst, something she does willingly but not wanting others to know. She would be a traitor to her race, for some, and risk ridicule from both sides of the racial divide. But Melanie wants this to be public and so she had waited for the moment to share the good news with her rector and the rest of the university community. I placed a picture of the two of them on my Facebook and Twitter avatar for more than a year, to share leadership pride in the two students and to signal through this powerful symbolism the kind of relationships that matter.

What makes nearness as a deeply personal, respectful even spiritual relationship possible?

Explaining the capacity for nearness

Looking across the many sincere and enduring relationships among black and white students, I sought in vain to find comprehensive theories that could shed light on how such a transformative closeness, or nearness, becomes a reality in young lives. We do, however, have a number of cues from both the student cases and the sparse literature on race relationships in divided communities.

It makes a difference, first of all, what kinds of homes the students come from. Students from deeply conservative and racist homes struggle more than most to make the transition to normal relationships with black students. Students from rural, agricultural communities, where the dominant relationships between masters and servants are largely undisturbed since the end of apartheid, struggle with the suddenness of integrated living. Until this time, their only sense of black people is as illiterate, inarticulate labourers to be commanded from day to day. There is no vocabulary for speaking differently to blacks as peers or as authority.

The three white male students outside the agricultural building knew I was the rector but they were struggling to look me in the eye. I recognised the problem and felt a warmth and closeness to them even as they tried to respond to the unexpected meeting on the stairs. "How are you?" I asked the young men. "*Alles reg, en met jou?*" (All well, and with you?). Innocent in English but hugely troubling in Afrikaans. "Jou" (You) is not a word you use with older people and certainly not with the rector of your university. Where they grew up, and indeed where I grew up, my mother would have administered a swift "klap" (smack) to the head. If I was a white stranger, at my age, I would be called "Oom" (Uncle), a universal form of address to an older person whether you know them or not. "*Jou*" is completely unacceptable, an overly casual "you" reserved for your friends. I smiled and walked away, hoping that time on campus would enable them to find another language of approach to all citizens, black people in particular.

By contrast, students who come from homes where black friends and black associates of their parents are an everyday experience, or where more open-minded parents allow for reason and offer explanation for social realities that are not driven by racial bitterness, the young people make their transition to university with much greater ease. The most intimate relationship with black people, in such contexts, is the domestic worker and where that person enjoys a measure of dignity and where disrespectful forms of address by the children are frowned upon, the students from such homes have an advantage when it comes to integration on campus.

Your school of origin also makes a big difference. Integrated schools begin to develop integrated minds and hearts. The difficult issues of co-living and co-learning are dealt with, if not resolved completely, at school. There are confrontations and conflicts, make no mistake, but the students begin to work through them and start to make lasting friends across the colour line. Coming into university, black and white students from well-integrated schools not only know white friends from 5–12 years of primary and secondary education, they are much more at ease with them on campus.

The two white women students on our Study Abroad programme even looked scared when I visited their group at their placement institution, Cornell University. It was the first few days of the programme and even though their UFS group was racially diverse it was clear that these two souls had great difficulty leaving each other's sides. I watched them throughout the combined breakfast with Cornell faculty and staff; they sat clinging to each other in one corner, before and after the meal, while the other white and black students mixed freely. They had come from conservative white schools in the previous year.

The churches in which students assemble make a huge difference. The largest and most integrated church in Bloemfontein is the CRC, or Community Revival Church, a charismatic community of believers composed largely of university students and community members, black and white. When the church first desegregated, the senior pastor – a trim and muscular man – made a courageous choice and told his fellow white congregants that they could stay or leave but he was going to remain faithful to the Word. The church is, and would be, one. Some wealthy congregants left but others stayed, and this assembly remains the only Free State religious community which is so thoroughly integrated on this scale. On Sundays, hundreds of UFS students stream to the CRC and fill campus buses on their way to worship. Students in this church come onto campus with strong bonds of friendship based on their transformed spiritual lives. This is not the case for black students from township churches or white students from the Afrikaans churches.

In general, therefore, your home, school, church and even geographical community (urban or deep rural) make a great difference in terms of your capacity to overcome prejudice, as a first step, and to embrace otherness, as a second step. But that does not explain Melanie, and many others, who in terms of these sources of socialisation were supposed to act differently. This is where we do not have, until now, accumulated data or refined theoretical insights that can offer answers except that we know there is something deeper within the capacity of such human beings that enables them to move beyond tolerance.

Which returns us to the key question in this study: how do black and white students come into close human relationships with each other despite their own biographies of segregation? The answers to the question hold considerable significance for race relations on university campuses and, by extension, in the broader society.

My starting point is that "sheer contact"[3] is not good enough. Merely placing black and white students into the same residential spaces, as we have seen, can trigger the kind of conflict and violence that culminated in the horrific racial abuse of the five Reitz workers on a university campus. A long time ago there were theorists who actually claimed that conflict between groups was, in fact, inevitable because most "ingroups" believed they were superior to "outgroups".[4]

Then came something called contact theory, advanced in a remarkable little book by American psychologist Gordon Allport in 1954 titled The Nature of Prejudice. With unusual insight, prescience and simplicity, Allport put forward the hypothesis that under certain conditions the interaction between groups can reduce prejudice. Those conditions were equal status in the contact situation, intergroup cooperation, shared goals and the support of authorities. What followed down the decades was a never-ending slew of studies that tested Allport's thesis especially in relation to each of those four "optimal conditions" and, while new ideas and controversies emerged, most studies confirmed that in general, he was right – contact, under certain conditions, reduces bias. In perhaps the most comprehensive review of research ever done on the subject, a staggering 515 studies, it was found that "greater intergroup contact typically corresponds with lower levels of intergroup prejudice".[5]

One of the elaborations on his ideas was the extended contact hypothesis, which held that simply knowing of a close, positive relationship with an outgroup member can reduce inter-group bias. By way of example, if one white person knew of at least another white person who enjoyed a close friendship with a black person, that knowledge in itself reduced bias in the white group.[6] What held for interpersonal relationships also seemed to apply to groups, and what applied in race relations also appeared to extend to other kinds of group differences.

What happens when these contact hypotheses are brought down into the real situations described in this book on a university campus and, in particular, when it comes to residential integration? One of the finest studies[7] on this question – "a natural field experiment" – randomly assigned white first-year students to either a white ($n = 136$) or a black roommate ($n = 126$). The students reported on their relationships during the first two weeks and then during the last two weeks of the academic quarter on three main issues – satisfaction, anxiety and racial attitudes. On the satisfaction index, the results were not encouraging; students in interracial rooms were less involved with their roommates and less satisfied with the relationship than those in same-race rooms. But what became clear was that racial attitudes and anxiety about the other group definitely improved over time for those students in interracial rooms, but not for those in same-race rooms.

So far, so good.

The problem with measurement-oriented studies of contact is that they cannot really tell you much about what happens to and inside human beings as they encounter each other in racially divided communities and on racially divided campuses. What is it about these human encounters between white and black students, for example, that accounts for shifts in attitudes and behaviours over time? "How do you now feel about X?" and subjecting that response to some measurable index of human behaviour is a very different question to "What happened in your relationships with X to bring about these new bonds of friendship or love?" The contact theorists do not go down this latter road in part, I suspect, because such transformations are difficult to "measure" in an empirical tradition that is much more inclined towards valuing the discretely observable rather than the ambiguities of qualitative encounters. Maurice Natanson's remark would probably sit uncomfortably with measurement scientists, that "intersubjectivity is experienced in a primordial way rather than known through proofs".[8]

The stories shared in this book are, however, intended to be deep and textured enough to begin to yield insight into what happens in these human encounters. Something transpires here that goes to the core not so much of "what we see" but "how we see" in the encounters between white and black students. "We recognised early on" says the white Afrikaans-speaking student (let's call the white student Clarie and the black student Andri), "that we shared the same values" and from that point of recognition would hardly be seen apart whether in formal university gatherings, informal "hanging out" sessions or on their many Facebook photograph postings. "Sisters", I once called them in light of their inseparability. There was no racial reference here no matter how often I tried to coax it from them in conversation; what they enjoyed was something much deeper, tied together by shared values.

Not all such deep human encounters, where conflict and distance separate lives, start with such clarity and seamlessness as in the case of these two students. Many of us experience specific turning points, dramatic incidents which come down to "seeing a significant other 'as if for the first time'".[9] As recounted in my earlier book, *Knowledge in the Blood*, for me it was the moment of encounter with a very poor white student – let's call her Marietjie – and her father, dressed in threads, in my dean's office in Pretoria where he was almost begging for a bursary (financial support) to enable his daughter to pursue her lifelong dream of becoming a teacher one day. As the smiling, upright young girl sat across from me, fitted very modestly in a colourful dress, I knew that the rest of her life, and that of her poverty-stricken family, rested solely on the decision I would make that evening.

Then something happened which to this day I cannot explain. In a flash, I saw my father, not a white man. I saw myself, not a young woman. My mind rushed back to the late 1970s when my father was in exactly the same position and told me that if I wanted to go to university, I would have to find my own way. I remembered how his heart broke, and what it must have meant for "the man of the house", to tell his son that whatever his dreams of higher education might be, it was not going to happen; or at least not with any resources this unsuccessful hawker (his job at that time) of fruit and vegetables could afford.

Of course I had seen this young woman before and thousands of her race every day on this largely white campus of the University of Pretoria. She was not unfamiliar, even though her plight was not as common to most of the white students in this teacher education facility. But now, with the flashbacks to my own past very much present in the conversation, I began to see her "as if for the first time". Until recently I had no conceptual apparatus for making sense of that turnaround experience, except for my more earnest evangelical friends who would find adequate explanation in other-worldly intervention.

Such a rare conceptual framework came to my attention through the research of Arthur Aron and his colleagues, which explains how through close human relationships we come to see and include the other person in the self.[10] Their explanation comports well with the two cases – Clarie and Andri at the UFS and Marietjie at UP:

> If I am concerned about your outcomes, I am evaluating the world as would you, I am holding your perspectives. Similarly, if the material, knowledge, and social impact of events that happen to you are happening to me, then your place in the material and social world is my place in the material and social world, I am holding your identities.[11]

This process of identifying deeply with the different *Other* is obviously much more than can be accounted for through mere physical proximity (the contact hypothesis) and offers a powerful set of insights into how cross-racial identification becomes inter-human identification with your brother and sister. But none of this is possible only at the level of emotional or even spiritual awareness, and so something else happens at the intellectual level, "a restructuring of the cognitive system" such that "people may come to take on the perspectives and identities of the other as one's own".[12]

I can at this point hear my conservative white students on both campuses (UP and the UFS), when the dialogue and discussion venture onto the terrain of the intercultural experience as offering great value in the process of becoming more fully human. The student then goes on the defensive – "but I am Afrikaans and I do not want to give up my identity" for the sake of what must be, for them, a strange and threatening multiculturalism.

The Aron schemata offers relief: "It may be as if we also desire to *be* the other, not to lose one's self, but to add "substance" to it, to make it richer, more complex" (emphasis in the original quotation).[13] In the same vein, Miroslav Volf in his exceptional book, *Exclusion and Embrace*, refuses to frame this problem as one of loss but rather a constant movement between coming close and standing back from one's culture:

> Both distance and belonging are essential. Belonging without distance destroys . . . But distance without belonging isolates . . . Distance from a

culture must never degenerate into flight from that culture but must be a way of living in a culture.[14]

Once again it bears emphasising that what I am proposing as a theory of nearness, drawing on these insights from social psychology, is not simply intimacy or the superficial knowledge of the other person that comes from being physically near. The white student who therefore claims, often defensively, that I *have* black friends might very well know where those friends were born or what they study or the kinds of careers they wish to pursue. What is at stake here, however, is not buddy knowledge that happens through the exchange of information, for "including other in the self is different from familiarity and similarity"[15] and encompasses deeper bonds of knowledge that comes from the closeness of individuals with implications for groups.[16]

There remains nonetheless one gap in the theory of nearness so far and it is this: what motivates the other person, whether in the case of Clarie and Andri, or the dean with Marietjie, to be drawn into such close relationships, consciously or otherwise? This is where my notion of nearness is more fully explained through the concept of transcendence not as something abstract, remote or religious and spiritual – as in everyday assumptions – but as revealed in "the concrete lives of human beings".[17] Here Steen Halling is helpful in distinguishing two meanings to this slippery concept – transcendence as our *capacity for openness* and as our desire to *connect with something larger than ourselves*.

There is visible in the case observations a tremendous capacity for openness among incoming students. As I have observed over and over again, young 18-year olds entering university half expect to be challenged and, even though they sometimes carry a bitter, second-hand knowledge of a past they were never part of, they are prepared to listen, to evaluate and then to decide for themselves on how to live their lives in relation to other people. This is the main reason why it is so much easier to change young students than older staff – the capacity for openness is still there. It comes with bright and dark sides – the desire to experiment, try things out, often away from home. "What would happen if" results in daring exploits the same students would never venture while at home.

Consider the case of the conservative white student with deep religious attachments who drinks himself into a stupor in his residence but arrives promptly at church on Sunday to participate in the "*nagmaal*" (communion). This is not an evil or dysfunctional person but one who is open, willing to test the limits of what is possible in campus life.

Remember the case of the young black woman in an earlier chapter who runs onto the rugby field to congratulate the white player who had just scored the winning points in the game. Her capacity for openness entails great risk for rejection by the white player and even ejection from the field as an interfering supporter, both reasonable outcomes. But her willingness to test those lines of separation between black and white, or between players and spectators, represents precisely the kind of openness that is *transcending* (moving forward, open with possibility) in nature.

Or the case of the young black woman who completely caught me off guard during one of my lunches with first-year students when I was dean; at that event, due to some fault in the organisation of the lunch, only black students showed up. After some discussion, a beautiful young woman confronted me with some urgency in her voice: "Professor, I have a real problem." I was bracing myself for another explosion of anger or anecdote of mistreatment. Then this: "could you help me find a white boyfriend?" I do not for one moment believe she was looking for a life mate, but rather to experience what it means to be open in relationships and not tied to the social expectation of race-confined devotions.

The capacity for openness is unequally distributed. While many students allow for openness to learning, whether pedagogical or social, others are super-cautious, trapped in the confines imposed by their own socialisation. But here is an opening to be seized on divided campuses – the capacity of hundreds if not thousands of students who are willing to step up to, and explore, those boundaries constructed by men and to determine what lies on the other side. It is this capacity for openness – "our forward moving nature [as] transcending beings"[18] – that is one condition for enabling nearness in human relationships.

The second meaning proposed is the desire to reach *for something that lies beyond us*, the transcendent. This, explains Hallet, is that:

> [...] sense of transcendence, of the future opening up, of a sense of presence, not of a personal being, but of connecting with something larger than myself.[19]

It is this sense of a bigger reason, a larger purpose, which drives many young conservative white students into church missions. While these youthful Christians would be desperately uncomfortable in forming genuine relations, let alone romantic ones, with black students in everyday on-campus experiences, the drive for outreach to save souls or mend soles is something that comes with the Dutch Reformed Church's longstanding civilising mission. The issue I wish to focus on is not the misguided Christian adventurism, in this case; it is about the capacity to sense a larger purpose that is shared among young university students wanting to make a difference in communities for something bigger than themselves.

The steady stream of students who march through my office with proposals to save the world forced us to open an innovation hub in order to manage these wonderfully idealistic commitments of youth. They wanted to solve the problems of illiteracy in the rural areas or provide tampons to high school girls so that they do not drop out of school, or rebuild dilapidated pre-school buildings so that poor children would receive a head start of decent education. Talk to any of these students and they speak in utopian terms of transforming not only individual lives or whole communities but the future of the country. Probe further and you discover a sense of being drawn by something outside of themselves, and much bigger than themselves, whether it is the 67 minutes of service every year to honour Nelson Mandela or the life of the soul.

I am moved, therefore, by the many gatherings of students on campus earnestly engaged in prayer and worship, not only over weekends but at night in home cells or early morning prayers in classrooms. These are the same students who are among the most committed when it comes to public duty inspired, as mentioned earlier, by a sense of calling far beyond the modular requirement of hours to be completed in a professional service learning course. It is often in the face of overwhelming need, even as they prayerfully serve, that students come to experience "a radical openness" that reveals their vulnerability.[20]

The critics

Contact theory, say some of its critics, is too soft on race and racism. It is therefore reformist rather than transformative because of its failure to address the politics of race. By taking race as given rather than a social construct subject to change, it accepts rather than challenges common sense racism.[21]

I would agree that contact theory holds a particular perspective on race relations that certainly does not operate in the vein of critical theory or from the perspective of the politics of race, and so some of these criticisms are well made. But gaining a solid empirical grip on measures of race relations through studies of prejudice and closeness in fact provides the kind of data required to be able to inform critical inquiries into the meanings of race within schools, universities and society. A one-dimensional approach to studies of race and racial prejudice impoverishes the field.

I also do not see how it is possible to deny the reality of race in the meanings assigned to this construct by the participants in these studies. This is a difficult position to take, since all my life I have fought against fixed racial categories and how we constrain the emergence of a humanism that does not remain trapped in official designations of who we are, or might become.

But that is a very different matter when it comes to how participants in my study see themselves and how difficult it is to convince them otherwise – that they are not white, African, Coloured or Indian, those four ubiquitous apartheid categories. By imposing our own categories of meaning on the subjective meanings of race to the subjects of study, we in fact distort those meanings as a starting point – not a conclusion – for a critical analysis and a more progressive practice.

There should therefore be a way of accommodating participant realities within a critical frame; this I believe is what Arun Saldanha offers when he argues that instead of running away from "race" we should examine its possibilities for the transformative project:

> Race should not be eliminated but proliferated, its many energies directed at multiplying racial differences so as to render them joyfully cacophonic ... What is needed is an affirmation of race's creativity and virtuality: what race *can be*. Race need not be about order and oppression, it can be wild, far-from-equilibrium, liberatory.[22] (original emphasis)

There is an equally powerful criticism that it is simply not possible to have "equal status" as an optimal condition for reducing prejudice through contact when, in fact, students in our case *come into* their campus relations from very different social statuses as black and white citizens. There are two problems with such a position.

First, it assumes status as static or fixed whereas black and white students coming into campus learning experiences in places like the Free State are constantly changing status. Black students are increasingly part of the burgeoning middle classes, the result of two decades of open access to the best schools and universities alongside an aggressive policy of black economic empowerment (BEE in South African parlance). White students, on the other hand, are increasingly visible, as in the case of Melanie, as working class and poor. This is not to ignore the national demographic picture that most black people remain poor and most white people remain relatively well off. I am simply asserting that, especially for university students, these statuses are in flux, changing slowly in favour of the black middle classes, and that this creates opportunities for a more equal dialogue.

Second, it reduces status largely to economic criteria as opposed to political voice. In a black majority country – and this situation could well be different in a place like the USA – black students know they are dominant in the political space and make their voices heard loudly on all campuses. They are disproportionately the necessary beneficiaries of state largesse, largely through a massive plan (the National Student Financial Aid Scheme) allocating scholarships and loans in favour of the poor. They control student political organisations by numbers. And they can demand the kinds of institutional attention in terms of resources that white students no longer can. Black students are not helpless victims dominated by those with greater access to resources. It simply is not the case.

Finally, the criticism that contact theory does not deal directly with racism lies beyond its very functional purpose. Contact, of the kind described by Allport and those subsequently, is a necessary but not sufficient condition for dealing with racism. You cannot engage the problem of prejudice and bigotry outside of contact. Put differently, you cannot achieve "emotional closeness" without first attaining "behavioural closeness".[23] This is where, perhaps, Allport's fourth optimal condition should put on more flesh than simply to signal "support by authorities". By this I mean much more than supportive laws and policies, for what is required is a range of critical interventions in and outside the classroom that both instruct and model anti-racist relations as a condition for prejudice reduction. But again, for this to even begin happening, you first need to bring human beings into the same physical spaces.

Summing up: A theory of nearness

Young people starting off university have extraordinary capacity for binocular vision; that is, "the art of gaining clarification of thought by perceiving through the other person's way of being".[24] On racially segregated campuses it is possible, therefore, to build a sense of social cohesion among black and white students even though they might come from largely segregated communities and find themselves inhabited by segregationist ideas. For some the adjustment of the binocular lens to gain a full and clear picture of the distant other happens quickly; for others it takes longer, and for a minority it might never happen. Under the right institutional conditions, most students will come to find the "racial other" closer than they thought.

But desegregation is not enough; in fact, it could be downright dangerous. What is needed is unambiguous commitment to changing the rules of the game.[25] That game concerns how black and white students come to interact in the newly desegregated space. This cannot be declared through policy and regulations alone, important as those instruments might be as signals of institutional direction; what is needed is a comprehensive set of strategies focused on breaking down barriers to human interaction. Such strategies include curricular interventions as well as a range of co-curricular plans that introduce new knowledge, confront stubborn stereotypes and create cosmopolitan canopies[26] (the photograph of the two girls in a concentration camp) on campus under which uncommon human relationships are engaged, negotiated and transformed in the course of time.

Mere tolerance as an approach to building interracial community will create superficial and strategic (while on campus) changes to human relationships. What is required is an approach that goes beyond simply "getting along" as the predominant strategy to one in which the understanding of others is itself transformed; in other words, a shift from intimacy to nearness. Nearness requires depth contact over time. It demands a campus discourse that constantly points out the limits of tolerance or intimacy. It comes from stressing what is common to human dilemmas rather than racial differences. It becomes possible through exposure to others and to other worlds beyond campus. It derives from black and white students working together on common projects. It flourishes when the co-curricular (outside of the classroom) opportunities for engagement happen often and in ways that create opportunities for dialogue. It takes place when those in conversation include black and white students sharing equal status – social, economic and academic – beyond their identities as students on the same campus pursuing the same degrees.

Student inclination to undertake the movement from segregation to intimacy to nearness depends on personal, familial, geographic and school-background factors. As a general rule, students who attended integrated schools, come from urban communities, attend integrated churches and grew up in open families where black and white friends of parents and the children move through the home are much more likely to initiate and sustain deep friendships across the colour line. Women students make such transitions to nearness more easily than men. Black students are more likely to accommodate interracial intimacy than white students.

By contrast, white students from rural communities who attended white schools and white churches, and whose parents do not have close friends of equal status from black communities coming through their homes, struggle at the very first hurdle – from segregation to intimacy. Those from isolated agricultural communities, where race relations and labour relations remain largely unchanged since apartheid, are most at risk of igniting dangerous interracial conflicts in intimate spaces such as university residences. It is, however, among these students that when the shift is made from segregation it is deep, sincere and transformative, with lasting personal and institutional benefits.

Black students from township communities who attended all-black public schools and black churches, whether from rural or urban areas, also struggle with the demands of integration but remain open to its possibilities. These students are generally very poor and often frustrated with their academic progress as a result of educational disadvantage from the school environment. Such students are preoccupied with the financing of their studies and academic progress, and much less obsessed with whether or not their residence or campus lives are integrated. This group of students is much more comfortable in the relatively stress-free relationships that come with being among black students, especially since they are more likely than black middle-class students to have experienced racism and racial distress from their contacts, or those of their parents, in off-campus engagements with white people.

Racial politics is a decisive factor in student capacity for moving from segregation to intimacy and nearness.

Black students who are very active in black nationalist politics generally smirk at efforts towards racial rapprochement or racial reconciliation. While nominally "non-racial" in the approach of the mother body, students from dominant parties on the outside tend to frame their politics narrowly as black politics with the emphasis on justice and redistribution. There is little appetite for conciliatory politics around issues like Afrikaans language accommodation, for example. Choices are presented starkly, as one of "them" versus "us". For the more radical among these students, their racial attitudes are formed in the cauldron of black poverty and often inflamed by more senior leaders on the radical edges of black politics. Depending on the national mood in black politics – such as periods of aggressive campaigning ahead of elections – this group becomes a major challenge to building social cohesion.

White students who are active in nationalist politics drive a parallel white-interests agenda. Their battleaxe is defensive – attacking any signs of distributive actions that appear to remedy black disadvantage or that threaten to diminish white cultural assets. The issues are commonplace across the historically Afrikaans universities – the preservation of the Afrikaans language, the progressive placement of more black students in medical school; changes to names of buildings or residences named after white supremacists; and perceived unfair treatment of white students or faculty as "minorities".

In institutional contexts that remain untransformed, black students and white students tend to migrate into these radical spaces where they become re-racialised as students and from which quarters it is very difficult to advance an agenda of integration let alone one that encourages nearness. The interaction between these two groups, in universities that remain largely unchanged, inevitably leads to confrontation that is sometimes violent.

Where institutional conditions create common spaces for interracial dialogue and discovery, these two political camps remain on the margins of university life and the majority of students seek the middle ground, a progressive politics by other means. Where students, black and white, sense a communal environment which does not prescribe their campus identities as simply racial and therefore oppositional, they are drawn to and inhabit such safe emotional and physical spaces where they do not feel the pressure to be one thing only – a political race.

Intimacy, and hopefully nearness, is seldom achieved in contexts where moral or political positioning is instantly judgemental and dismissive of young people who come from divided communities. Human beings anywhere, and especially in racially divided communities, do not come to their senses as a result of being preached at by posturing politicians or through the self-righteous judgements of the enlightened. Intimacy, as a first step, is achieved by working with woundedness, acknowledging one's own struggles and finding within this mutual vulnerability openness and opportunity for talking through and dealing with racism.

Migrations to nearness are achieved through leadership which is neither top-down nor bottom-up; transformation demands both. Student leaders under supportive institutional conditions tend to lead once they understand what the goals are, and commit to them. Senior leaders in university management must lead in ways that make those goals clear, but they need to do so through a model of exemplarity. Their visible lives as leaders, when consistently embracing other human beings regardless of race, signal powerful messages downwards that transform the ways in which students think of themselves and others.

Nearness requires role models, not only at the level of senior leadership but in the daily examples of students who reach out beyond the limits of the epidermis to affiliations which are not simply physical and strategic but deep and enduring. This comes from the ability of some students "to see the other in oneself" and to make the cognitive and emotional shifts that transform black and white relationships and, in the process, change institutions. Such exemplarity must be made visible for nearness to become a more distributed form of student interaction.

The pursuit of intimacy and nearness does not happen in a vacuum. Racially divided campuses exist inside racially divided communities which compose a racially divided country. In largely rural settings where the primary commentator on change is a racially conservative newspaper, intimacy will be ridiculed and resisted alongside any changes that threaten the racially privileged estate. Students come from and re-enter such communities; the real test of the durability of new relationships formed on campuses will be the extent, therefore, to which these ties and understandings last into the world of work and outside of it.[27]

Nearness is dangerous for it threatens the core commitments of segregationist thinking, where many layers of sediment which underpin such beliefs and practices have shaped the lives of communities and campuses over centuries. It is an approach to interracial community that will inevitably be non-linear in its unfolding. The quest for nearness will be circumvented, challenged, abused, undermined and ridiculed. There will be losses, even tragedy. But nothing provides a more lasting touchstone of institutional transformation than the deep transformation of student lives inside changing institutions that set multiple years as the timeline for change.

Racism and intimacy have always coexisted mainly in forms that are dangerous and divisive. Yet inside these fraught relationships are found countless examples of tenderness and trust, companionship and communion. Think back to the domestic labourer who expresses "genuine love" for the children and family under her care even as she shows awareness of difficult working conditions and unequal relations.

It is in fact the very closeness of these human relationships that provides the opportunities for nearness. The outspoken emotion of resistant hearts expresses at the same time the vulnerability that allows for change. Think back, for a moment, to the student lashing out against integration on the one night and shortly afterwards pleading for forgiveness and asking to be made part of the solution.

The racist, acting largely out of a learned ignorance while professing friendship with the victims, should be called to account on the racism even as the claim to intimacy is recognised as a powerful starting point for rebuilding the broken relationship. Not knowing is not the same as wilful ignorance, and should be accepted as sincere especially in cases where there is remorse and recompense as the truth begins to dawn on the perpetrators.

Immediate victims of racism are often more likely to forgive and forge renewed ties with those who did them harm than more distant accusers, whether family members or indignant scholars or political activists. That is because the immediate victims know something more about the twisted affection and personal vulnerabilities of those who did them wrong; they sense, in other words, new possibilities for black–white relationships through the power of pardon.

None of this is possible, however, without risk.

Notes

1 Lewis, C.S. 1960. *The Four Loves*. New York: Hartcourt Brace.
2 See Spalek, B. and Imtoual, A. (eds) 2008. *Religion, Spirituality and the Social Sciences: Challenging marginalisation*. Bristol: The Policy Press. Recognising the divergent roots of science and spirituality, the editors nevertheless argue for scholars "journeying between world views" and assemble case studies which show what happens when "the spiritual dimension of our existence is acknowledged and the result is social science is reconfigured", p. 113.

3 I borrow this handy term from the classic study on intergroup contact: Allport, G.W. 1979. *The Nature of Prejudice*. Boston, MA: Addison-Wesley Publishing Company, p. 261 (original publication 1954; this quote from the 25th anniversary edition).
4 Sumner, W.G. 1906. Quoted by Pettigrew, T.F. and Tropp, L.R. 2005. In Dovidio, J.F., Glick, P. and Rudman, L.A. (eds) *On the Nature of Prejudice: Fifty years after Allport*. Malden, MA: Blackwell Publishing, p. 262.
5 Pettigrew, T.F. and Tropp, L.R. 2008. How does intergroup contact reduce prejudice? Meta-analytic tests of three mediators. *European Journal of Social Psychology* 38, 922–34. Available from: www.interscience.wiley.com
6 Wright, S.C., Aron, A., McLaughlin-Volpe., Ropp, T. and Ropp, S.A. 1997. The Extended Group Contact effect: Knowledge of cross-group friendships and prejudice. *Journal of Personality and Social Psychology* 73(1), 73–90.
7 Shook, N.J. and Fazio, R.H. 2008. Interracial Roommate Relationships: An experimental field test of the contact hypothesis. *Psychological Science* 19(7), 717–23.
8 Quoted in Halling, S. 2008. Intimacy, Transcendence, and Psychology: Closeness and openness in everyday life. New York: Palgrave Macmillan, p. 1.
9 Ibid., p. 15.
10 Aron, A.P., Mashek, D.J. and Norton, E.N. 2007. Closeness as Including Other in the Self. In Mashek, D.J. and Aron, A.P. (eds) *Handbook of Closeness and Intimacy*. Mahwah, NJ: Lawrence Erlbaum Associates, Publishers, pp. 27–42.
11 Ibid., p. 27.
12 Ibid., p. 28.
13 Ibid.
14 Volf, M. 1996. *Exclusion and Embrace: A theological exploration of identity, otherness, and reconciliation*. Nashville, TN: Abingdon Press, p. 50.
15 Ibid., p. 32.
16 Ibid., p. 32.
17 Halling, S. 2008. *Intimacy, Transcendence, and Psychology: Closeness and openness in everyday life*. New York: Palgrave Macmillan. p. 185.
18 Ibid., p. 184.
19 Ibid., p. 185.
20 Ibid., p. 186.
21 For an excellent summary of the position of some of the critics, see Erasmus, Z. 2010. Contact Theory: Too timid for 'race' and racism. *Journal of Social Issues* 66(2), 387–400.
22 Saldanha, A. 2006. Reontologising Race: The machinic geography of phenotype: Environment and Planning D. *Society and Space* 24(9), 9–24 (quote on p. 21).
23 See Berscheid, E., Snyder, M. and Omoto, A.M. 1989. The Relationship Closeness Inventory: Assessing the closeness of interpersonal relationships. *Journal of Personality and Social Psychology* 57, 792–807.
24 I borrow this beautiful expression of binocular vision, and its definition, from the book *Distant Neighbours* describing through letters a relationship between close, but different and distant, friends: Wriglesworth, C. (ed.) 2014. *Distant Neighbour: Selected letters of Wendell Barry and Gary Snyder*. Berkeley, CA: Counterpoint Press.
25 I am grateful to the historian Mahmood Mamdani for this simple but powerful point, made in casual conversation on the occasion of his visit to campus after the reconciliation gesture at the UFS: "You now need to change the rules of the game."
26 The Yale sociologist Elijah Anderson distinguishes between the ethnocentric and the cosmopolitan in how people occupy common areas such as restaurants. In his work on Philadelphia in the USA, the cosmopolitan canopy refers to public spaces in the city "where diverse people converge, defining the setting as belonging to everyone and deemphasising race and other peculiarities. No one group claims priority", Anderson, E. 2011. *The Cosmopolitan Canopy: Race and civility in everyday life*. New York: WW Norton & Company, Inc., p. 5.

27 Amy Wells completed a fascinating study on the durability of race relations among high school graduates in the first wave of desegregation following Brown versus Board of Education in the USA, the legislation that ended segregated schooling. What she found was disappointing – that while black and white students did in fact enjoy interracial community while learning together, they re-segregated after leaving high school. The question is whether this will be true for university students in a black majority country like South Africa on a campus like the UFS.

11 A near and present danger

Introduction

By sheer coincidence two of the students, one black and one white, came from the same small town of Pongola on the north-eastern coast of South Africa, 800 kilometres away from Bloemfontein. They would meet one fatal night on a dark campus road in an event that would severely test the strength of the transformation accord at the University of the Free State. It was February 2014.

I was returning late that night from a school hall meeting where I had addressed the farming community of Theunissen, a rural town about 1 hour north-west of Bloemfontein. After a long day at work nothing gave me more joy than to travel into the rural hinterland and talk, as in this case, to mainly white and some black farming families about the state of education in the country, the university from which many of them had graduated, and how we could work together across racial lines to repair schools and human relations in our fractured country. There would be earnest questions and intimate conversations afterwards in the communion of food and friendship. Everybody seemed really optimistic about the future of campus and country at this event.

We left at about 21h30 that evening for the drive back home to Bloemfontein. My dean of students, Rudi Buys, who accompanied me, was a fellow speaker at the event, and in the driver's seat. I enjoyed travelling with him to the rural communities because in our close friendship the communities could bear witness to the strength of the ties between the young, white Afrikaans-speaking head of students and the older, black rector of the university. I was the godfather of his newly born son and our families had bonded immediately since our arrival on campus.

I was responding to the usual flow of student queries on Twitter when my stomach turned. "Do you know about this?" I asked the dean. "No," he said.

A black student had posted on Twitter an emotional and angry message about two white students who had allegedly driven their "*bakkie*" (pick-up truck) over the body of a helpless black student and, when the student stood up to complain to them, the two white men beat him senseless. "Do you know about this?" I asked again, now in a state of shock. Twitter had lighted up with tweets and re-tweets, and the undiluted message was now travelling fast and furiously across the campus community and into the big cities. Here was a firestorm coming if ever I saw one.

We started to call secretaries and student leaders and other campus administrators to find out what on earth was going on. By this time the car was picking up speed as we raced towards Bloemfontein in the dead of night to get to the campus, deal with the crisis and attend to the victim. Within minutes, the name of the student was tweeted to me. "Do you know him?" I asked Rudi. "Yes, I think so; he left a message wanting to speak to you but it was not clear why or what it was all about." The dean thought it was a routine student inquiry because no details were left. I had just changed my mobile phone number which I had had for about a decade; every journalist had the number, and seemingly everybody else, so I changed it just to get some privacy back into my life. That must have been the reason the student victim had not contacted me directly.

By the time we drove through the campus gates, sweating, the following was communicated to us. A black student was hit by a "*bakkie*" driven by two white men who came through the main gate on the north side of campus. The "*bakkie*" had then driven to and stopped at one of the former white male residences, presumably to visit friends. The black student stumbled towards them, confronted them about the vehicular assault and was beaten for his troubles. The men in the pickup truck then escaped in their "*bakkie*" by driving through the medical school gate on the west side of campus. The "*bakkie*" had false licence plates and could not be traced. The victim had been taken to hospital, treated and then released, meaning that his injuries were probably not life threatening. Before going home I instructed campus security to work through the night, with the police, to track down the strangers who had come onto campus and assaulted the student.

The senior leadership of the university had an early meeting scheduled that we used to deliberate on this tragic event. I called in campus security and asked for a progress report. I was told they still could not track down the vehicle because of the false number plates. There was a question buzzing in my head at that time. Why, if the strangers did in fact knock down and run over the black student, would they stop at a men's residence? Surely in a hit-and-run accident you try to escape as soon as possible? And why stop at that particular residence? So I called in the prime, the student head of the residence where the "*bakkie*" stopped, and asked whether he knew the men. I put it quite bluntly: "Do not lie to me." He was actually quite forthcoming. They were in fact students, former campus residents who now lived off campus. He himself did not see much of what happened; the confrontation was over quite quickly and he had heard that the black student had approached the two men in the "*bakkie*" with a broken bottle to fight. But he knew little else because he was still inside the building at the time and what he got was largely from hearsay.

Two students? This changed the entire scenario from searching for two white strangers. The prime gave their names and then, to my shock, informed me that one of the students was already sitting outside in the waiting room. "Where is the other student?" I asked. "He is writing a test," said the prime. "Go and fetch him." In the meantime, campus security was called to my office.

When my secretary informed me that the two students had arrived, I went outside to confirm their identities. I was careful not to talk to them because in a disciplinary case I am the last court of appeal and, consistent with every case, whether staff or students, I do not therefore engage the campus persons against whom allegations are made.

They were taken by campus security to obtain a full report and, by this time, the black student had already laid criminal charges against the students, including attempted murder, and so the two also had to report to the Park Street police station. One of our senior colleagues made sure they had legal representation. In the meantime, and on the basis of the evidence in hand, we suspended the two students pending the outcome of the criminal case and for another good reason: their lives were now in danger on campus.

At this stage I was emotionally devastated. We had toiled so hard, day and night, weekends and holidays, to bring the campus out of Reitz; now this. "How was this possible?" I would ask myself over and over again, having witnessed first-hand the steady shifts in institutional culture and the gradual embrace among students of each other. It simply did not make sense, but here we were – back where we started. It was a thoroughly demoralising experience.

As if on cue, the Johannesburg media screamed "racism" from the moment the event happened and before a single investigative reporter had even hit the campus. "Another" racial scandal, repeated almost every media station, with the unforgettable Reitz incident taken from the archives and replayed on television as if there was a straightforward logical connection between the two events. "A leaking water bag," our brand specialists used to say in the early days to indicate that for all the good work going on, a single negative event would leak our best efforts. That is how it felt, and the toll on leadership was palpable throughout the main building.

The greatest damage was done by a prominent radio personality in Johannesburg. He posted on his Facebook a photo of the black student's injured face and questioned support for the racist university from prominent personalities. Student leaders from our campus jumped right in and joined the accusatory crowds; the university managers were to blame for not stamping out racism. Government officials could not restrain themselves from pointing the finger straight at the rector – this is what happens when you let students off lightly through forgiveness and reconciliation. A very prominent struggle activist lambasted me in person on Twitter and at a Johannesburg university forum; she made sure I also got a personal summary of her remarks:

> Dear @JJ_UFS I argued it is unhelpful to deny racism in our society. I also said as VC it not your place to tell us what to think.

It is still not clear to me where the denial of racism ever took place or the telling of people what to think, but it was open season on the university and the "driving over the body" of a black student who is then viciously assaulted immediately afterwards – with a picture of his wounded face – was too compelling and emotive a case to answer through calm deliberation and logical argument. "It might well be a case of racism" I argued in public, "but we do not know that yet." In the court of black public opinion, the case of racism was sealed. I refused therefore to go onto any radio or television shows, despite repeated demands, knowing that to even ask that prominent people withhold judgement until the facts were in would be dismissed as the denial of racism.

I did, however, have immediate responsibilities on campus, and so the first thing I did was to ask to speak to the victim. He wanted to come with a group of black students and I declined; this was a personal meeting. From the moment of our first meeting in my office I started to have my doubts about his case.

"First of all I want you to know that I am deeply sorry for what happened to you." He nodded his head. "And I want you to know that we will do everything we can to support you during this difficult time." He started to tell me hair-raising stories of his upbringing and my eyes stretched when he said that he was thrown into crocodile-infested waters in his coastal village by white people who then laughed at his dilemma as he tried to escape.

Suddenly he stood up and asked to use my office toilet. "Sure, this way." I had no reason to suspect anything and waited for him to return as we talked about the experience, what he went through and his disappointment that he could not reach me; I explained the recent change of my telephone number and gave him the new one. "Is there anything more we can do for you?" I asked.

"I can make this problem go away," was his surprising answer.

I was absolutely stunned by this very strange response. "I can deal with X and Y," he said in reference to politically active students. "So you know what to do Prof." At this point a mix of anger and disappointment started to set in, but I had to keep a straight face. "No, I don't know what to do. What are you talking about?" By now of course I realised he wanted money. In his mind I might be willing to pay for him to be silent and not embarrass the university. "No, I don't know what you mean. You have to be explicit about your needs for me to be able to respond." At this stage he stood up and headed back to the toilet. By this time it was clear to me that the toilet was an opportunity to consult his handlers. Back he came and I told him to go home and we could continue the discussion at some future time.

What was going on here? Was he genuinely knocked over and beaten up and now looking for financial compensation? Or did the foul act not happen at all and the entire drama a scheme to extract money from the university? I did not know but at that stage, with the initial evidence available, I had to treat him as if he was a victim. The truth will come out, I remember telling myself. I called some of my trusted senior staff together and told them about the event. Just as well because when he realised later that I was not giving him money he went to the *Saturday Star*, a Johannesburg newspaper, and twisted the contents of the meeting to suggest, inter alia, that I doubted the seriousness of his injuries and tried to keep him from speaking to the media.

By this stage pressure was building on campus for the university management to be seen to be more angry, more visible and more vocal on the matter. There were other black voices on campus making the same point – condemn the act outright and distance the university from any acts of racism. I did, but more than that I could not do given that we simply did not have enough evidence at the time. I then put out a statement that spoke to the growing angst on campus, and wise voices urged me to announce a university assembly to address student concerns.

In the meantime the Student Representative Council had requested permission for a march on campus which would end with the presentation of a memorandum to the rector. Of course permission was granted and on the day a group of students arrived at the front entrance to the main building. It was a smaller crowd than I expected, maybe about 150, but the pleasing thing was the racially diverse character of the marchers. In the midst of the crisis I could see a breakthrough. In previous years this would have been an angry black crowd including outside agitators, with the real threat of violence at any moment.

In fact, the last time there was a protest march on Red Square, the ironic name of the red-paved bricked flooring, strangers were bussed in, bricks flew and teargas sprayed; that seemed a long time ago. This protest was peaceful, consisting only of students and, even though one or two students had threatened disrespect, it was a well-organised and well-managed event. I was expecting an emotionally charged statement on racism as the SRC President started to read the memorandum through a loudhailer. Demand Number 1? Better and cheaper food on the Bridge.

I accepted the "memo" with gratitude, promised to respond within two weeks and announced the university assembly as the place where the response would be read.

The *Callie Human*, the largest auditorium on campus, was packed. We had not had a university assembly like this before but the idea was appealing – a regular meeting place of the academy to address problems of concern or to spell out a vision for the future. Here was a crisis, and what better way to engage the community than to call them together to talk. The large audience was remarkably calm and respectful; any student who had ideas of disruption, and there were a few, would find little support in this hall. I spoke to the issues captured in a circular to the campus community:

Dear University of the Free State Students

In the past four years there has emerged a new consensus on the UFS campus about the things that divide us such as racism, sexism and homophobia. Students and campus leaders have worked hard to develop this new consensus in residences and in the open spaces on campus. There can be no doubt that new bonds of friendship have developed across the markers of race, ethnicity, class, religion and sexual orientation. I bear witness to these new solidarities everyday on the campus.

You chose a white student to head up the transformation portfolio on the SRC. You chose a black captain to head up the university's first team in rugby. You chose a white "prime" as head of residence to lead a predominantly black men's residence. You chose a South African woman of Indian descent as Rag Queen and last week, a black student from Cape Town as the men's Rag winner – choices not possible and never made before in our campus history. Many of you have intimate friends who come from different social or cultural or religious backgrounds. You learn together, share rooms together, pray together and party together. In other words, in the day to day workings of this university campus, you have demonstrated to campus, city and country that we can overcome the lingering effects of racism and other maladies in this new generation.

I have said this repeatedly that *from time to time this new consensus will be tested* when a minority of students, and they are a small and dwindling minority, still act as if these are the days of apartheid. And when that consensus is tested as it was this week, and as it will be in the future, only then we will be able to assess the strength and durability of our progress in creating a new South African campus culture of human togetherness based on respect, dignity and embrace. The real test of our leadership, including student leadership, is how we respond when our transformation drive is threatened.

Let me say this: I have absolute faith in you, as students of this great university, to stand together in your condemnation of these vile acts of violence and to move together in your determination to maintain the momentum for the human project of the University of the Free State. We have come too far to allow a few criminals to derail what you have built together in recent years.

There will, no doubt, be unscrupulous people on all sides of the political spectrum wanting to milk this tragedy for their own narrow purposes. There will be false information, rumours and exaggerations by those who wish to inflame a bad situation to gain mileage for their agendas. That is inevitable in a country that is still so divided.

I ask you, through all of this, to keep perspective. Two or ten or even twenty students behaving badly do not represent 30,000 students; a minority of violent and hateful persons do not represent the ideals, ambitions and commitments of the majority. At the same time, let us be realistic – anyone who thinks you can drive transformation without resistance clearly does not understand the difficult process of change.

The events of the week remind us, however, that we still have a long road to walk in deepening social and academic transformation at our university. Yes, we have invested hundreds of hours in training and mentorship; we have created new structures – such as the Institute for Reconciliation and Social Justice – to capture the energy and imagination of students driving transformation; we have created many opportunities for students to study and travel on this and other continents to enable cross-cultural learning; we have established formal and informal opportunities to dialogue about difficult issues on and off campus between students and their leaders; and we crafted new curricula to enable teaching and learning on the big questions of our times.

The rest of the communication talked about further steps to be taken to deepen transformation at the UFS and expressed the hope that the students involved in this violence would come to see the error of their ways and return to study, "for that is the kind of university we are". There was a dignified end to the large assembly; we had managed to calm the rage that was building and now the really hard work was before us – to deepen the transformation with added emphasis on the quality of human togetherness among all students, especially the ones on the margins of the change project.

Deep reflection

The crisis more or less under control, I asked a group of about 20 university leaders and thinkers, students and staff, and two community leaders – one from a black church in the township and one from a white church in the suburbs–to assemble for a full day in an off-campus resort to reflect together on this dangerous bend in the transformation road. We needed, all of us, to understand how this could even happen given the change trajectory we thought we were on. The instruction was to be honest, to put everything on the table; we desperately needed to understand what was going on. Were we victims of our own marketing? Why did nobody see this coming? Yes, we were used to occasional reports of "micro-aggressions" in which students or staff would report being slighted because of difference – gay and lesbian students, black students, students with disabilities – but nothing as aggressive and violent as the vehicular assault and the physical encounter that followed.

We talked about lingering traditions from the past, those untransformed spaces on campus. In some male residences students still wear uniforms; whereas in the non-Afrikaans universities students came to escape the rigidities of school and home, like the uniform, in our institution, and similar ones, this was in fact a way of clutching onto culture, memory and tradition in the face of change. We talked about a strange space outside one of the men's residences called the "*tiekie*" (once the name for the now discontinued two-and-a-half cent coin), a traffic roundabout painted brightly. When a woman student stood on that sacred place, the men from the residence would drag her into the men's showers where she had two choices – a hot shower without clothes on or a cold shower wearing her clothes.

We stood aghast at this childish, sexist and offensive behaviour in the twentieth century until several senior leaders reminded colleagues that women students came to complain that they had heard rumours that the "*tiekie*" was to be banned; "we want to be *tiekied*", they argued. "Don't take away everything from us. We are students. We like our traditions."

All of this was tolerable, of course, until a black student or a progressive white student inadvertently stepped on the *"tiekie"*. Then all hell broke loose, as happened recently. A black woman student stood on the *"tiekie"*. A white first-year student, on instruction from his seniors in the men's residence which claimed the piece of concrete, runs off to catch the young woman and bring her indoors to be showered. The black woman, unaware of the tradition, runs for her life with the white man in pursuit. Instantly, a ritual that existed for whites before desegregation is interpreted as a racist attack by the black woman who has no other meaning for the pursuit than racial violence. Other examples were raised in this Bush conference of how the little things that remained unchanged scuppered the big things that were changing.

We delved deeply into white masculine behaviours. One white man around the table told the harrowing story in few words: "When I was 18 I went to Tsumeb and I never came back." Of course he came back physically but here he sat with us acknowledging that the compulsory military service that put white men into war zones in Namibia, in this case, destroyed their emotional, psychic and spiritual selves and that such trauma lives on in them and their sons even to this day. Few black people allow for such empathy and insight when it comes to our white compatriots and yet, without excusing violence or racism, here is a trauma and victimhood nobody wants to talk about.

We talked therefore about whether it was possible to change a campus without changing a community. This was an important question because, from the moment the violent encounter happened, the white Afrikaans community imputed guilt on the black student and innocence on the two white students. None of the Afrikaans newspapers carried the bruised face of the victim, which they would have milked for all its worth if it had been a white student. How then do we deal with the issues of anger, guilt, shame, bitterness and aggression of especially white men or, what Michael Kimmel once called "aggrieved entitlement?"[1]

These were complex issues in a relatively isolated, rural university surrounded by white graduates of the university and descendants of its long history and culture. In the city and throughout the rural areas of the Free State, white alumni and parents felt very strongly that this was *their* university. As one angry old white alumnus wrote to me: "we built this university with our sweat and blood, not you, so know your place." It remains for many a great difficulty understanding that the UFS is and was a public university, and that the racist exclusion of blacks over almost a century was a point of shame, not of pride.

Having lost political power, and control over most public institutions – the national government, the parastatals, the municipalities and even most of the schools – the only places in which white South Africans could still exert some authority were the churches and the universities. The churches remain relatively uncontested without any interference or pressure from the state. The universities, on the other hand, were fair game for an unrelenting contestation from Pretoria in the north to Stellenbosch in the south and, in between, the North West University and the University of the Free State. At Stellenbosch, an overwhelmingly white, Afrikaans-dominant university, the push-back is organised – at least in formal terms–around the protection of the Afrikaans language.

How would the UFS speak to and include the concerns and anxieties of the broader white community while still pushing forward with the important task of an inclusive transformation that not only brought black and white students and staff together, but kept them together? It would be easy to bulldozer the change process, as happened at some of the other former white universities, but that kind of mean-spiritedness hurt human beings and alienated white citizens in favour of black citizens. That is not what the UFS was about. A firm conclusion was left on the table – that campus transformation would always be affected by, and affect, broader community perceptions about change at the university. We needed to be "out there" raising support from and positively influencing both black and white communities about the change processes.

It was clear from our research data that the UFS had broad-based community support for its transformation direction. Beyond the Free State, the UFS had solid support and indeed won multiple awards for the transformation process in South Africa and internationally. It was the minority voices of white conservatism and black radicalism that constituted the noise. It was, however, the voices that carried in the Afrikaans newspapers, for whites, and in the predominantly black newspapers, for blacks. Organised, these voices did great harm especially with those Afrikaans newspapers that made no secret about the fact that their constituency was that hard-core conservative voice. Their noise outstripped their numbers. After clearly malicious reporting on the UFS transformation, we had no choice but to take our case to the ombudsman who ruled on all three of our cases against the local newspaper, declaring that its unfounded reports "did great damage to the UFS".

We left the meeting in the Bush with a clear path as to how we would take forward the university in the light of the tragic event that had placed the UFS back in a negative media spotlight. In these moments of collective reflection by a cross-section of black and white staff and students, with leaders from the community, there is an invaluable sense of honest, critical support that an organisation's leadership so desperately needs, not only in times of crisis.

The victim

On a Saturday morning, while recovering from the emotional drain of the campus assault, my mobile phone rings. It was the victim. He needs help. He has no food and his body is hurting from the attack. Could I arrange for medical assistance? I rushed to his off-campus rental house which he shared with other students within walking distance of the university. I felt strange. His dark bedroom had some young men in there looking morose and whom I did not recognise as students. I wondered, even then, whether these were among his handlers. Before leaving for the home of the victim I had called a young doctor, also a colleague at the university, and he was already in the room examining the student's injuries and prescribing medication. I rushed to the chemist and returned with the medicines and bags of food. He appeared grateful and I asked him to call at any time should he need anything. It was after this visit to his home that he went to *The Star* with the concocted story of being pressured not to talk to the media and that our goal was to push him towards reconciling with the perpetrators.

I was beginning to lose patience with the young man and refused his requests to see me. How could I trust him? He meets with me and then turns the conversation into serious personal accusations in the media. I declined any further meeting requests. Then the abuse intensified through personal emails and Facebook postings, at some point leaving me with no choice but to consult our lawyers. We decided not to act even as the abuse continued: "you are my project", he writes, "and I will not rest until I get to you", and worse. By this point I realised that the man was possibly disturbed and that his case now proceeding through the courts might be on thin ice. He was going to collapse his own case, I thought.

The first signs of trouble came from the South African Human Rights Commission (SAHRC), a body that had spent considerable time and resources investigating public complaints of racism especially in schools and universities. It had taken a special interest in the UFS after the Reitz incident and was hypersensitive to any and all incidents rumoured or reported from the Bloemfontein campus. The complaint in this case was that the victim had claimed to being called by the derogatory term "*kaffir*" (nigger, equivalent) by the assailants and it was said that some women students were in the area at the time of the vehicular assault and had heard those hateful words spoken. So apart from the criminal case, the commission had to rule on whether the dignity of the victim had been trampled on in the course of the assault. From what I had experienced I thought the conclusion was far from clear.

I was not completely surprised, therefore, by the short letter from the local office of the SAHRC that landed on my desk:

> The South African Human Rights Commission has completed its investigations into this matter. After careful review of the information gleaned from the investigation, we wish to advise you that there is no corroborating evidence to make a conclusive finding of racism and violation of human rights . . . In view of the above, the Commission will close the file in this matter.

But worse was to come for the now questionable victim when the local magistrate ruled on his case barely a few weeks later. The court ruled that the black student was an unreliable witness; that he had changed his story several times; that he was prone to anger and exaggeration; and that on the balance of evidence presented, the magistrate said he could not find the two white students guilty.

The victim did not even bother to show up in court for the ruling, and when a newshound tracked him down he declared that he did not know what happened in the courts since nobody had bothered to tell him.

"Tawana Brawley" was my immediate thought when I heard the Bloemfontein magistrate's verdict. This was the black American teenager who, in the late 1980s, claimed to have been abducted and raped by a group of white men. She was found in a dumpster disoriented and dirty with the words "nigger" and "KKK" printed – upside down – on her body. Black activists from everywhere came out in her support and the case raised racial tensions throughout New York and the USA as 1000 people marched through the local streets in protest. The courts found she had fabricated the entire story in order to escape a beating or worse by her father for being out late. Tawana Brawley was already a troubled teenager by that time. But the harm she did to race relations in her community was incalculable.

Something did happen on that fateful night on a dark street on the campus of the University of the Free State. The evidence at hand at the time certainly suggested that the white students had a case to answer. But court evidence suggested that other scenarios were now possible: that the black student might have been drunk and not fully aware of what happened that night; that he was not in fact hit by the "*bakkie*" but thought so; that he then approached the two white students, attacking them physically; that they then turned on him and got the better of the physical altercation; "self-defence", their lawyer would argue.

I called a news conference in the main building in response to the decision from the magistrate's court. The local Afrikaans press came out in full, fuming, as if this was a personal matter to be taken up on behalf of their own. The contempt of some of the journalists present was undisguised. The black student was always guilty and the white students always innocent. In all the incidents of alleged racism on or around campus, this was the only one that came out in favour of the whites, and they were going to milk the case for all its worth. The next day's headlines were not surprising and warned of dire financial costs to the university as if the institution, and not the state prosecutor, had presented the charges.

But the damage was done and I announced that the suspended students were free to return to study and that we were considering action against the so-called victim, pending the release of a transcription of the magistrate's ruling. I publicly apologised to the two white students and their families for what they had had to go through in this process.

How could one student do so much harm to two other students and their families, to race relations on campus and to the institution itself? Could one student, with such serious allegations, scuttle the transformation trajectory of a university that had made such great strides to overcome its distant past and the recent scandal of Reitz?

One national television station coaxed me into a live discussion on race relations on university campuses. Towards the end of the interview, and in relation to this new scandal, the Johannesburg journalist asked me: "and how is the victim doing?" I had a full go at the ridiculous question. "Which ones?" I thought.

The dark side of intimacy

> And stand together, yet not too near together. The pillars of the temple stand apart, and the oak tree and the cypress grow not in each other other's shadows.[2]

"Is there a dark side to intimacy?" ask Mashek and Aron in their massive compendium of research on closeness and intimacy.[3] The question is largely rhetorical, for we know this to be true from spousal abuse to parental abuse of children to the abuse of a loving partner. But this case is different in that the intimate spaces opened up on campus become abused by the very victims of apartheid. Whereas this victim would not have been able to access the university as a black man until recently, he now abuses his newfound status to concoct stories of racist abuse. This is the dangerous flipside to white racism at close quarters – when black victims imagine racism for their own benefit.

This of course is dangerous territory and no self-respecting social scientist wants to go down this very rocky road for one simple reason – the pervasive and lasting influence of colonial and apartheid racism is so severe, and so long denied, that we tend to overlook or minimise those cases in which previous victims cry wolf. For example, virtually none of the English-language media that had so lambasted the white "racists" from the university carried any prominent stories about the findings of either the SAHRC or the criminal courts. None of our personal critics who took to the airwaves as soon as the story broke came back and apologised for their angry, outrageous pronouncements on the white racists or the institution and its leaders. Total silence.

But as we saw in this case, the damage done to real people – in this case the two white students or in the Brawley case the falsely accused white junior assistant attorney general – is severe. Then there is the damage to fragile institutions trying to rebuild broken human relationships and create intimate spaces. This is the dark side of intimacy – when victims cry racism for their own ends.

It remains the most powerful weapon of black South Africans in public argument or private differences – to dismiss white opponents with the charge of racism. Given our racist history, and the unyielding structures that sustain racist practices, it is easy to fall into this trap of quickly dismissing individuals or groups as racists. The charge is powerful in its ability to completely undermine any grounds for further argument; it is psychologically and emotionally an instant and deep wound from which it is difficult to recover, especially for a sensitive person. It renders the white voice voiceless.

There is an even darker side, so to speak, to the reckless charge of racism which has at times been very personal. Because I was classified as Coloured by the apartheid regime, a tag I hated since the day I became aware of it, this meant that you were deemed somewhere between pure white and pure black (*African*, in current South African usage). I used the word "pure" with considered disregard, contempt actually, because in everyday usage Coloured is defined as "mixed race" – a designation that is fraught with all kinds of ideological assumptions about race and purity, on the one hand, and quite simply wrong-headed given the centuries of intermingling across human categories.

In official reckoning, nonetheless, you were deemed marginally better off than "Africans" but less privileged than whites. This is the way people who accept the Coloured tag tend to put it today: "under apartheid we were not white enough and under democracy we are not black enough." There were surely material differences created by apartheid to separate Africans and Coloureds – such as labour preference areas favouring Coloureds in the Cape and greater per capita expenditure on education – but in a strict class analysis, those distinctions sometimes blurred between Coloured squatters and African squatters, or not, in the case of the African professional classes and the Coloured factory workers. It was the harshness of the pass laws, reserved for Africans, and the slew of petty apartheid provisions – Mandela, for example, would not get shoes or bread in prison, but Coloured and Indian comrades did – that really imprinted in memory the gratuitous and oppressive hurts that linger to this day.

It is an enduring tribute to the Black Consciousness Movement that it saw through these manufactured racial categories and collapsed apartheid distinctions to declare African, Coloured and Indian people as one group, black, against the divide-and-rule tactics of the apartheid regime. This new sense of black was a solidarity that remained "thick" throughout the long years of struggle, but has become razor thin as many African activists and colleagues – like their white nationalist counterparts then – see distinct material advantages in reinserting the essential African identity back into public discourse.

Perhaps the most brutal expression of racial essentialism came through the voice of a presidential spokesman at the time, Jimmy Manyi, who declared that there was "an oversupply of Coloured people in the Western Cape". It was without question one of the lowest points in the racist rhetoric of the essentialist African voice and led a "Coloured" cabinet minister to lambaste Manyi's racism in an open letter to the press. What remains disturbing from the incident was that the presidency did not denounce, let alone fire, its spokesman, as would have happened in any decent democracy; it was, in fact, to castigate the Coloured minister for speaking about the matter outside of his political party.

The "African" academic colleague who therefore charged me with "hating African women" after the decision to offer institutional forgiveness to the white students in the Reitz affair knew exactly what he was doing. The Coloured man, in his definition, is not one of us; he is biologically and politically a different category of person. In essence, he cannot be trusted to love outside of his own and that is what explains his behaviour. I was somewhat amused by his racist essentialism when he published "research" on the different meanings of headaches for Basotho, Coloured and other species of humanity.

These examples of the dark side of intimacy draw attention to the fact that simply placing human beings in physical proximity to each other does not, in itself, resolve deep differences of history, ideology and memory. In fact, it could inflame old conflicts and lead to dangerous situations in which "victims become killers" as one of Africa's foremost historians once put it.[4] This turning of the victim into perpetrator was in fact witnessed much earlier at the University of the Free State in a devastating challenge to the new intimacy being established in the residences.

Villa Bravado

We had hardly come out of the Reitz scandal – and now I *was* on the job – when "another video" was leaked into the public space. All residences were warned against initiations. Training was provided on racism, stereotypes and the enduring harm of initiation. Clear lines of discipline were communicated if any residence again overstepped the mark as far as these rituals were concerned. Of course we had hoped that the very public consequences of what could happen to students, as in the Reitz saga, would discourage continuation of the tradition. No student wants to lose their place at university.

The puzzle was that Villa Bravado, the short-hand reference often used in relation to this former white residence, was now for all intents and purposes a black residence. Its prime, head of residence and most residence committee members were black. It was black students who complained about these strange and savage rituals of humiliation, something completely unfamiliar to them from either schools or the historically black universities in the country. Why, we asked ourselves as leaders, would an initiation video emerge from a black residence?

The real horror was yet to come. In a bizarre twist on the Reitz scandal this was a case of black-on-white initiation. How did this happen? In response to the university's drive to de-racialise the residences, progressive white students started to filter towards the black houses. The three white students in the video were told, accurately, that all newcomers to the Villa residence had to undergo the same initiation treatment. Leading the ceremony is the prime, a young black man called Chris, who appears to be reading from a white page instructions as to what is about to happen. The three white male students stood with their heads down awaiting their initiation fate, surrounded as they were by a loud group of black students.

Suddenly, the white students had water poured on their heads and which splurged onto the tiled floors. They then went down on all fours and eventually flat on their stomachs and imitated swimming movements on the floor. Some students tried to grab their legs. One tried to kick in the direction of their bodies. Others did grab their legs and pulled the bodies a short distance. More water was poured on the floor. One student can be seen filming the episode and there is raucous laughter in the semi-circle around the male bodies on the floor. The white students were now fully fledged members of Villa.

Without a video, this incident, as in the Reitz case, would have been a non-story. If the students being initiated were black, there would have been strong management action – as in other cases – but nothing more sensational than that. But the imagery of white students dragged on the floor by black students in the wake of Reitz was explosive stuff, and true to form, the local Afrikaans newspaper had a field day reporting the initiation to its conservative reading base, with all the comparison to boot.

Distasteful as this was, the incident was not Reitz. The white students participated voluntarily *and* with clear knowledge of what was happening. The initiation was a common event applied to all Villa students. The initiation was not an anti-integration statement; it was, in the twisted minds of male students, a bonding ritual for newcomers. But even the surface parallels with Reitz were simply too much to ignore for an ever-vigilant press and a conservative community that wanted tit-for-tat justice at the slightest hint of black wrongdoing.

That said, there were clear rules and constant communication from the senior leadership on the undesirability of initiation, and action had to be taken. We disciplined the black head of the residence who, by all accounts, was aware of, if not actually present at, the event. Despite constant threats and mobilisation of black sentiment against the university on his side, the discipline resulted in his departure. We disciplined the prime and he was removed from his position in the residence and suspended. Villa itself was put on serious notice of much more severe consequences if this happened again.

How does one explain such quantum entanglements (see epigraph at the start of the chapter) when black students begin to see others in themselves in this destructive way? When the very things you rebelled against become part of you as a black student or black student leader once you assume the same powers? Here the power of "social structures", as sociologists like to put it, is much more powerful than explanations that are reduced to individual or group pathologies. Deep within the fibres of the organisation are memories, traditions and histories that envelop and shape the behaviour of residents. Even those who resent these initiation rituals often come to embrace them, as with the black students in this account. Having come in with no power as first-year students they now, as seniors, have access to that power and are willing to impose it on newcomers. The newcomers are not strangers but the most intimate of friends, members of the house whose loyalty is being secured through rituals which, to the outside observer, are humiliating and demeaning; but not to the students.

This dark side to intimacy has a curious twist, therefore, because it builds a fraught solidarity among students who are actually worlds apart in terms of politics, culture and ethnicity but bound together as members of a house. In the metaphor of quantum entanglement, they are actually distant but because of bonding contact begin to behave as one. This is only one of many bizarre attachments where because of a "higher" principle of intimacy – house membership – black students would come to defend white students, and white students their black mates, even when the issue on the table is a violation of the rules.

Does the dark side of intimacy yield transformation possibilities?

The two examples raised on the dark side of intimacy are similar but different in important ways. In the case of the false allegations of assault and racism, it is almost impossible to reconstruct race relations among the actors within this drama. This is especially true in the early months, even years, after the formal findings of the courts. The white students, at the time of writing, together with some of the parents, are patently angry. They denounced the university for "not hearing the students' side of the story" ahead of the suspension and for judging them as racists before the evidence was in. At one stage they suggested legal action on prompting from the local press, but did not pursue this course. In a fit of anger the students indicated that they did not want to return to the university to complete their studies. The university cleared their financial obligations for the year in which the incident happened and kept the offer on the table for a return to studies.

The black student does not appear to have the capacity or inclination to approach the white students to apologise for his actions. In his mind, he is the injured party despite the rulings of both the Rights Commission and the courts. Those around him sustain that belief in his victimhood, and his unremitted anger and aggression through social media postings do not suggest any likelihood of conciliation in the near future.

Where hurt runs so deep, where one or more of the actors in a race drama are emotionally immature, or where there are strong political motives on the part of one of the parties, it is impossible for the dark side of intimacy to progress towards light. That was not the case in the Villa incident.

I have to confess that I was angry with the black leadership of the residence, the head and the prime in particular. Surely they know what humiliation means from recent experience as black people? They were not raised in these kinds of initiation rituals. I had expected, perhaps naively, a kind of comradeship among those of us who had lived through the bitter struggle, and understanding that we knew what was at stake in the transformation of this important university. It would be a hard lesson I would learn over and over again – transformation is not something "done" to whites, it is something we all need. Apartheid destroyed that inner sense of wholeness for black and white alike.

After the head of residence left I still had to deal with Chris once his suspension was lifted. He came back into the university and I avoided intimate conversation with him. I was surprised by how hard my own heart had become in relation to this young man; it was not easy to let go of that deep sense of disappointment, that feeling that "he should have known better". Truth is I had always dealt better with white racism than black prejudice. With white South Africans under apartheid, you knew what to expect. You understood the terms of the relationship. This helped you prepare, emotionally and spiritually, for the onslaught when it came. You were always ready as a black person, your sensitive racial antennae alert to any abuse. When the acts of prejudice come from those you know intimately, it hurts in a different and deeper way. This was the reason I had difficulty having a normal relationship with the former prime of the house.

But something was happening to him in spite of my distancing behaviour. He was going through a deep and sincere transformation himself, largely a result of the big-hearted dean of students who took Chris under this wing. This transformation was something to behold. Gone was the arrogance of the former leader, the heavy-handed coercion of younger students. He carried so clearly in himself a new humility that spoke of remorse and reflection. Still, I kept my distance while quietly observing Chris at one public student meeting after another in which he was playing the subdued role of mentor and support staff on the various transformation projects under Student Affairs.

Then things came to a head. It was yet another student leadership training session during which I was to speak. Chris was central to the organisation of the event and it was no longer possible for me to continue carrying this hurt and disappointment within me. Right there, and in front of all the other student leaders, I apologised to Chris and asked his forgiveness for the bitterness that separated us from each other. I expressed appreciation for his recovery and his quiet but firm role in the transformation of the student body. He had made the transition from a dark and dangerous intimacy to something much more profound, nearness.

At that moment I was aware of course that this was an act that would demonstrate to these young student leaders the importance of three things – recognition of a near but distant colleague, the need for contrition as leaders and the capacity to forgive. But right now my goal was not to teach others; it was to teach myself submission and seek that sense of nearness to a better leader than myself. In this case, and through our complex entanglement, it was possible to move from that dark side of intimacy.

"There is a crack in everything. That's how the light gets in."[5]

Still, I have not given up on the possibility of a transformative outcome even in the assault case. What I have learnt, as a leader, is that timing is everything. You cannot insist on conciliation. Time heals and sometimes it does not, as was clear in the many cases from the Truth and Reconciliation Commission. It depends on the personalities involved, the politics of the time, the leadership available, the patience exerted, the opportunities afforded and the cultural contexts of the country and the people caught up in the particular drama.

In this latter sense South Africa has had one considerable advantage at its disposal for dealing with the dark side of intimacy; in formal terms, it is a deeply religious country for both black and white citizens. However troubled the state church was under apartheid, and continues to be in its post-apartheid traumas, formal religion left within its white community a spiritual understanding of wrongdoing and an emotional capacity for forgiveness. In the more charismatic

Afrikaans churches, such as the AGS (Apostolic Faith Mission), this kind of openness was particularly evident through the leadership of the white pastor, Isak Burger and the black pastor, Frank Chikane – the latter nearly poisoned to death by apartheid's agents.[6]

It is this religiosity that made it possible for one of the most hated ministers of police under apartheid, Adriaan Vlok, to go on his knees before the black mothers of a Pretoria township and wash their feet, asking for their forgiveness for the murder of their sons by personnel under his command. They did.

"Darkness cannot drive out darkness; only light can do that. Hate cannot drive out hate; only love could do that."[7]

This is why one of the most powerful images in the immediate aftermath of Reitz was that in Figure 11.1, black and white staff and students holding each other in prayer.

Here spiritual light is cast over the darkness of dangerous intimacies and brings campus citizens into communion. This is an under-utilised resource in campuses torn about by racial division and in which the claim to spiritual lives is constituted in formal religious ceremony. The UFS is at the moment a largely white and black Christian community, so the spiritual resources drawn out would differ from one university to the next. Some universities are consciously avoiding religiosity of any kind, such as UCT, whereas others are self-consciously multi-faith by virtue of their histories – such as UKZN (University of Kwazulu-Natal), where many students and staff are from Hindu, Muslim and African traditional

Figure 11.1 Uniting in prayer

religious communities. It does not matter what the religious configurations might be in various communities; the opportunity for leadership is to discover its rhythms on campuses and draw this resource into the task of conciliation and communion.

Yet another student came through the "open door" early one morning, clearly rushed and on her way to her first class. She sat down immediately looking flushed and immediately told me she had no problems. This morning the young white first-year felt the need to say "thank you" for the good things happening on campus. I thanked her for saying "thank you" and was about to rise when she asked whether she could pray. She took my hands and in the softest and most beautiful Afrikaans I had heard, asked for blessings on the day. This happened all the time, and every time it did, I felt a lighter load to carry and a brightness in a sometimes dark and difficult management space.

Nothing, however, came close to matching the spontaneity of a bright freshman from an isolated, rural town in the north-west of the country called Klerksdorp. I was rushed on this day and running to my office and, as I was about to pass the massive and iconic campus statue of the Boer President Steyn, I heard a voice coming up behind me and calling me to stop. "*My ouma is in die hospitaal*," she said in Afrikaans. I was not sure why this information about her grandmother being in hospital was so urgent to me when she explained: "and *ouma* (grandmother) insisted that I come and greet you on campus". I was thrilled. "What is *ouma*'s cell number?" I asked. Right there we sat down together on the lower platform of stones around President Steyn and called "*ouma*" in her hospital bed. She had fallen in old age. When she heard the rector was on the phone I thought she was going into another shock. We had a pleasant conversation and a few months later I visited her in her home with the family. But as the young woman stood up where we were sitting on the base of the monument she came close and asked: "Please do not forget to pray for *ouma*." I promised to do so. And so the light provided by student spirituality shines through the student life experience and creates binding possibilities, if taken, without which dark intimacies would remain hidden, obscure and dangerous. In such circumstances one becomes conscious not of leading but of being led, by the generosity of students – as in the case of Moses.

Moses was actually his real name, the first black president of the SRC in the history of the UFS, and he had a crisis on his hands. It revolved around the upcoming inter-varsity between the UFS and its neighbouring cousin and sporting enemy, the North West University. The black-dominated SRC wanted these sporting ties broken, arguing that they merely perpetuated relations with a still largely untransformed white university with which the now dominant black student body of the UFS could not relate.

Some of these points were valid. The UFS was changing at pace and the sporting relationship with NWU, with its emphasis at the time on "white sporting codes" – especially rugby – was fast becoming an anachronism on our campus. The senior leadership of the university heard the complaint and had already taken steps to broadening the sporting partnership to include other universities and to extend the range of sports to include, for example, soccer, a very popular "black" sport in South Africa. I asked the students to stay in the transformation process and not to scupper the fragile negotiations already underway. I also told them there would be consequences if they disrupted an official university event.

But some of the angrier black student leaders wanted to make a political point so they violently stormed the most vulnerable of sporting events, the netball competition, causing mayhem on campus including violent confrontations with the white students. I suspended the SRC and its members from attending classes. This was, as indicated earlier, one of the consequences of what was still at the time the party political structure of the student leadership body. It was the one action that stopped once and for all the tendency towards violent student actions on campus and led to the transformation of the SRC itself to what it is today – a highly political student body not constituted in terms of parliamentary political formations but in terms of broad issues of concern to students, even as political parties are allowed to be active and registered on campus.

Moses and the other students eventually returned to campus after the suspension was lifted to continue their studies. He married a white American woman who, like him, was active in the evangelical churches including the CRC in Bloemfontein. On a subsequent visit to the University of Washington (UW) in Seattle, USA, I became aware of the fact that Moses was a youth pastor in the area churches of that region. We were on our way to the university car after a day of building relations with UW staff when a desperate call was made to one of my staff – Moses wants to see you urgently. We waited and waited, and eventually he arrived. I was wondering what could be so important, especially since he had after all left with that violent incident still in both our minds.

He arrived, took me by the arm, and asked whether he could speak to me separately from the group. We walked about 10 metres away and then he said: "I really want to apologise for my immature behaviour when I was a student. Please forgive me." I know for sure that generous act on his part would have been much more difficult were it not for his spiritual life.

Notes

1 Kimmel, D. 2013. *Angry White Men: American masculinity at the end of an era*. New York: Nation Books.
2 Gibran, K. 1923. *The Prophet*. New York: Alfred A. Knopf.
3 Mashek, D. and Aron, A. (eds) *Handbook of Closeness and Intimacy*. Mahwah, NJ: Lawrence Erlbaum Associates.
4 Mamdani, M. 2001. *When Victims become Killers: Colonialism, Nativism, and the Genocide in Rwanda*. Princeton, NJ: Princeton University Press.
5 Cohen, L. 1968. *Selected Poems, 1956–68*. New York: Viking Press.
6 Chikane, F. 2002. *No Life of my Own: An autobiography*. Johannesburg: Picador Africa, an imprint of Pan Macmillan.
7 King, M.L. Jr 2003. *A Testament of Hope: The essential writings and speeches*. Edited by Washington, J.M. New York: HarperOne; reprint edition.

12 The intimate observer

Introduction

Early every morning, without asking for it, somebody tosses a newspaper across the high gate of my home on Whites Road where it lies in the driveway waiting to be picked up. On sunny days it is unwrapped but rolled into a tight bundle by a single rubber band. On rainy days it is covered in plastic and, when the newspaper delivery sometimes miscalculates on the weather, the paper is soaking wet by the time it is collected. I have a strange relationship with this bundle of news. At first I used to read it because there was almost always a story about the university, if not on the front and inside pages, invariably in the *Letters to the Editor*. I wanted to know what the readers of the paper thought about this provincial university. Over time I would ignore the newspaper for I found its reporting superficial, sensational and almost always negative about the institution. But to understand the University of the Free State you simply could not ignore its most intimate observer.

This is *Volksblad*, a regional read (Free State and Northern Cape provinces) that claims to be the oldest Afrikaans newspaper in South Africa. Its roots lie deep within Afrikaner nationalism since its labelling as a "rebel newspaper" following the Anglo-Boer War; in fact its founders and first editors knew each other as British prisoners of war in one of the St Helena camps. With an explicit mission as a "Christian national" newspaper committed to love and protect "*de Afrikaander natie*" (the Afrikaner nation), it survived initial hardships to become a respected source of news in the north-western town of Potchefstroom.[1]

Started in 1904 as a Dutch weekly *Het Westen* serving the two former Boer Republics after the South African War (1899–1902), its name changed to *Het Volksblad* in 1915 to signal its broader ambitions as a paper for the "*volk*" (nation, in it's ethnic sense). In 1917 its name changed simply to *Die Volksblad* after moving its headquarters to Bloemfontein the previous year, where it now exists with the University of the Free State on opposite ends of the same long road, Nelson Mandela Drive. Since then it has never abandoned its primary audience – white, Afrikaans-speaking citizens – even under its new name since 2001, simply *Volksblad*.

"Is it an accident," asks the Chairman of its holding company, Naspers, in the *Foreword* to a biography of the newspaper:

> that the University of the Free State celebrates its centenary in the same year [as *Volksblad*]? Clearly not. Both institutions were born out of the difficult struggles [versugting] of the Afrikaner to take its rightful place in its own land. This was done hand in hand with the rise of Afrikaner nationalism after the devastating experience of the English War [*sic*] of 1899–1902.[2]

Many of its editors and editorial staff are white, Afrikaans-speaking people who studied – or dropped out of – the institution. "What a privilege to have been a Volksblad-man and a Kovsie-man" writes one of its editors on the inside cover of its centenary publication, and: "It was a pleasure to share Volksblad 100 with UOFS 100" says the Naspers chairman on the same page of congratulatory handwriting.[3] The two institutions were inextricably bound together in birth and in life for over one hundred years.

Many of those who worked for *Volksblad* lived in the university residences and were enculturated into its rituals, habits, traditions and bygone memories. They were both the subjects and the dispensers of initiation. They only know Afrikaans as the language of the institution. This is where their grandparents, parents and other relatives studied when the place was all-white and for Afrikaans speakers. Here, on their campus, the most intimate bonds of friendship, and friendly rivalries, are replayed in public and private stories to this day.

Now these alumni work at the Volksblad. When they report on the UFS they do so with partisan passions. They remember how their treasured university used to be, unencumbered by the kinds of tumultuous changes that seem to be reverberating through the institution. These are not distant, unaffected reporters without a stake in the course and destiny of the university; they are the university, holders of its fondest and purest memories. Successive editors would often tell me about the dismay with the university among alumni described as "lojale Kovsies" (loyal Kovsies).

With varying degrees of intensity, this kind of loyal attachment is also the case in the relationship between *Die Burger* and the University of Stellenbosch, and *Die Beeld* and the University of Pretoria – and by extension in the case of the latter newspaper, the more distant University of the North West more than one hundred kilometres from the Pretoria offices. The same dynamics apply in these other two regions – the staff members of the newspaper are often graduates of the nearby institutions on which they report and any university publicity, especially negative, would quickly make it onto the pages of the respective regional papers.

Perhaps only *Die Burger* newspaper in Stellenbosch has as intimate and intense a relationship with its local university as *Volksblad*. One of the main reasons for this clutching intimacy between the newspaper and the university in the Free

State is the sparsely populated province, where little else happens except for the dramas of provincial government, the university, the region's rugby team and the lives and deaths of ordinary citizens.

Stellenbosch is part of the larger Western Cape, which hosts the national parliament, and Pretoria is the administrative capital of the country, home to all the national government departments; there is much more to report on. But Bloemfontein and the Free State is minute in comparison, both in terms of population density and major industries. That is why reporters from the *Volksblad* often roam the campus in search of stories or call colleagues asking for any stories, especially scandalous ones.

Why? Because the newspaper knows that its core readership is conservative, concerned and anxious about the transformation of the UFS, in colour and character, away from its more consoling past. For both commercial and political reasons the newspaper therefore binds tightly the relationship between the university and its readership of *"lojale Kovsies"*, creating an intimate scrutiny that has as much to say about the politics of the present as it does the history of the past. The *Volksblad* not only therefore captures the anxieties of its readership about university transformation; it often leads with crushing editorials lampooning change at the beloved university. It allies with the white Right and nowhere was this more evident than in the Reitz saga:

> The local Afrikaans-medium newspaper [Die] Volksblad effectively became a platform for opposition to the transformation initiatives at the university. A conservative all-white political party, the Freedom Front Plus, also actively mobilized white students against the integration policy.[4]

That anger and anxiety from the readers is unleashed on one page of the newspaper, the *Letters* section.

The media, emotions and politics

Letters to the Editor has long been recognised as "a genre of political speech"[5] and therefore attracted the attention of researchers interested in what a collection of letters tell us about readers, ideology and society.[6] This line of research has also been pursued in South Africa and especially in relation to the Afrikaans newspapers and the question of race, identity and transformation.[7] What is different about this particular analysis of *Letters to the Editor* in this book is that the focus of the *"Letters"* targets one source, the University of the Free State, and together serves as a collective commentary covering a period 2009–2014 that witnessed the most fundamental changes inside this century-old institution since the end of apartheid.

The letters are almost exclusively written by white, Afrikaans-speaking readers who have ties to the UFS as alumni (*oud-Kovsies*[8] is a familiar reference in many of these letters) and/or through their children. A total of 354 letters were analysed over the approximately 5-year period from June 2009 to July 2014

(62 months or about 5.7 letters per month on average).[9] A vast majority of the letters (about 70 per cent) were highly critical of the university, and many of these correspondences were in the form of ad hominem attacks on individual leaders of the university, often laced with bitter sarcasm and always deeply emotional.

My intention was not to do a simple content analysis but to ask what the tone and content of these letters might reveal about this very intimate audience, and its newspaper, for whom the university is a large fish bowl being goggled for running commentary on campus and community, government hospitals and the medical school, the past and the future.

The content analysis revealed several recurring themes in these letters that yield startling information on issues of race, intimacy, proximity and distance among white Afrikaans speakers with various kinds of affiliation to the university.

For that small minority of the population which reads both the English and Afrikaans press in South Africa, you might as well be in two different countries. The *Sowetan* and *City Press* clearly speak to a largely black, English-reading audience, on the one hand, and *Die Burger* and *Beeld* to a mainly white Afrikaans audience. The same is true of the Sunday newspapers; the *Sunday Times* has a broader English-speaking black and white audience compared with *Rapport*, which speaks to a largely white, and to a lesser extent, black Afrikaans-speaking audience. The *Mail & Guardian* still positions itself as the struggle newspaper that every Friday used to break political stories of atrocities under the old apartheid government and now of corruption among the new leaders of the post-apartheid state.

Across newspapers, their commentary on national issues, such as corruption in government, is often very similar. But their judgement on race – from racial quotas in rugby to racism on university campuses – is a difference that can be measured in planetary time. However, even within the Afrikaans newspapers, for example, there are sometimes differences on racial judgements; *Beeld*, for example, would take an editorial stance condemning the racism of an iconic figure among many white Afrikaans speakers, the popular singer Steve Hofmeyr; not the *Volksblad*, easily the most conservative of the main Afrikaans newspapers.

The *Volksblad* therefore makes for special reading from a critical analysis of news because of its primary audience, the mainly conservative, white Afrikaans-speaking readership of the *platteland* (rural farming areas) in middle South Africa and its concentrated focus, more than any other regional paper, on the University of the Free State and its change trajectory.

The *Letters to the Editor* are in almost all cases a response triggered by an article carried by one of the *Volksblad* journalists on the front or inside pages of the newspaper. Occasionally, a self-initiated letter would be a parent's concern about parking on campus or an alumnus' attack on an academic department or an applicant's complaint about not getting a job he believes that he is better qualified for than anyone else. Most of the streams of letters, however, respond to a newspaper report published a day or so before.

Not all letters are published; there are often complaints from more liberal colleagues that their letters are ignored despite repeated submission. In other words, there is widespread suspicion that letters are not simply ignored for technical reasons common to newspapers all over the world – length, racism, sexism, unfairness or complete anonymity – but for ideological reasons; that is, the letters favoured are those conforming to the ideological conservatism of the *Volksblad*, with very little space for letters of liberal or radical opinion on a matter. By carefully selecting what to publish, the *Volksblad* therefore plays a *political* role and not simply a technical, editorial role in what takes to print. The analysis that follows does not therefore only reflect the hearts and minds of the readers of the newspaper, but largely captures the editorial position of the *Volksblad* as well. The *Volksblad's* nominal audience is white, Afrikaans and conservative and the newspaper plays directly to the fears, anxieties and prejudices of that group of citizens.

It is important, in this respect, to understand that in both the caption to an article and the content – quite apart from the screaming headlines on the advertised posters adorning the lamp poles of the city – the *Volksblad*, perhaps even more than other mainstream newspapers, not only takes sides, it unashamedly stirs emotion and shapes opinion[10] by virtue of what it reports, what it leaves out, which letters it selects to publish and how it orders the news.

Media researchers call some of these practices stereotype activation by priming audiences towards particular interpretation of messages.[11] Priming is defined as the effects of the content carried by a media report on the subsequent behaviour, thoughts or judgements of people.[12]

Consider as an example of priming a complaint I shared with the then editor of the newspaper about how it reported a tragedy:

> I was dismayed as usual by the incipient racism of the Volksblad in how it reports death, this time on the front page of the newspaper on Tuesday 27 May 2014. Once again, for reasons only your newspaper will understand, a heart-breaking story of white death is reported – and specifically white people with Afrikaans names – as this group of citizens are the only South Africans who tend to die on your front pages.
>
> You tell this tragic story of death with moving colour photographs of the white family and a lengthy narrative about the father and child who died. Then of course the singular lines that a black man also died in that "*bakkie*" [pickup truck]; he has no family or photograph or moving story behind his name. He just happened to be on the "*bakkie*". This pattern of racist reporting is not dissimilar to the way Afrikaans newspapers reported death in the days of my youth – "*drie mense het gesterwe en 'n kaffir*" ("three people died and a kaffir"). In fact, this pattern of reporting is consistent from the past into the present in that some people become visible and draw empathy, and others fade into the background as an afterthought.
>
> This has to stop.

> You expressed regrets to me, directly, for placing racist student accommodation advertisements in your newspaper; I appreciated that candour and that is why I did not report your newspaper to the SAHRC [South African Human Rights Commission]. However this kind of racism is more subtle, it will try to defend itself, and it will deny intent; that is what makes such reporting so dangerous.
>
> We work very hard at the University to bring all our people into communion in a conservative, unequal and deeply divided province and country. We spread the benefits of funding and advancement equally to all students and staff. Everyone is treated with dignity and respect. Coverage of staff and student tragedies and successes enjoy equal coverage. Despite the relentless pressure from politicians to bend in favour of a new one-sidedness, we have resisted any attempts to undermine a generosity of institutional spirit in everything we do.
>
> A major institution like your newspaper could, in this city and province, help build decency, democracy and the dignity of all our people, working with the university, or it could undermine these important goals in our young country. I need to tell you as a fellow institutional leader that this kind of reporting is deeply offensive, and undermines that quest for decency, democracy and dignity for all South Africans.

To this day there has not been a response to my correspondence. This is only one of the many ways in which an important institution makes some citizens visible and devalues others simply by ordering the news in line with a racial stereotype of who is important and who is not. When this takes on racial meanings, newspaper reporting prepares the grounds for a very dangerous separation.

The *Letters*, however, run perfectly in line with such stereotypic depictions of black people and the one-sidedness of reporting on institutional transformation. What follows therefore are thematic issues expressed on "the university and transformation" in a content analysis of *Letters* to the *Volksblad* (VB).

"Integration is unnatural; against the predestined order of things"

Much of what is published in these *Letters* is unashamedly separatist and against the integration policies of the university. It is difficult to imagine any post-apartheid newspaper publishing such vitriol. Sometimes the racist charges stretch credulity. *Boerseun* writes:

> somebody must explain to . . . supporters of forced integration that South Africa is the end-product of the unnatural and coerced putting together of a dozen different nations (*volke*). One of these is the Boer nation to which I belong . . . the Boer nation has its own history, culture, anthem and flag.[13]

While this kind of extreme ethnocentrism revealed by *Boerseun* is certainly a minority opinion when it comes to conservative association with such notions of "the Boer nation", his racist views on integration as unnatural and compelled are not, as many other letters to the VB would reveal.

For Dr Theron, integration is a form of "spiritual violence" and he is clear, in the unsubtle language of National Socialism that "experiments with racial integration and the philosophy of racial mixing" would be "catastrophic" given the inevitable tension that will result from inherent differences between white and black students in the same space.[14] In the same vein, Andre van Zyl continues the refrain of "unnaturalness":

> The more I read about what is happening at the University of the Free State, the more I realize what an unnatural community is being created ... The students of the UFS are being changed into an unnatural community. Any unnatural relationships lead to hypocrisy ... I hope the UFS will one day *again* be a *normal* community where free association is allowed (emphases added).[15]

Not everyone resorts to such a raw, racial essentialism to make the same point; it is sufficient to make the case for "free association" through an appeal to the Constitution, where van Zyl concludes his complaint.

The case for "free association" came up in heated responses from the VB readership when we decided to report a private provider of student accommodation in Bloemfontein to the South African Human Rights Commission (SAHRC) for racist advertising of a residence in the same newspaper at the beginning of 2014.

"Safe accommodation for non-affirmative action women students within walking distance from campus", the advertisement read, with a photograph of a smiling white woman student alongside. In response, our black and white students – who found this offensive – decided to test the claim. Of course, when a black student called, she was told there was a long waiting list; when a white student called immediately afterwards, there was ample space available. The newspaper response to our action was swift, as in this letter from *Hartseer oud-Kovsie*:

> The question arises why Prof Jansen challenges the right of a private owner to free association? The application of race-based racial quotas is after all the norm in South Africa, or is that only the right of the government? Racial quotas apply in universities, the civil service, municipalities and in sport ... His interference in the choice of a private provider screams against the heavens.[16]

The South African Constitution of course does not allow for discrimination of any kind when it comes to access to commercial facilities, whether for white or black citizens. Even so, it is hard to believe that affirmative action intended to open up access to black citizens after 300 years of colonialism and apartheid can be equated with such a racist advertisement that shuts down accommodation access to black students under the guise of "freedom of association". Unless, of course, there is no history.

In this logic, no university has the authority to change or challenge the rights of students to choose their residence mates, not only because it is unnatural but because the Constitution defends free association, as a regular letter writer put it:

> The rector ... has already demonstrated with his forced integration in residences that he simply steamrollers over students who want certain choices (also provided through the Constitution as the right to free association) on grounds of language, culture and religion.[17]

In sum, whether through brash assertions about the natural order of races or through appeals to freedom of association as the authors claim to be promised in the Constitution, a repeated commitment among letter writers is that of separation rather than intimacy – a theme that persists over the five-year period of this analysis.

"I am so tired hearing about race I want to scream!"

There is a paradox that runs through many of these Letters. Not only do they insist on separating races, they do not want to hear the word race (or racism) itself – terms which are used interchangeably in the complaint. No other issue generates more emotion than the university's naming of race and racism as problems to be overcome. This of course is odd.

For generations, white South Africans made a fetish of race through the most inordinate policies, laws and practices that regulated every single aspect of life according to race. Codified in the word apartheid, white Afrikaner nationalists voted the National Party into power precisely because of its obsession with race as an organising frame for everything from where you were born to where you would be buried. It was race that privileged generations of whites to create the kinds of inequalities that mark every aspect of black life to this day. So why now this emotional reverberation when the "R" word is used?

Anti-ras (anti-race) wants to know why on earth "race must always be dragged along" in every conversation and expresses great exasperation which emotion the English translation does not capture as well: "*ek is so gatvol daarvoor ek wil gil*" (I am so fed up with this I want to scream).[18]

One of the regular letter writers, Ann from Douglas (a small town in the rural Northern Cape), expresses the same exhaustion when she says:

> The normal South African does not work, eat and sleep racism. All this does is to help those with an agenda to keep racism alive. For who will carry the blame for South Africa's problems if there is no race card to play? ... The big "R" is used too quickly and too easily. Most times for own benefit.[19]

By a cruel twist of logic, the blacks who bring up race are the real racists, as van den Heever argues in reference to one of my newspaper columns in which I wrote on racism: This is just another example of a racist stripe ... he should rather stay quiet about things that bothered him in the past [for] then his true colours would not come to the fore so easily.[20] Nelisbloem agrees: "He is apparently loved by his students; just a pity he has to keep bringing up the race thing."[21]

There is no race because there is no history, or at least no reprehensible history, as Simon van Leeuwen points out in his desperation to get away from the racist past:

> I am tired of the University's constant exposure of the Afrikaner's "ugly past" through compulsory first year courses such as UFS 101 and residence policy. I am tired that the Afrikaner's history ... reflects them as "violent cowards".[22]

This is the same reason the young Johan du Plessis describes himself as "*woedend*" (extremely angry) because, he believes: "My country's progress is being held back, because my people's history is being denied and twisted." While he recognises the good and bad in his people's history, he is adamant that that history is misrepresented and his God-given race, colour and culture are being denied. "I can remain quiet no longer."[23]

Apartheid, in this reasoning, was buried a long time ago, and that is even more reason not to bring up race over and over again, as a regular puts it in an astonishing interpretation of history:

> Poor apartheid which already died off in the 1960s and was replaced with separate development in which the human dignity of nations were recognised in order to rule themselves [the TBVC countries][24], is still being dished up as an "evil monster."[25]

"There is no racism – students are just having fun"

There is a prominent thread running throughout the *Letters* that the university is a place for undergraduate student fun. Any constraints placed on student fun – such as our decision to ban the use of alcohol in residences – is seen especially by male alumni as overly restrictive, an overbearing management style that inhibits student life among adults. "We are just students having fun", would be the response from even current students in response to what they see as any infringement of established traditions.

Not only do the letters reject the portrayal of the past as an "evil monster", there is a tremendous nostalgia for that past where student fun marked university life and carries the memories of alumni to this day. "Not Reitz again", starts Markus Gertenbach in his letter titled "Wish life was still like that."[26] He then launches into a lengthy description of the affable black man – "a proud

Xhosa" – who served as their gardener in his student residence at Stellenbosch, who played along with their student traditions, and was, actually "like family". There are warm-hearted stories of students "arrested" and sentenced to a mud bath then hosed clean and applauded. "No court cases, no suspensions . . ." says the letter writer, in reference to Reitz: "I wish life was still like that."[27]

In the same vein, also writing from another university, an *Oud-Ikey* (former University of Cape Town student) recalls that the public also accepted "*studentepret*" (student fun) and spoke with emotion on how students "got away with murder".[28] With the inter-varsity against Stellenbosch University, students "broke into the residences" of the UCT residences to "steal" their trophies and shields, which were returned after the inter-varsity. A *Matie* (Stellenbosch student) that caught an *Ikey* during inter-varsity would strip the offender down to his underpants and then promptly dump the student into the Eerste River, from where he had to hike back to campus.[29] And so on.

These stories of student fun from a distant past, on two white university campuses, is told with one purpose in mind – and that is to reduce the racial humiliation of older black workers to exactly the same class of actions, *studentepret*. This is what Herman Wasserman, in his extensive analysis of how the Afrikaans media treated the Reitz incident, calls the *trivialisation* of racism so evident in these *Letters*.

There are three common expressions in the *Letters* trivialising racism in relation to Reitz – "blown out of proportion", "making a mountain out of a molehill" and "children will be children". In this process, the five black adults so "initiated" are reduced to children in the same way as 18-year-old first-years, the annual and ultimate target of this abuse. The infantilisation of black adults is a particularly odious form of racism yet not at all inconsistent with the kinds of treatment of black South Africans especially in rural, agricultural settings. Having reduced the adults to children – people young students can play with – there is no offence, and this is one of the most disturbing aspects of the Reitz matter; it also explains the tenor of the *Letters* to the Editor. What's the fuss?

And so the nostalgic stories in various letters about campus life at the UFS, and other universities, continue to recall a perfect, wholesome, unencumbered past in which apartheid leaders, like President C.R. Swart, are deeply missed. One reader recalls how "*Oom*" (Uncle) Blackie (a reference to Swart) was honoured by his school choir with the song: "When you come to the end of a perfect day."[30] From these *Letters* the song might well have had another meaning – the end of that perfect day of white life under apartheid.

"We are actually the real victims"

There is a strong sense of victimhood throughout these *Letters*; real victimhood, that is. Whenever there is a charge of racism or any wrongdoing taken to be a commentary on the group – white Afrikaans speakers – there is a reflective "turning around" of the charge towards others, the ones who *actually* deserve to be blamed or charged with doing harm to this group of victims. When a few black students are applauded at a graduation ceremony since they had overcome great difficulty to eventually gain their degrees, a letter is written to indicate that everybody, including whites, worked hard and struggled financially to reach the graduation platform.[31]

Elsewhere I referred to this phenomenon, drawing on the work of Eva Hoffman in Poland, as the clash of martyrological memories among two groups of people who both believed they were harmed by another party.[32]

Naturally, the English is the real perpetrator. While serving as dean at the University of Pretoria I was asked to join an evening meeting of conservative Afrikaans speakers who had gathered, it turned out, to lambaste me for daring in one of my columns to appeal to the new black government not to discriminate against white youth wishing to serve in the democratic civil service. One of my many arguments was that a broader intercultural work experience would help erode destructive behaviours such as initiation. An angry man spoke out, to some applause, making sure I knew "it was the English who started with initiation, not the Afrikaners".

In this vein, Jaap Steyn protests that:

> Jansen speaks of the imposition of Afrikaans but no language in our history has been imposed to such a great extent as English in the past 200 years – especially in the last fifteen years.[33]

Of course, English was never "imposed" on any group in the sense that Afrikaans sealed its own long-term fate, and arguably that of the Nationalist Party itself, when through a gross political miscalculation the Afrikaner government decided in 1976 to extend instruction in the language to additional subjects in black schools – an event that sparked the Soweto Uprisings and, in the estimation of many, the beginning of the end of apartheid following the long political lull in the resistance after the Sharpeville Massacre of 1960.

But the author's complaint lies much further back in the Anglo-Boer War and the abiding hatred of the English and their language, and periods after Union in 1910 when Afrikaans children were required to speak English in some schools. The new South Africa has 11 official languages and the choice of most South Africans, at school and university, is to study in English. While it is true that Afrikaans no longer enjoys the dominance it once did under Afrikaner nationalism, students still attend schools and universities in which they can pursue instruction in Afrikaans. The point here is that there is a complete denial of the imposition of Afrikaans on black people under apartheid – many of whom have no capacity in the language.

The reflexive impulse to blame some other target sometimes takes on bizarre comparisons. James Kemp, for example, writes in his *Letter* that while the Human Rights Commission (HRC) was preparing itself to bring the Reitz Four before the Equality Court, it had not responded to a complaint that lay dormant for more than a year charging that the University of Cape Town was practising unfair "blatant racial discrimination" by requiring white students to obtain higher school marks to enter medical school than black candidates. Here again, as in the *Letters* regarding the racist advertisement for student accommodation, a strangely illogical connection is made between a charge of racism and affirmative action.

"It would appear to me," says Kemp, "that the HRC (Human Rights Commission) only considers race discrimination and human rights violations when it has to do with white on black racism. Yet the violation of a prospective student's rights is less important than when somebody refuses to cut the hair of Mr Jody Kollapen."[34]

Mr Kollapen, a black South African of Indian descent, was the Chair of the South African Human Rights Commission at the time and who was subjected to racism when a white Afrikaans owner of a barbershop refused to cut his hair – as he did another black customer whose case Kollapen had gone to verify. This clearly racist incident, for Kemp as it is for many *Letters* writers, is no different from affirmative action. It is whites who are the real victims of racism.

This "deflection" of racist wrongdoing is especially common in relation to whites as victims of crime. So Ben Neethling, in responding to one of my statements that we would not tolerate another year of apartheid at the university and its discourse of essential "cultural differences", takes off on a racist chant that links violence to black culture:

> I plead for attention to one little cultural difference. The final examinations are in sight. This is the season in which a certain group of students begin to protest about increases in residence fees, tuition fees, etc. Then follows protests. The campus is subjected to vandalism. First the garbage bins are overturned and rubbish thrown about. What follows is the throwing of stones and tyres burning with buildings that burn with millions of Rands of damage.[35]

Of course there was no such chaos that followed, but for the *Letter* writer this is black culture in operation and it is this inherent inclination towards violence that should be taken into account and not the charge of abiding apartheid.

Hammoerabi went to great lengths to protest the court's finding of guilt in the case of the Reitz Four and then, over several paragraphs, describes in unusual detail the case of a woman who had her handbag stolen out of her car when she stopped at a traffic light. He did not know the woman but spent much of a page describing her presumed trauma and what she might go through in the future as she remembers this act of theft. Then the deflective charge:

> There was no prominence in the media, no overwhelming cries of loss of dignity; no emotionally charged court appearances; no accusations of racism, no claims for compensation. Why not? Because the political ideology of the day decides what is a mountain and what is a molehill, and wants the human rights violations of the Reitz-Four "actors" to be considered more serious than that of the poor victim of theft.[36]

It is very difficult to understand the moral equivalence being drawn here by a planned act of racism in Bloemfontein against four black workers, who are intimate acquaintances to the four white students, and the random theft of a handbag in Alexandra township in Johannesburg more than 440 kilometres away, where the criminal deed took place. But that is the familiar deflection from the racist charge in Reitz that this *Letter* writer believes, with so many others, was nothing serious to begin with.

The Reitz Four were, after all, innocent and the workers had a choice to refuse the so-called urine-laced food and drink – and then the deflection: other than the white farmers who are mutilated on their farms and down whose throats boiling water is sometimes forced.[37] This is what troubles Jannie Maree, also: "Are we as whites the only sinners? It is very clear that 'white against black' is a much more serious transgression than 'black against white'."[38]

No other claim to victimhood is so emotionally explosive in countries coming out of long periods of white supremacy as the "our women will be harmed" trope or worse, "our women will be raped". Rape has long been a "black peril narrative" in South Africa, the USA and in colonial settlements everywhere. Social hysteria fed by images of hyper-sexualised black men raping pure, innocent white women lies deep within our racist history but surprisingly extends into post-apartheid South Africa, as Lucie Valerie Graham so disturbingly portrays in her book *State of Peril: Race and rape in South African literature*.[39] By invoking images of vulnerable white women victims at the mercy of rapacious black men, the *Letter* writers effectively exploit this dangerous emotion.

No rape of white women by blacks occurred on campus; it was simply the alleged threat of rape, reported the previous day in *Volksblad*, that was sufficient to get *Demokraat* to publish this extraordinary letter in reference to white women students:

> Volksblad reports ... about a racial incident at the University of the Free State in which women were threatened with rape, sworn at and threatened with bricks. Now we are waiting for the singing of the choir which for years now has so lustily busied itself with the so-called Reitz-race video. Will they make just such a fuss over this? Or do they first want to see a video? Will someone not just make a documentary video about one campus rape or one farm attack on one of our students' parents? This will, after all, be democracy.[40]

It is this exploitation of the rumour of rape, when in fact nothing of the sort happened, that is so pernicious, on the one hand, but also so effective in tapping into raw white emotions about black peril. Where there are no details of allegations of rape, race is assumed to be present and, in S.J. Fouche's outrageous letter, rape on campus and rape in the broader society blend seamlessly into one:

> In the past few weeks there have been several reports in Volksblad regarding black on white violence – white UFS women attacked by black students

and a white woman allegedly raped by policemen (although the newspaper in the latter case did not mention skin colour, I conclude that the policemen were black) to mention only two cases ... The message or dictum seems to be that it is right for blacks to rape and murder white parents, women and children but a white must just dare to wee (urinate) into the food of blacks.[41]

Rape, in such contexts, is playing the ultimate race card.

"Sort out your own mess first"

There is no easier target for deflection of any charge of racial wrongdoing than the black government itself. Even under Nelson Mandela, the government could do nothing right. As if to say "I told you so," the lead articles and the *Letters* would describe the failings of the black government on everything from official incapacity to control crime to the rampant corruption within the state to the failings of the education system. Things worked so well under the white government, in other words.

My bi-weekly columns for *Die Burger* newspaper, once the official mouthpiece for the Afrikaner Nationalist Party, would normally be taken up in the regional Afrikaans print media belonging to Media 24, the company controlling these outlets. Week after week I would be hailed for being open, honest and direct in my criticism about the failing school system – until I wrote about racism and this dangerous intergenerational inheritance parents leave to their children. Then the tide of opinion in the *Letters* shifted instantly in a tirade of personal abuse; there was very little argument, only personal attacks. Any criticism of government in relation to education was, however, very welcome.

Even the parliament has now joined the "choir" of condemnation, writes Jannie du Toit in response to criticism from "leftist racists" about the innocent Reitz incident; they ought rather to be more concerned about corruption and scandals within their own ranks, which the country cannot afford.[42] To really grab the attention of that segment of its readership, the clear intention of the newspaper is to consistently show decay, dysfunction and distrust. The same is true of the provincial and, by extension, national government. It is corrupt and incompetent, and nothing good comes from the political authorities as an informal sample of leading news items will show. Against this picture of black decay, it is the white Afrikaans-speaking citizen constantly portrayed as the vulnerable victim of urban home invasions, farm murders and affirmative action quotas in areas like sports, jobs and medical school admissions.

The *Letter* writer S. Moller does not therefore stand alone when he links protests on campus to barbarity in black culture when he asks:

> I wonder why there is a culture among those appointed into high positions to enrich themselves and do they in fact care a damn about service delivery? In the event that they are caught, why are they not called to account but rather redeployed to continue stealing? Do they perhaps know too much,

and must their mouths be kept shut, otherwise the rot would be opened up even further?

And then the racist jibe:

> Is this the result of a lack of education, a lack of training, or is this part of a particular culture? Is it perhaps an incapacity for strong control? Has somebody ever sat and thought whether a cause can be attributed to this barbarism . . . Just a pity that this beautiful God-given country that was so carefully built up through blood, sweat and tears is being broken down by barbarians.[43]

I cannot think of another South African newspaper that would dare to publish such undiluted racist attacks on black people and can get away with it. Which raises the question: why does the *Volksblad* actually print such racist invective without fear of retribution? There are two reasons – it is in Afrikaans and therefore the vast majority of South Africans, black and white, who would otherwise wade in against such racism and discipline the newspaper and its *Letter* writers, are blissfully unaware of this kind of vulgarity.

The other reason is that the drama is being played out far away from the major cities in this largely rural, middle-of-the-country region in which there is very little national interest to begin with – except when there is some spectacular racial incident – at which point every big city commentator from radio to print to television dives in as if there was no steady build-up to create and sustain such racist cultures as reflected in this and other *Letters* to the editor.

The general criticism captured in these emotional rants remains true. Especially since the government of Nelson Mandela, South Africa has fast lost its reputation for good governance under successive administrations. The wholesale denial of causality in the link between the HIV virus and AIDS, and the official questioning of the efficacy of anti-retroviral drugs by Mandela's successor, led to the deaths of tens of thousands of South Africans. The rampant corruption under the current government, with no sense of accountability even within party ranks and elites, has done immeasurable damage to the international stature of the country and to trust among its citizens. All of these issues continue to lead front pages in all the print media, English and Afrikaans, black and white, across South Africa; what makes the *Volksblad* and its *Letters* different are the racist chants that accompany these complaints about corruption and inefficiency in government.

The Reitz Four scandal at the UFS was in fact a comical event but what should rather focus our attention, Jannie Maree writes, are the greater crimes in government and the barbarism of the blacks:

> What has happened in the country to much worse humiliations, destruction of people's future and lives, through the barbaric actions which time after time happen in the country and which has never been given the same public attention.[44]

"We are losing everything"

Consistent with the projection of whites as victims, a recognisable trope throughout the complaints in the *Letters* is the notion that "everything" is being lost. One change in a residence or an alteration to the university motto is often met with the proverbial throwing of the hands in the air: "we are losing everything." Of course this is exaggeration in a country that still remains highly unequal along racial lines and in which there has been no wholesale transformation of anything – whites still own their land and property, white schools still operate as before and white persons are five times more likely to find a job after graduation than any black student. It is not only the political Left that argues very little has changed.

The same is true of the former white universities. Colonial and apartheid symbols still mark prominently the landscape of all the former white universities, from the statue of the imperialist Cecil John Rhodes on the campus of the University of Cape Town to apartheid's political founder, who has a major building named after him, the D.F. Malan Memorial Hall at Stellenbosch University. There is even a university in the name of Rhodes and an "*oxwagen*" of the "*Voortrekkers*" continues to mark the emblem of the University of Pretoria.

The vast majority of professors at the former white universities remained white and male 21 years into South Africa's democracy, where more than 80 per cent of citizens are black. There are campuses with majority white students, like Stellenbosch and the Potchefstroom Campus of the University of the North West. On all the campuses of the historically Afrikaans universities, Afrikaans is still taught and there is no prescription over what should be taught in the curricula of the white universities. Lower levels of non-academic staffing at the historically privileged universities are largely black, while higher levels of administrative personnel are largely white. But you would not know this from the *Letters*, for "everything has changed" and "we are losing it all" in the words of the *Letter* writers.

There are three reasons for the slow pace of transformation of campus and country. One has to do with the unparalleled generosity of the founder of South Africa's new democracy, Nelson Mandela. He relentlessly pushed, in public policy and personal example, his mission of reconciliation. From his calculated appointment of a white Afrikaner woman as his very public personal assistant to putting the brakes on calls for radical land distribution, President Mandela went out of his way to ensure that citizens choose the path of conciliation rather than conflict in the aftermath of apartheid.

A second reason has to do with *realpolitik*. As many scholars and observers have already pointed out, South Africa's transition to democracy came at the very point that the Cold War had ended and radical models for transforming societies and economies no longer enjoyed as much credibility as they did in the period immediately following post-colonial independence rolling down the African continent from North to South. Powerful, capitalist institutions of the North had in turn advised and warned the fresh-out-of-prison Nelson Mandela the disaster that would befall South Africa if it even considered radical transformations of the national economy. "Why are you not taking money from the World Bank," Mandela asked some friends of mine who were among his prominent advisors, after complaints from the elites in the Bretton Wood institutions. "They are not giving us money for free Madiba," they gently coaxed the ANC President; "these are interest bearing loans; we have to pay it back, and much more."

There was a third reason, which had to do with the interdependence of white and black South Africans. No other post-independence African country had a significant white contingent (15 per cent) within its borders. As a result of apartheid-inspired privileges, many of these white citizens occupied major positions in the private and public sectors throughout the country. They had built great schools, profitable companies and leading industries with their advantage. To move in with a heavy hand would collapse those many islands of privilege and advantage, especially for the emerging black elite, their families and children. Rather than "take over" or destroy any of these privileged institutions, a better strategy was to call for inclusion and the opening up of access. This kind of reasoning comported well with the negotiating position of the major white opposition parties in the run-up to the first democratic elections in 1994 – no radical transformation of the economy; the retention of cultural privileges such as white schools and the Afrikaans language; and a rights-based Constitution that affirmed a longstanding credo of the new ruling party, that South Africa belonged to all who live in it, black and white.

In the state of anxiety expressed in the *Letters*, though, there is no sense of ethnic accommodation or political generosity on the part of the progenitors and beneficiaries of apartheid. In their minds, everything is lost. *Diep Seun* is terribly upset about the discussion I launched on what to do with the massive statue of the Boer Republic President in front of my office. In a letter that combines genuine inquiry with personal insult and sarcasm, he asks:

> Prof Jansen, pres MT Steyn now really has nothing to do with your so-called reconciliation gestures. The statue troubles nobody but you. If the statue is one-sided, that is also good; our country needs many things such as statues and more, which mean something for one or other component of the nation. The country has seen many governments come and go and all of them left something behind. *Must everything be removed, Prof?* (emphasis mine)[45]

Boerseun, recognisably among the more virulent of letter writers, puts it even more bluntly:

> By this time it is already very clear to readers of the Volksblad that Prof Jansen has been tasked by the ANC to *wipe out all remnants of Afrikanerdom* that still remains [*sic*] at the University of the Free State. (emphasis mine)[46]

As a non-member of the ANC and one regularly attacked in public by its politicians, I have often wondered whether the comrades really knew that I was regarded in some quarters as having been "sent" or, in the language of the movement, deployed to do my work as a university leader. They would no doubt be amused.

A "trotse Kovsie-student" joined the fray, complaining bitterly about the threat to traditions:

> Mention the word tradition and you are looked at as if you were mad. Residences have become a housing block but *this does not mean everything must change*. (emphasis mine)[47]

Möller, a regular writer, extends this complaint of "everything lost" to discussions at that time (2010) to review the historical inter-varsity held annually with Afrikaner cousins at the University of the Northwest, with a swipe at the rector and dean of students:

> It would fit them perfectly to break down and destroy the total culture, traditions and values of the "old" Kovsies.[48]

Johan du Pisanie acknowledges that sometimes things have to change but insists that:

> to totally remove a culture is wrong. As an Afrikaner man in 2014 I am proud of my history. And even if I was not proud, it is still my history. (emphasis mine)[49]

The "everything lost" trope should not be read as a commentary on the specific incident being addressed by the letter writer. It is an emotional state, a reference to changes in the country as a whole since the legal end of apartheid in 1994. More than what happens at the university from one day to the next, the authors are expressing a general unease with what I elsewhere called "loss and change"[50] – that sense that everything familiar and true is being taken away. The fact that most things dear to the individual have not been removed is not the point; it is that sense of existential dislocation, and what better target on which to inflect this sense of total loss than the dearest possessions of the *Letter* writers, the university which belonged to them as white Afrikaans speakers, their families and friends.

Underlying this "total" sense of loss is a larger complaint that the university as cultural property has changed hands. That is why the most emotional tirades were directed against me for speaking in many public addresses of "my students" or "at my university". Several times I would hear "it is not your university!" or, as expressed in some of these *Letters*: "It was the Afrikaner who built the UFS, then UOFS."[51] And then the routine insult, that the rector sits in a "nice warm office and soft chair of an institution (actually one of many) pushed under his backside for him by white Christians".[52]

I wrote back in fury at one of these letters that landed on my desk, laced with unbelievable racism referring to me as "*Hotnot*"[53] and written in old cursive form on wrinkled paper by someone who clearly was very old. For some strange reason such *Letters* normally come with a return address:

> First you exclude me from this university because of my race, and then you blame me for not being here to build it. How dare you. I would have you know that since the day I started working for my country I paid taxes to build this university. Like everyone else, therefore, it belongs to me because it is a public institution.

Sometimes, you just lose it.

I knew that by responding in my home language, English, to his Afrikaans letter, the poor man must have had an added fit.

"I should have gotten the job"

The sense of racial entitlement runs consistently through various *Letters* when it comes to jobs at the UFS. Some context is necessary. There is no other public sector employer as readily available to white South Africans in the Free State province than the university. Whereas white Afrikaans speakers dominated the civil service for decades under the most expansive programme of white affirmative action under apartheid, that privilege came to a grinding halt when black nationalists took over national and provincial government, quickly changing the complexion of the bureaucracy at all levels. Every government department was affected, from housing to education to transport and agriculture; black nationalism effectively did what white nationalism had so effectively secured – a racially dominant civil service. Whites were still hired in the new civil service but in very small numbers.

The impact of this sudden and swift change to the complexion of national, provincial and local government in poor provinces like the Free State was severe. There are no major industries in the region and the once-powerful mining industry has become a very small part of the regional economy. Even the major banks in the Free State were under pressure to hire more black staff, and private companies found themselves lacking access to competitive tendered projects unless they had significant numbers of black employees in their ranks – something monitored through Black Economic Empowerment regulations.

In this context, where the UFS is considered still to be the one area relatively free from government interference, and in which whites could, as before, still find and retain their jobs, much of the emotion in various *Letters* centred on whether an applicant was in fact successful in his or her application. When somebody failed to qualify, a torrent of emotion and abuse would be unleashed at the university in ways that would not happen if the application was for a job in a government department. After all, the university, in the minds of angry applicants, *should* hire them.

Underlying this sentiment is a deep sense of white entitlement, captured so elegantly in Michael White's book *Angry White Men* through his construct of "aggrieved entitlement".[54] The first assumption behind such entitlement is that the white candidate is always better: "I have more experience; the other person is a junior; my qualifications are superior; the other person does not carry merit."[55]

In considering how to respond to such aggrieved responses, the university is often at a disadvantage. Should we reveal the real reason the person did not get the job? Should we talk openly about poor performance in an interview? Should we compare curricula vitae and list the many ways in which the successful candidate was in fact better? Should we make public the negative letters of reference on file? Should we enumerate the actual criteria for the job – not the person's own sense of qualification – and why the other candidate was in fact better? We often ponder giving out such responses, but there are very real legal threats surrounding the confidentiality of persons and processes despite the urge to set the record straight when *Letters* condemn the work of selection.

The second assumption driving entitlement is past practices. It used to be so easy to find a job as a white, Afrikaans male in these universities. But policies had changed. Now there was a very demanding research profile that had to be met especially in senior positions. In the new country, positions were open to competition from black and white, local and foreign, Afrikaans speakers and non-Afrikaans speakers; now the candidate had to actually compete but the assumption is that it should be as easy now as in the past when racial privilege assured access to university positions for the few.

The third assumption driving the anger is that it is all politics; political decisions scuppered employment possibilities. Not a single university appointment is adjudicated on grounds of politics, but the argument is nonetheless made with some venom, as in the words of Jan Greyvenstein as he defends an embittered man who did not get the job:

> Botties, old friend, your politics tripped you up . . . your political opinion does not make you a weaker or stronger lecturer. That you rather resigned than compromise your conscience demands the highest respect.[56]

Gerrit van Tonder, without a shred of evidence, agrees: "Maybe your politics was too far to the right because academic merit could surely not have played a role[57] in the decision." Affirmative action is to blame, even when, as in one of these cases, the preferred candidate was also white. "Real value-added considerations," he continues, "alongside exemplary academic qualities should be non-negotiable with any academic appointment at any university."[58] Of course it never was the case under apartheid, in which white privilege and ethnic loyalty counted more – as van Tonder concedes in relation to the once-favoured appointment of whites loyal to the Afrikaner secret society called the Broederbond, only to insist that affirmative action explains the lot of the complainants.

Racial entitlement not only overlooks any objective criteria in appointment, it also lacks any sense of generosity to those so long excluded from access to personnel positions at the UFS as in the case of former white universities. There is no sense of injustice because, once again, there is no history. The reasoning goes something like this: "I got the job before so I am entitled to get it now and, if you do not give it to me, it's because of politics." In this context, *any* black appointment is non-meritorious as T.J.K. Visser asks: "The appointment of the Rector, was it quota or merit?"[59]

The truth is that more than 95 per cent of the professoriate at the UFS remains solidly white and male. Blacks remain a minority at every level of academic appointment despite being the excluded majority in the national demographic. But you would not know that from the stream of letters to the *Volksblad*. It is impossible, in such a context, to have a logical and reasonable discussion about competence or diversity or even standards.

Standards. It is by far the most common assumption informing aggrieved entitlement in the *Letters* and that is that standards are falling. It is a claim that requires no evidence; it can be safely assumed that if as a white man I did not get the job, the conclusion is obvious – standards dropped. "Our university standards in South Africa have never been high," I argued in a late-2014 seminar on transformation at the University of Cape Town, arguing that unless you travelled across the world, you would not know what a truly high academic standard composes.[60]

This was certainly the case at the UFS when I arrived in 2009 – there were no A-rated scientists, we had one of the lowest pass rates for undergraduates in the country, our institutional research performance was paltry, admissions criteria were so low it attracted the most mediocre white and black students, and the criteria for academic staff promotion were "average" at best. All of that changed dramatically over the five-year period, with every one of the issues just raised showing marked improvements, in both numbers and quality. None of this matters of course in "the standards are falling" argument because it is an emotive appeal not an empirical one; it is a defensive political posture not a fact-based statement.

It is sufficient to make the falling standards argument through the *Letters* pages of the *Volksblad* to safely assume that the readership would take this to be true, regardless of the evidence. Standards, in this usage, is code for whiteness. T.J.K. Visser's letter could not be clearer on this point: "I can state without reservation that the overwhelming majority of whites stand for merit."[61] Blacks, in other words, do not.

Sanctuaries of meaning

The range, depth and complexity of emotions found in most of the *Letters* speak to very intimate bonds that continue to exist between white Afrikaans readers and their historical university. The stories contained in the submissions to the editor recall "perfect days" of nostalgic memory that were so cruelly interrupted by new regimes that threaten to overturn the natural order of things. Everything before was good, wholesome and true; everything now is bad, broken and lost.

Nostalgia restores a measure of control in periods of uncertainty, even as it offers an escape, however temporary, from the chaos and confliction of the present. Roger Aden, quoted in Wilson (2005), captures the functionality of nostalgia this way:

> Nostalgic communication provides individuals with a means of symbolically escaping cultural conditions that they find depressing and/or disorienting. Using communication to move through time allows individuals to situate themselves in a *sanctuary of meaning*, a place where they feel safe from oppressive cultural conditions. (emphasis in original quotation)[62]

In these depressing and disorienting "cultural conditions", the real victims are poor whites who suffer because of a gross misrepresentation of the past, a cruel exclusion from the present and a dark future. New regimes threaten treasured traditions, culture, memory and identity itself. In the process, races which should remain separate from each other are now "forced" to share the same living and learning spaces.

The racial animus seeping through the *Letters* still represents what one colleague calls "primitive forms of racism" where *disgust* drives commentary about biologically inferior groups and, as elsewhere, "anger now serves as the primary emotional trigger of whites' negative racial attitudes".[63]

There are several retributive responses to these perceived attempts to break such intimate bonds. One is the threat to withdraw alumni contributions. In this part of rural South Africa, alumni donations are normally very small ($20–80 on average) and, as often discovered, those who threaten to withdraw were not donors to begin with. But it is the threat that counts, not the magnum of any personal contribution.

Another retaliatory response is the threat to send white Afrikaans-speaking children elsewhere and, to rub white salt into the transformation wound, to the auld enemy, the North West University (NWU). Beyond anecdote, there is no evidence of such migration. In fact more and more Afrikaans students from other provinces now come to the UFS. Incidentally, that kind of threatened destination might change now since the appointment of NWU's first black vice-chancellor who, from the day of his appointment, has been lambasted in the Afrikaans press for not being sufficiently pro-Afrikaans. Still, it is the threat that counts.

And the third and most persistent of all retributive actions is to write stinging letters of criticism and denouncement to the local Afrikaans newspaper. An applicant who did not get a job at the university writes to the newspaper. A staff member who is disciplined rushes off an anonymous letter to the editor. A parent whose child cannot find parking on campus in the immediate area where they want to be calls the newspaper. A group of alumni that do not like the possibility that their old residence might be renamed flood the newspaper with denouncements of the university leadership. A Christian who is deeply offended by the changes to the university's motto would have no shortage of company decrying "the removal of God" from the institution. The idea with the *Letters* is not simply to complain in a public space about what is happening on campus; it is to shame and belittle what happens at the university, to discredit leaders and, in doing so, to find affirmation in a chorus of support.

There is a symbiotic relationship between the newspaper and its readers. In the frequent headlines about "loss and change" at the university, the *Volksblad* would prominently place an invitational block near the often provocative, if not inflammatory, article: "*Wat sê jy?*" (What do you have to say about this matter?). The invitation is taken up promptly online and in print the following day on the *Letters* page. The letters on the subject can be kept running for days, and sometimes weeks, often being followed by an editorial piece making pontificating comments on the terrible wrongdoing by the university. There is not simply ideological reinforcement of conservative, often racist, opinion on university transformation, but an interdependence of customer and company that keeps the newspaper afloat.

Why would a reader run to the newspaper on everything from the content of a graduation ceremony (blacks are too loud in their adulation) to the core curriculum for first-year students (indoctrination)? It is quite simple: there is no other place, any more, in which your political commentary as a conservative white South African will be taken seriously by others. During apartheid, when blacks had no representation in government, whites found their voice within the state and its extensive networks of power and patronage. Jobs were reserved for whites, as were university places.

The racially exclusive right to vote meant direct access to parliamentary authority and the local councillor down the street. No such privilege or power exists any more; the white conservative vote might be exercised dutifully but it carries no power to change anything given the very small slice of the vote garnered by the white exclusive parties. In these circumstances the Afrikaans newspaper has become the sole repository of white anxiety about everything from corrupt government to prejudiced courts to "reverse racism" (affirmative action) to changing universities.

But as can be seen from the many *Letters*, the relentless criticism of the university is, in fact, an alibi for criticism of state and nation at the same time. The emotional outpouring of grief and loss, often in extremist and abusive language, "turns in" on the nearest possession of heartfelt value, the local university.

To dismiss all such deeply expressive emotions of grief and loss as the voices of racist lunatics or right-wing conservatism is to miss an important challenge for leadership in the aftermath of the cataclysm called apartheid – how to respond in ways that turn those very vulnerabilities of emotions, hurtful as they might be, into a passion for something bigger, an inclusive transformation that gives equal weight to conciliation and correction. That is only possible through leadership.

Notes

1. I acknowledge that much of this information was initially drawn from a set of historical commentaries on the origins of the *Volksblad* by Jaap Steyn, then a professor in the Department of Afrikaans and Dutch the University of the Free State. These sources are: Steyn, J. 1990. Nie Sonder rede rebellekoerant. *Die Volksblad*, 29 July, p. 15; Steyn, J. 2004. Koerant wys hy kon altyd druk hanteer. Volksblad, 18 November 100: 4; and Steyn, J. (1990). Volksblad se pad lank met nasionalisme. *Die Volksblad*, 29 September, p. 10. Since then Barnard, S.L., Stemmet, J. and Volksblad *'n Lewe van sy eie: Die biografie van Volksblad*. Kaapstad: Tafelberg-Uitgewers Beperk.
2. Vosloo, T. 2004. Foreword. In Barnard, S.L., Stemmet, J. and Volksblad (newspaper). *'n Lewe van sy eie: Die biografie van Volksblad*. Kaapstad: Tafelberg-Uitgewers Beperk. p. 7.
3. Ibid.
4. Suransky, C. and van der Merwe, J.C. 2014. Transcending apartheid in higher education: transforming an institutional culture. *Race, Ethnicity and Education*, p. 5. Available from: http://dx.doi.org/10.1080/13613324.2014.946487.
5. Wahl-Jorgenson, K. 1999. Letters to the Editor. *Peace Review: A Journal of Social Justice* 11(1), 53, 59.
6. See the excellent account of the production process itself with respect to letters to the editor, in Wahl-Jorgenson, K. 2004. A "legitimate beef" or "raw meat"? Civility, multiculturalism, and letters to the editor. *The Communication Review* 7(1), 89–105.
7. Wasserman, H. 2013. Discourses of race in the Afrikaans press in South Africa. In Mano, W. (ed.) *Racism, Ethnicity and the Media in Africa: Mediating difference in the 21st century*. London: I.B. Taurus. Available from: www.academia.edu/1809499/Discourses_of_Race_in_the_Afrikaans_press_in_South_Africa; and Steyn, M. 2004. Rehabilitating a whiteness disgraced: Afrikaner white talk in post-apartheid South Africa. *Communication Quarterly* 52(2), 143–69.
8. Kovsies is the affectionate name of the University of the Free State used over many decades. The word is derived from the origins of the older universities in "colleges" more than a century ago. The University of the Orange Free State, as it was then called, originated out of Grey University College which became College of the Orange Free State (Kollege van die Oranje Vrystaat) with the acronym KOV, which became KOVsies; just as the Transvaal University College became TUC or the Afrikaans Tuk-ies, rounded to Tukkies, as the University of Pretoria students are known.
9. The monthly density of "*Letters*" given here is a little misleading since our graphs show the months of November and December to contain very few, if any, letters since South African universities begin to close down for the summer holidays around that time.
10. Nabi, R. and Wirth, W. 2008. Exploring the role of emotion in media effects. *Media Psychology* 11(1), 1–6.
11. Mastro, D.E. 2009. Racial/Ethnic Stereotyping and the Media. In Nabi, R.L. and Oliver, M.B. (eds) *The SAGE Handbook of Media Processes and Effects*. Washington, DC: SAGE, pp. 377–91.
12. Roskos-Ewoldson, D.R. and Roskos-Ewoldson, B. 2009. Current Research in Media Priming. In Nabi, R.L. and Oliver, M.B. (eds) *The SAGE Handbook of Media Processes and Effects*. Washington, DC: SAGE, pp. 177–92.
13. Boerseun. 2010. Dan Roodt is nie Julius Malema nie. (Letter to the editor). *Volksblad*, 31 March. Available from http://152.111.11.6/argief/berigte/volksblad/2010/04/01/VB/14/aabriewedinsdag.html
14. Theron, J.A.L. 2010. Vraagtekens oor Jansen. (Letter to the editor). *Volksblad*, 8 September. Available from http://152.111.11.6/argief/berigte/volksblad/2009/09/09/VB/6/aakkorterbrifffuv.html

15 van Zyl, A. 2014. UV se verpligte assosiasie. (Letter to the editor). *Volksblad*, 24 March. Available from: www.netwerk24.com/stemme/2014-03-23-sanral-ontgroening-en-tuie
16 Hartseer oud-Kovsie. 2014. UV, MRK en vrye assosiasie. (Letter to the editor). *Volksblad*, 24 January. Available from: http://152.111.11.6/argief/berigte/volksblad/2014/01/24/6/briewe24jan_22_0_436722157.html
17 Lambrechts, J.v.N. 2011. UV, verskaf regte inligting, asseblief. (Letter to the editor). *Volksblad*, 20 January. Available from: http://152.111.11.6/argief/berigte/volksblad/2011/01/21/VB/6/briewe20.html
18 Anti-ras. 2009. Prof Jansen praat self baie oor ras. (Letter to the editor). *Volksblad*, 29 August. Available from: http://152.111.11.6/argief/berigte/volksblad/2009/08/29/VB/13/satbrifffafff.html
19 Ann van Douglas. 2009. 'R' vir eie gewin. (Letter to the editor). *Volksblad*, 30 July. Available from: http://152.111.11.6/argief/berigte/volksblad/2009/07/30/VB/10/aaaann.html
20 Van den Heever. 2010. Ons is nou dik vir hierdie gesanik. (Letter to the editor). *Volksblad*, 26 March. Available from: http://152.111.11.6/argief/berigte/volksblad/2010/03/27/VB/8/aadonderdagbriewe.html
21 Nelisbloem. 2010. Jansen en die ras-ding. (Letter to the editor). *Volksblad*, 27 March. Available from: http://152.111.11.6/argief/berigte/volksblad/2010/03/27/VB/13/satkorttbriwwwe.html
22 Van Leeuwen, S. 2013. Afrikaner-identiteit en UV-naamsverandering. (Letter to the editor). *Volksblad*, 21 March. Available from: http://152.111.11.6/argief/berigte/volksblad/2013/03/28/VB/6/briewe21mrt.html
23 du Pisanie, J. 2014. UV-transformasie: Trots of nie, dis my geskiedenis. (Letter to the editor). *Volksblad*, 20 March. Available from: http://152.111.11.6/argief/berigte/volksblad/2014/03/20/12/briewe20mrt_23_0_5974444.html
24 The TBVC refers to the apartheid reserves, which were designed by the apartheid rulers to isolate "non-urban" black South Africans in impoverished rural "homelands" rather than have them work and trespass in white areas; the four referred to here as TBVC were the Transkei, Bophuthatswana, Venda and Ciskei.
25 Lambrechts, J.v.N. 2011. Is dit nou boodskap van versoening. (Letter to the editor). *Volksblad*, 3 February. Available from: http://152.111.11.6/argief/berigte/volksblad/2011/02/04/VB/10/briewe4.html
26 Gertenbach, M. 2009. Wens die lewe was nog so. (Letter to the editor). *Volksblad*, 25 November Available from: http://152.111.11.6/argief/berigte/volksblad/2009/11/26/VB/8/brief525.html
27 Ibid.
28 Oud-Ikey. 2009. Dit was studentepret. (Letter to the editor). *Volksblad*, 9 December. Available from: http://152.111.11.6/argief/berigte/volksblad/2009/12/10/VB/6/grysbrief9.html
29 Ibid.
30 2011. Ek mis ook vir Oom Black. (Letter to the editor). *Volksblad*, 6 June. Available from: http://152.111.11.6/argief/berigte/volksblad/2011/06/07/VB/6/briewe6junie.html
31 van Rensburg, R. 2012. Skaam oor UV-plegtigheid. (Letter to the editor). *Volksblad*, 12 April. Available from: http://152.111.11.6/argief/berigte/volksblad/2012/04/12/VB/6/brief12.html
32 Hoffman, E. 2004. *After Such Knowledge: Memory, history, and the legacy of the Holocaust*. New York: Public Affairs (Perseus Group).
33 Steyn, J. 2009. Hieroor is Afrikaansstryd. (Letter to the editor). *Volksblad*, 14 August. Available from: http://152.111.11.6/argief/berigte/volksblad/2009/08/14/VB/6/brieftaal.html

34 Kemp, J. 2009. Verstom oor Reitz-vier in gelykheidshof. (Letter to the editor). *Volksblad*, 26 August. Available from: http://152.111.11.6/argief/berigte/volksblad/2009/08/26/VB/13/satbalkonbrifff.html

35 Neethling, B. 2009. Gee aandag hieraan. (Letter to the editor). *Volksblad*, 9 September. Available from: http://152.111.11.6/argief/berigte/volksblad/2009/09/10/VB/8/aakkorterbriffuv.html

36 Hammoerabi. 2010. Reitzvideo: Berg en molshoop? (Letter to the editor). *Volksblad*, 3 August. Available from: http://152.111.11.6/argief/berigte/volksblad/2010/08/04/VB/6/briewedinsdag3.html

37 Venter, E. 2009. Praat van toeval. (Letter to the editor). *Volksblad*, 17 September. Available from: http://152.111.11.6/argief/berigte/volksblad/2009/09/18/VB/4/aakorterbrifff.html

38 Maree, J. 2010. Genoeg is genoeg. (Letter to the editor). *Volksblad*, 6 August. Available from: http://152.111.11.6/argief/berigte/volksblad/2010/08/07/VB/8/briewevrydag6.html

39 Graham, L.V. 2012. *State of Peril: Race and rape in South African literature*. Oxford: Oxford University Press, p. 4.

40 Demokraat. 2009. Bohaai hieroor ook? (Letter to the editor). *Volksblad*, 27 October. Available from: http://152.111.11.6/argief/berigte/volksblad/2009/10/28/VB/6/aauvvroueaanval.html

41 Fouché, S.J. 2009. Dubbele standaarde. (Letter to the editor). *Volksblad*, 3 November. Available from: http://152.111.11.6/argief/berigte/volksblad/2009/11/04/VB/6/aakorterbriffffff.html

42 du Toit, J. 2009. In plaas van kruisiging moet Jansen lof kry. (Letter to the editor). *Volksblad*, 27 October. Available from: http://152.111.11.6/argief/berigte/volksblad/2009/10/28/VB/6/aahoofjansen.html

43 Möller, S. 2011. Eendstert betogings by UV en elders barbaars. (Letter to the editor). *Volksblad*, 19 August. Available from: http://152.111.11.6/argief/berigte/volksblad/2011/08/20/VB/6/brief19.html

44 Maree, J. 2010. Genoeg is genoeg. (Letter to the editor). *Volksblad*, 6 August. Available from: http://152.111.11.6/argief/berigte/volksblad/2010/08/07/VB/8/briewevrydag6.html

45 Ann van Douglas. 2010. Krap waar dit nie jeuk nie. (Letter to the editor). *Volksblad*, 24 March. Available from: http://152.111.11.6/argief/berigte/volksblad/2010/03/25/VB/8/briewebladdinsdag.html

46 Boerseun. 2010. Jansen se stellings is aanvegbaar. (Letter to the editor). *Volksblad*, 14 May. Available from: http://152.111.11.6/argief/berigte/volksblad/2010/05/15/VB/8/briewevrydag.html

47 Trotse Kovsie-student. 2010. Kampus: Geskok oor die dinge. (Letter to the editor). *Volksblad*, 17 August. Available from: http://152.111.11.6/argief/berigte/volksblad/2010/08/18/VB/6/briewedinsdag17.html

48 Möller, S. 2011. Intervarsity met Potch, Joburg. (Letter to the editor). *Volksblad*, 17 February. Available from: http://152.111.11.6/argief/berigte/volksblad/2011/02/18/VB/8/briewe17.html

49 du Pisanie, J. 2014. UV-transformasie: Trots of nie, dis my geskiedenis. (Letter to the editor). *Volksblad*, 20 March. Available from: http://152.111.11.6/argief/berigte/volksblad/2014/03/20/12/briewe20mrt_23_0_5974444.html

50 See chapter in my book by that title in *Knowledge in the Blood* (2009). The reference to "loss and change" actually comes from a book on the psychology of grieving personal or social loss; see Marris, P. 2015. *Loss and Change*. (Revised edition). New York: Routledge.

51 Van Leeuwen, S. 2013. Afrikaner-identiteit en UV-naamsverandering. (Letter to the editor). *Volksblad*, 21 March. Available from: http://152.111.11.6/argief/berigte/volksblad/2013/03/28/VB/6/briewe21mrt.html

52 de Klerk, J. 2012 Jansen-rubriek eenogig. (Letter to the editor). *Volksblad*, 8 September. Available from: http://152.111.11.6/argief/berigte/volksblad/2012/09/08/VB/6/briewe8sept.html
53 Derogatory name for a so-called Coloured person, some of whom have *Khoisan* roots in the larger Western Cape; the old colonial term for this group of First Peoples was *Hottentot*, and its bastardisation as "*Hotnot*" is intended as a racial insult.
54 Kimmel, M. 2013. *Angry White Men: American masculinity at the end of an era*. New York: Nation Books.
55 See, for example, Dr L.J. Bothma's bitter account of his experience of alleged discrimination as he responds to another white male who also complained to the *Volksblad* about himself not getting a job for which he was, obviously, the best candidate; Bothma, Dr L.J. 2012. Wagner nie al een wat onder UV-bestuurstyl ly. Available from: http://argief.volksblad.com/cgi-bin/volksblad.cgi
56 Greyvenstein, J. 2012. Wagner-geval is skokkend. (Letter to the editor). *Volksblad*, 9 May. Available from: http://argief.volksblad.com/cgi-bin/volksblad.cgi
57 van Tonder, G. 2012. Regstellende aksie se rol by UV word nie genoem. (Letter to the editor). *Volksblad*, 12 May. Available from: http://152.111.11.6/argief/berigte/volksblad/2012/05/12/VB/6/brief12.html
58 Ibid.
59 Visser, T.J.K. 2010. So kan SA 'n wenland word. (Letter to the editor). *Volksblad*, 12 October. Available from: http://152.111.11.6/argief/berigte/volksblad/2010/10/13/VB/6/briewedinsdag12.html
60 University of Cape Town South Africa's Channel (2014). UCT Transformation Debate 2014, Prof Jonathan Jansen, 6 November [Video file]. Available from: https://www.youtube.com/watch?v=CsXL6sKmT5k
61 Ibid., endnote #25.
62 Wilson, J.L. 2005. *Nostalgia: Sanctuary of meaning*. Lewisburg, PA: Bucknell University Press. p. 34.
63 Banks, A.J. and Valentino, N.A. 2012. Emotional Substrates of White Racial Attitudes. *American Journal of Political Science* 56(2), 286–97.

13 Nearness in leadership

Introduction

Russell Hayman Botman was the first black rector in the 150-year history of Stellenbosch University. He would also be the first to die in office. Botman would not, however, be the first to depart under fire for not sufficiently protecting the interests of racial conservatism at his university.[1] First appointed in 2007 and then reappointed for a further five years, the activist theologian was one of the most gentle and kind-hearted of university leaders. Black, Afrikaans-speaking and a churchman without rancour, he was instantly acceptable to racial conservatives even as he took on one of the most difficult jobs in higher education – the academic leadership of an overwhelmingly white-dominated institution that vigorously defends its untransformed position through a mix of anti-ruling party rhetoric and a near-obsessive defence of its self-apportioned cultural asset, the Afrikaans language.[2]

Situated in the picturesque wine land areas of the Western Cape, Stellenbosch University is a venerable Afrikaner institution that traces its roots to the mid-nineteenth century and its subsequent baptism as Victoria College in 1887. The quaint old town of millionaires and paupers, affectionately known as *Eikestad*, is surrounded by majestic mountains and seems almost secluded from the hurly-burly of race politics in the rest of the country. Yet scratch the epidermal surface of the City of Oaks (*Eikestad*) and this little space of heaven reveals a tragic history of racial violence, gross inequalities and university segregation.[3] It was, after all, the university that produced some of apartheid's most notorious political leaders, such as Prime Minister D.F. Malan, and the kind of racial knowledge modelled on Nazi science which was recently (2013) uncovered on campus through a tray of glass eyes alongside a human skull and "30 differently coloured locks of hair".[4]

Now as the coffin of this relatively young (60) black university leader was slowly hauled up the long aisle separating the crowd inside the D.F. Malan Memorial Centre, I was surprised by how angry I was; after all, we were not close friends. Yet men of that age do not normally drop dead without reason. Yes his body was compromised by diabetes and hypertension, and he had gone to see the doctor in the week that he died. But the immediate biomedical cause of death does not explain itself, an insight I gained long ago from scholars in the health field who work at the intersection of social science and medicine.[5]

Botman had lived through one of the most trying periods of his life, as a university leader in a very public spectacle as the local Afrikaans newspaper turned up the heat through relentlessly negative reporting on the beleaguered rector. He would constantly be harassed by alumni and complaints from inside his own council that not enough was being done to "protect" Afrikaans. Any sign that more black students – or "the Natal English",[6] as one of the "*taalbulle*" (literally *language bulls*, or fighters) once put it in a radio debate with me – were being admitted was read as compromising the position of Afrikaans on campus since more English would have to be taught.

This was polite racism at its best. Instead of making the case for fewer blacks on campus, the argument could be made for more Afrikaans in classes. This was, after all, an official language recognised in the post-apartheid Constitution. No doubt there are those Afrikaans cultural activists for whom the language is regarded as an important cultural property, but there are others for whom it is the perfect wedge against becoming like all the other universities – majority black. This will happen anyway over the next decade or longer, but for now it is a life-and-death fight for racial domination masquerading as cultural preservation.

Russell Botman was up against it. So when he proposed on this lily-white campus a rather mild and moderate proposal to formally establish a centre for inclusivity, all hell broke loose. That week, ahead of the meeting of his council, the Afrikaans press lay into him with headline articles speculating about his imminent demise. The local newspaper carried rumours that he was about to be fired at that Monday meeting of the council for controversies around the centre. It had in fact come to light that on the Friday following that council meeting, one or more persons had laid a complaint against the rector calling for his resignation. Members of the council itself – something highly unusual in South Africa's Afrikaans universities – were routinely taking on the rector they had appointed in the press. He survived that Monday meeting only to be found dead on his bed at home after calling in sick during the previous days. A courageous journalist chronicled these and other events in the days leading up to his death in the online newspaper, the *Daily Maverick*.[7]

I had reason to call Rector Botman in the days before he died on a matter completely unrelated to these squabbles. Before we had even completed the formal exchange of greetings, he took off with a long list of his concerns about what was happening at the university and the efforts even among his own colleagues and council members to undermine transformation. He never spoke like this, at least not to me, for he was always cautious and reticent when we had occasion to meet. At that point I knew my fellow rector was taking strain. What I could not foresee, however, was that he was already in his final days on earth.

In time I would come to understand my anger on the day of his funeral. I had seen this movie before. The kind of animosity stoked by the press quoting any number of anonymous sources was familiar to me. I recognised the well-orchestrated racial conservatism that drives the toxic mix of rumour and fact on matters of transformation, and the highly personalised assaults on your dignity and humanity as a leader. And I knew, also, how one's body begins to become frail under the relentless pressure surrounding you. I knew, in other words, how he died.

Leadership issues

Nobody tells leaders about the high costs of transformation, especially for black leaders of historically white universities. There are costs to the family that come through the constant exposure in the conservative media. There are costs to your reputation as nameless individuals take their case public, not on public argument but on personal assault.

Here, incidentally, is a big difference between the white English universities and the white Afrikaans universities; in the case of the former, debates are largely argumentative and rival ideas are presented, defended and taken on in public forums and on the institution's website. The University of Cape Town is a good example of such a tradition. At the historically Afrikaans universities, it is personal and it does not take long for differences about transformation to descend into an assault on your race.

You walk a tightrope between the incessant demands of government for more transformation and the constant reminder from your conservative community that there is too much transformation. Under an activist minister of education, "race" is constantly inflamed by reckless statements and context-blind pronouncements from on high that in fact undermine your own efforts as a leader to create within the contexts of your own work the drive for transformation that both corrects the past and holds together the present.

How then does one lead under the burden of the past, given such volatile contexts in the present and where the future of both the university and society is at stake?

Friends in a rainy season

I wish to suggest specific leadership strategies that enable the transition from intimacy to nearness in the course of the desegregation of a white university campus. These leadership reflections, drawn from the storied research in the book, draw on the metaphor of rain reflected in the title and cover photograph. In popular culture rain has a dual meaning – of both blessing and disaster. To the Free State farmer rain is a blessing in this drought-stricken part of the world but too much rain, or rain at the wrong time, can destroy sensitive crops. Rain brings relief to empty dams but also dangerous mudslides. Who can forget the Merriespruit dam disaster of 1994 when the suburb by that name in Virginia, Free State, was flooded when the dam broke following heavy rains, killing 17 people and washing away homes?

In times of crisis, the rainy reason offers hope even as it portends danger; the outcome depends on leadership. So how can leaders lead on racially divided campuses in divided communities and divided countries?

Start with your largest and most powerful constituency

This is the undergraduate student population. In this respect you have to start with the incoming first-year students and work with them over the three-, four- or five-year course of their degree studies. You cannot start with seniors; they are about to leave the institution and they would have imbibed all the negative experiences of race and remonstration that make them very difficult to change. Senior students, I often found, would have been traumatised by their multi-year experiences to such an extent that any rehabilitation would take time that neither they nor the institution had. If they came through the experience of living and learning on a divided campus relatively unscathed, that might be a valued personal benefit but not an institutional one. But in traditional universities, like the UFS, where longstanding traditions such as initiation rituals and separate living do great harm to individuals and institutions alike, there is little that can be done with or for senior students.

It is, in fact, almost too late for first year students as well. From Gordon Allport[8] in 1954 to Frances Aboud in 2005 and to the most recent (2014) developmental research on the subject,[9] the findings are remarkably consistent over more than half a century of research – children already learn the habits of prejudice in their earliest years. Many of our students come from racially broken environments in which they have lived and learnt, prayed and worked, separately from each other as young black and white adults. As would have been evident in the voices of students in the compulsory core curriculum, they already have firm views of the past, the present and the future by the time they set foot inside a place of higher learning.

They have learnt to be angry about poverty and dispossession, as black students, and about alienation and accusation as white students. Even as youth straight out of high school, their political antennae have been sensitised to the "r" (racism, as accusation) word as white students and to the "t" (transformation, as affirmation) word as black students. Having never lived under apartheid, they nevertheless behave as if they were there.

Still, most first-year students are open to change. They half-expect to be challenged and to learn new knowledge. Perhaps sceptical at first, in the right circumstances they begin to open up to new possibilities.

Adopt a set of simple, strong and consistent entry messages

When? From the moment the first-years step onto campus and as they begin to find their ways through residence halls and lecture theatres, on the sports fields and the campus churches, in the dining facilities and in the orientation venues. What are those messages that apply on a campus with a long history of racial segregation and animosity?

Start with the message that prejudice and bigotry are condemned in the strongest terms. It is an uncomfortable message and likely to get some parental reaction – *is the assumption my child is racist?* – but it must be done soon, often and always. Nothing works as well as a regular reminder as to what the institution stands for.

That message, however, needs to come from the top, meaning the most senior levels of leadership and, in institutions with rigid hierarchies, from the rector him/herself. That message cannot simply be about race, for while racism was the original sin of so many nations that held slaves and executed genocide against local populations, the original sin was *difference*. For this reason sexism, xenophobia, homophobia and discrimination against people with disabilities should be part of the anti-prejudice message. Every opportunity to do this should be taken by leadership, and advertisements for jobs or annual communication to students should contain a placeholder on the first page that states clearly the university affirms all its people.

Design carefully and with the best available talent the co-curriculum for student learning

Most institutions do this in a fragmented way, but *the overall model of education* to which students are exposed might be much more significant in how well prepared they will be as graduates to lead and serve in a divided country. It can safely be assumed on university campuses anywhere that teaching and learning around these difficult issues of transformation will not happen in most physics or accounting or labour law classes. For those overseas universities with a liberal arts foundation or the few with core curricula, there is some respite from the rigidity of disciplinary learning and vocational training. But most students do not engage with the difficult and controversial issues of their times, like racism, in the normal course of studies.

That overall model of education refers of course to orientation programmes before students start the first academic year; it includes residence education programmes after classes and over weekends; it refers to the steady stream of off-campus student camps whether by academic department or residence or religious community; it includes generic leadership training opportunities offered by more and more universities; it has to do with who is invited to speak at special ceremonies like graduation and what those messages are primed to communicate; it is, in fact, about the day-to-day interactions with students as the leaders rush to meetings and the students to classes. All of this requires planning and integration behind a clear set of goals, something we started to call the co-curriculum. Too many university programmes of this kind can be described as fragmented and opportunistic, on the one hand, or rule prescriptions ("this is our policy on . . .") on the other; you do many things all over the place for disconnected campus citizens and hope for the best.

Make visible actually existing exemplars of interracial solidarity and friendships

You need to show that the education model works and that there are powerful alternatives to divided community among staff and students alike. In this sense it is the task of leadership to draw attention to ideals in practice. As the desegregation of residences unfolded, and the students responded to cues about our new value system that publically prized courageous human relations, they would see the evidence of not only what was desirable but what was real. I would not skip an opportunity to talk well in public gatherings about Nida and Modeyi, or Clarise and Andricia, or Melanie and George, and the many other student leaders – Tanya, Michael, Sibusiso, Stefan and scores of others who openly embraced, lived with, and loved students who used to see themselves as other races. There is nothing more powerful than exemplarity, and simply seeing and knowing that such relationships exist carried powerful meaning for both black and white students whose own biographies tell only of separate and, often, resentful lives in relation to what social psychologists call out-groups.

Model what you want from students in your own leadership choices and example

In this respect you cannot change a campus without visible changes in the senior leadership team. I am always conscious of that profound observation of the Sizer's: *The students are watching.*[10] Few universities are privileged to have as diverse a team of senior managers – mainly women and black, national and international, gay and straight, and multilingual in terms of home languages. This was no accident; it was planned because we simply could not project to the conservative Free State and its main campus profound statements of vision and mission without demonstrating the same in our leadership practice. That is the first hurdle at which many university leaders fall flat. For what the students see is what they come to believe – the exemplar on display.

In this respect the combination of the white rector and the black dean of students would come to be a powerful symbol of love and togetherness in almost every public gathering on campus at orientation week or off-campus when addressing farmers. There are many other such examples in the senior leadership teams of the university that emerge from progressive hiring practices and conscious cultivation of the leadership diversity of the university in the public imagination. Here the social psychology research recalled earlier is clear – *the extended contact hypothesis* – that simply knowing somebody from your own group connected to an out-group reduces prejudice in the in-group. In leadership, as in life, symbolism matters; not the symbolism that can be found in those opportunistic headshots of the marketing catalogues of universities but real, genuine friendships forged in the heat of battle to transform a white university.

Find the creative resources that already exist within the student body to lead the transformation

Not all students are the same, even in the most conservative and isolated of institutions. And the one invaluable resource is those students who come into university from desegregated schools and from homes in which it was completely normal for black and white people to pass through and where interracial friendship was an everyday experience.

The emotional labour of working with students who have no experience of interracial friendships in an integrating university is tough. Nothing is more straining on the emotions than bearing students who not only lacked normality in interracial experiences but were in fact actively nurtured on a doctrine of defending whiteness. I was exhausted, therefore, when I invited to my office a very young first-year student whose educational experiences were locked up in schools called, without any sense of irony, *Christelike Volkseie Onderwys* (CVO, Christian schools for our own [read white, Afrikaans] people). She rattled off to me the doctrines of ethnic and cultural preservation, and explained why she was a student leader – to fight for the rights of her own people on a segregated platform. "You do not need a university," I said to the young woman; "you already have all the answers."

It is by no means a given that students who experience interracial friendships in home, at school or in church will migrate those values into a segregated university; as indicated in earlier chapters, students in these circumstances are often forced to re-segregate as happened in the early years of the UFS. But when leadership generates the institutional conditions for nearness, these students then find a place and position from which to lead with some advantage to themselves and great leverage for a changing university.

Yet few things bring more joy than those many moments of genuine change among students who emerge from racially segregated environments and make the shift, slowly at first, and then with strident enthusiasm, towards integrated living and learning on campus. Inside these students there is a gradual process of transformation as resident knowledge begins to engage with new knowledge. This is a disconcerting process for young students with open minds who now have to grapple with the unfamiliar and the uncertain. Moving away from the past carries all kinds of threats – the loss of intimate connections, friends and sometimes family, who would surely detest the embrace of difference. That is a hard choice for the in-group offers security, reassurance, nourishment and familiar defences against a hostile out-world. And yet there is a sense of a larger, welcoming world than what was once presented as threatening and alien.

The student leader sitting with me must have had one of the most harrowing experiences any young person could possibly encounter. As the head of one of the most conservative white male residences, he was confronted with great pressure from white male alumni who wanted to make sure that the deliberations on a change of name for his residence would be terminated. The call to him from the older men was interpretable as biological: "you are one of us, defend the House." He was taking strain, his medical school studies were under pressure and he was seeking advice. Of course he had the choice of siding with the conserving voices and bringing that voice as a unified complaint to the senior leadership. But he was torn between listening to the old men and responding to the arguments for change. My message to the young leader was intended to sketch a bigger picture:

> I want you to know that in these moments your leadership is being tested; how you decide will make you a future leader in this troubled country or you will simply be like so many other aspirant leaders, black and white, whom when under pressure to make difficult choices fall back on their race. I cannot tell you what to do, but think "big picture" and ask yourself in this trial what kind of leader you wish to be.

He was furious a few days earlier when I called all the student heads of residences together to express concern that one of the students in his house had secretly recorded a meeting with the members and sent off the recording to the local Afrikaans newspaper. The newspaper headlines, and emotional responses that followed, predictably vilified the dean and angry *Letters* against the proposed name changes would run for weeks. It would culminate in a meeting of Convocation (alumni) in which a small group of white male alumni, mostly older men, put on a display of angry, infantile rage – conscious of the local paper in attendance – to decry the name change of the residence, and just about everything else having to do with change at the UFS.

But then one of the campus-wide student leaders, an impressive black woman, sat down with the angry head of residence for several hours, and talked through the challenges and the choices of transforming a university with decency and inclusion in mind. Slowly, he began to change and was now in my office seeking guidance on leading for change. "Never tell a student what to do," is a mantra of leadership that I try to remain true to; "talk rather about choices, and the consequences of choices, in the bigger scheme of things."

The student leader then decided on a course of action that tore at the heart. He would, under the generous and gracious leadership of the student dean, mercilessly vilified in the press, call his young men in residence in together and talk through the desirability and direction of change. They spent hours together over the next few months debating whether and, if so, how to change the name of the residence so that it signalled and symbolised inclusion for the very diverse residence rather than be reminded of the legacy of a white supremacist.

In time he would bring to the university leadership a set of choices the students themselves had come up with as proposed name changes. I was quite sure he would be happy to escape the noose of leadership of this difficult residence as his term came to an end. To the shock of many, he wanted to stand as leader of his residence for a second time. The "circuses", as the students call the platforms in which prospective leaders present their candidacy, were merciless in their questioning of his leadership for a second term. But they voted him in by a comfortable margin to lead again.

It was hard to believe that this was the residence that once presented me with a swastika as a greeting call.

In short, student leaders are much more credible than senior managers or leaders in creating safe spaces for deliberation and action on togetherness among suspicious, cautious and divided student bodies. They are there late at night and early in the morning. And where they act in pairs, black and white, their example reverberates down the corridors of residences and onto the campus more generally.

Concede and convey a sense of your own brokenness

The question often asked is: "How do students, or adults for that matter, come into these changed spaces with the willingness to reconsider starting positions?" This is an important question that goes to the heart of the leadership approach at the UFS. It was to model, throughout, a sense of broken leadership; that is, rather than the "strong man" model of leadership so prevalent in both popular literatures and, sadly, in some of the business management or executive training wisdom on the subject, our approach was to begin with the notion of weakness.

No leader, whether in the corporate world or education, in the home or outside of it, leads with perfection. At the best of times leaders are uncertain and unsure of themselves. The notion of the strong-willed leader with perfectly packaged answers to every crisis scenario belongs in "he-man" comic books. Leaders, whether they are conscious of it or not, lead with their emotions not only with their minds; the two are intimately connected, as new research consistently shows.[11] Leaders lead through their biographies, their own struggles and efforts to "do right" in their lives; they bring those experiences of hurt and healing with them into their work spaces and, if mature, can draw on lessons learned to improve and influence the lives of others.

Broken leadership does not mean weak leadership, in the sense of having critical personality or managerial deficits that threaten the very survival of the organisation you are charged with leading. It means, rather, a leadership conscious of its authority and how such authority could heal or hurt an organisation if not wielded wisely. It implies leadership that acknowledges how the leader got there, through the sacrifices and the goodwill of others, and how such leadership should therefore demonstrate generosity especially in times of challenge from followers. It suggests leadership that acknowledges personal frailty and how on the path to leadership mistakes were made in the very nature of being human, and that therefore the judgement of others is never from the vantage point of self-righteousness but always from a position of humility. All of this is captured in that beautiful paradox of Pauline wisdom: "when I am weak, then I am strong."[12]

It means the ability to say sorry in public and in private. Some of my fellow leaders were concerned when they saw the draft press statement I would read after the findings of the magistrate in the case of the black student who might have lied in his accusation about being "driven over" by the two white students. "What are you going to apologise for?" That kind of reasoning makes sense.

I was not responsible for the mess caused by the accuser. What we did made legal and political sense at the time, given the clear evidence in hand. The magistrate did not say that nothing had happened, he merely declared he could not make a guilty finding based on the evidence before him. And there were possible legal ramifications for the university if I made an apology at that point. But it was clear that there was much more at stake than legal manoeuvre or personal pride; our students and the community needed to know that there was among us as leadership a generosity of spirit, a capacity to back down and say "sorry", a willingness to be vulnerable in a crisis. "You did not have to say sorry," said a white colleague, once the local Afrikaans paper, the voice of the "*volk*" (nation), had slammed the statement of remorse.

Such a position of brokenness, I found often, would be misinterpreted by some colleagues as leadership that tolerates wrongdoing such as racism, the mistreatment of students and junior staff or the deliberate undermining of management authority. Having done such things, and being disciplined, a colleague might complain that "the human project" does not apply in his or her case. Broken leadership does not mean silence or softness on injustice; it means being clear and resolute in condemning all kinds of bigotry and naming the particular kind of abuse in public and in private conversations on the matter. What broken leadership is committed to, however, is to find resolutions to wrongdoing that do not simply hand over wrongdoers to legal justice or expulsion and leave them there, but to work very hard at conciliation, at bringing human actors back into communion, if at all possible. And sometimes it is not.

Know when to move on and leave behind

The leadership literature talks about "balance" when it comes to leading racially divided organisations, communities and divided campuses.[13] That is, conciliatory leaders in particular try to balance out competing interests or perspectives in ways that do not collapse the organisation but give space for broad participation through constant dialogue and consensus. That is the ideal; it is not always possible.

In the context of the UFS it became clear to me that there was a level of vicious racism on the margins of the discontent with institutional direction for which no amount of talking or listening would convince such persons or groups that what is being done is in the best interests of our children and our country. I certainly had no intention of listening to disrespectful groups whose racial animus has driven them beyond the bounds of decency. "Balance" therefore has its limits. Sometimes, as a leader, you simply have to move ahead with the limited time and energies at your disposal.

Build allies – but always on the basis of interracial solidarity

You cannot lead credibly on divided campuses without building allies across racial and class divides. It was important therefore to make sure that both unions

– the one representing mainly white staff but open to all and where most of the professionals were registered, and the one representing mainly black staff working at lower levels of staffing – were on board, that progressive white and black staff were sought to rally behind projects and ventures that broke the cultural and curricular rigidities of the institution, that prominent white and black community leaders were drawn into key events on campus and sought after for advice in the normal course of running the university, and that all students were constantly engaged on critical issues.

The most important lesson of leadership on divided campuses and communities is that allies must be sought and nurtured during times of peace. That is, you cannot begin to scramble for support from allies only when an ugly crisis rears its head; the building of trust happens best when the waters are calm. Most importantly, the allies behind the struggle for transformation must at all costs represent black and white South Africans in all their diversities. This is not only the right thing to do as a matter of principle; it is also the wise thing to do as a matter of strategy. The struggle for transformation must carry within the very face of its organisation the ideals of inclusion and cooperation.

Determine what is common to student experience and ambition, not only what makes them different

It is important in leadership to introduce complexity into the often crude and ahistorical treatment of distance, separation and inequality as only *racial* problems. There is both intellectual validity and political advantage to recognising the many different ways in which students and communities are divided. The most important challenge in the rural Free State is the problem of both black and white poverty.

True, most poor people are black but colonialism and capitalism always ensured an Afrikaner underclass quite apart from racial advantage in terms of access to resources.[14] It takes some time to convince the more radical black students on my campus that apartheid was as much a system of capitalist exploitation as it was one of racial domination. Therefore, a more progressive approach to poverty would be to recognise both poor white and poor black students in the effort to overcome social and economic distress. This approach works well in South Africa in that the demographic distribution ensured that most blacks would gain from our generous bursary or scholarship programmes, but so would poor whites.

Clara (not her real name) attended a modest township school in a poor fishing village outside of Cape Town. She was so poor that her parents and then single mother simply could not afford to place her in the more affluent white school in the small town. "When I first attended the other school," Clara tells me, "I was really, really scared, surrounded by all black students; it was very difficult for me for a long time." In the course of time Clara adjusts to the school which, while disadvantaged, built a reputation for hosting an exceptionally strong academic programme under its determined principal leader.

Clara begins to make her closest friends among the black students at the school and becomes one of the academic stars of the establishment. She changes deeply through her closeness to black students in school. *Die Burger*, the main Afrikaans newspaper for the Western Cape, carries her story prominently – the poor white youth who cannot attend university unless she finds the funds to do so. I ask my colleagues to track her down and I ask her to join the UFS on full funding, including round-trip travel home at the end of every university term. This response to the poor young white student is published in the Afrikaans press and immediately any number of white members of the community begin to call to offer Clara material and emotional support during her studies in Bloemfontein.

"My white friends are uneasy with me," confides Clara. "They cannot understand why my best friends include white and coloured and black students on campus." If ever there was a case for fully desegregating primary and high schools, it can be made through the compelling story of a poor white girl's transformation. Students like Clara would save universities, and the country, much travail and tension if early desegregation happened for white and black students. The task of leadership is to recognise and utilise opportunities afforded through young people like Clara for recruiting sentiment and building confidence in an approach that demonstrates, in practice, commitments not based solely on race but also on class and other identities which separate and stereotype citizens of campus and community.

Do not mislead yourself about your own authority or capacity

Leadership for nearness requires enormous capacity in terms of numbers, quite apart from competence that comes from adequate preparation for the job. This is one of the more serious weaknesses in popular imagery and even in traditional school leadership research – that the single, charismatic leader can, by sheer force of personality or command of power, make things happen across complex and conflicted organisations. There is now, fortunately, a generation of research on what is called "distributed leadership"[15] which proves quite the opposite – leaders are dispersed across an organisation and only a self-delusional CEO or university president would imagine that authority is concentrated in the one person or office.

You soon recognise in running this kind of enterprise that in such a "loosely coupled" organisation, people down a university's chain of command enjoy considerable autonomy and wield enormous power, from the hiring of staff to the population of the academic timetable to the admission of students. Yes, there are policies and regulations; but there are also powerful traditions and habits that remain embedded in the day-to-day operations of a department or unit that no leader in the main building can "see", let alone control, in a massive organisation. For this reason alone, you are dependent on "stretched over" leadership – to use a specialist term from the research by James Spillane of the University of Chicago – involving an "interactive web of leaders" in the university, to begin to bring coherence and common purpose to the mission of integration and, more broadly, transformation.[16]

Here selection of the team is everything. You need a core team that is loyal to what you want to achieve in terms of both academic excellence and human togetherness; ambitious backbiters that undermine your authority will distract you from the main work at hand and drain much-needed energy from your own human capacities. You need team members who are better than you in core areas of competence; you hire them to complement your skills.

You need individuals in that team who are unafraid to tell you where you are messing up, especially in hierarchical institutions like the traditional Afrikaans universities. There are classical stories from aviation to the presidency of how in tradition-bound organisations planes go down and people die needlessly because somebody in the leadership team did not believe it was appropriate to speak the truth, upwards.

Your team must, most of all, share the core values agreed on with regards to the deep transformation of an old university; if you cannot convince the team of what's worth doing, you cannot convince the members of that small department you might never physically visit in a large university.

Even if agreed on the core values, the diversity of the leadership team is a crucial strength in divided communities. You need white colleagues with their unique insights into the minority (in South Africa's case) white community's fears, concerns, anxieties and hopes. This is someone who not only comes from the churches and lives in the marketplace with that section of the community, but knows how to translate their core concerns into a management context. Sometimes people confide certain kinds of information only to members of the in-group. What is said needs cultural interpretation, for the written or spoken word in itself might not convey the same meaning to insiders versus outsiders. The same is true of black colleagues who speak the regional African language, for example, and who can capture emotions about the university from among ordinary people in ways that the English language might not make clear. Your leadership team members therefore function as cultural interpreters of the environment.

"Where are the white students?" confides a colleague in the voice of a visitor to campus with her prospective student daughter. My initial inclination was to shoot back a slightly irritated factual response – "they're all over the campus; open your eyes." But it took me a while to understand that this was not a question about facts; it was a question about feelings. It was the expectation of dominance – that the university was not, like Potchefstroom or Stellenbosch, so overwhelmingly white that prospective white students from conservative communities felt much less threatened than when they were a demographic minority, as in the country. Misreading that message could have led to leadership blunders and insensitivities in *how* that prospective student, and all who felt like her, would be welcomed and embraced on this South African campus in the conservative heartland. Whatever the many other benefits of diversity in the leadership team, strategic insight was one of the most important which, when fed into the joint inputs and deliberations of the senior leaders, made for a much wiser set of decisions.

Give up power more often than you use it

Even within a diverse team of senior leaders there is, inevitably, a hierarchy that also applies in our relationships with colleagues and students. There is, in other words, a power differential. A hard-nosed reading of organisational hierarchies would insist, therefore, that no relationship can be equal and that no true consent can be achieved under such circumstances. This of course would be especially true in the case of traditional Afrikaans universities where the rector or "senior manager" could, without serious consequences, call the shots on everything from admissions policy to parking lots on campus. Where such a leadership practice has been allowed to embed itself in a patriarchal and paternalistic culture, the dangers of unequal relationships become especially serious. But the claim is a little more complex than the "no true consent" argument would make it out to be.

First of all, and as intimated earlier, it matters how you carry and exercise your authority. This is why in chairing a meeting it is so necessary to enable yourself, as the senior leader, to be overruled in the final decision. You obviously can and should make your inputs on institutional budgets and the hiring of deans, but you have to be aware of the fact that colleagues might yield to you not on the basis of argument but on the validity of your ideas. That takes time to accomplish but is necessary to build both democratic institutions and respect for decisions. Done consistently, followers begin to gain a sense of their own voice and vote in such circumstances. It is also important to respect your immediate senior leaders who act to moderate and redirect your own views on a subject. I do not accept the premise, therefore, that it is inevitable that "no true consent is possible" in hierarchical organisational structures and cultures; it depends how you wield your authority.

This should not be read as jellyfish leadership on things that really matter. You cannot leave a critically important decision such as the desegregation of the residences or the hiring of more black and women staff to a simple vote. Where the moral cause on the table is so fundamental to the long-term interests of the university, you do need to exercise your authority as a leader and point to the desired direction. But even in such cases, the ideal is to achieve that outcome through persuasion (moral authority) rather than through the all-pervasive "*opdrag*" (command, formal or legal authority) I found in the traditional Afrikaans universities. In rare cases, nevertheless, you have to go against the majority opinion – such as on residential desegregation – but those cases should remain rare. The way to ensure this is to make sure you are regularly outvoted.

I had already decided that the constant reports of humiliating initiating rituals in my first few months as leader were threatening to keep us in crisis management mode for a long time to come. Seniors simply took it on themselves, no matter what senior leadership said, to continue time-honoured traditions of sometimes violent initiation ceremonies. I discussed the matter with senior leaders and decided on that Friday morning to take to a critical council meeting a proposal to declare the most troublesome male residences as first-year residences and effectively eject seniors off campus into private accommodation. While seniors remained in residences, I argued, there was simply no chance we would turn around this devastating practice within residences.

Early that morning I was on my way from the parked car to my office for final preparations for the council meeting when I saw waiting for me along the walking path a group of student leaders from *Huis Karee* – at that stage one of the sources of several such initiation atrocities and just generally crude, racist behaviour on the part of often drunk seniors. They were immaculately dressed in the black blazers and dark yellow shirts and ties, hair flattened with an assortment of creams. They were on their polite best, and I joked whether male students had ever emerged from bed this early in the morning. "Sir, we would like to see you on an urgent matter," whispered one of the leaders. "Come inside, but I do not have much time," I warned, since the Council meeting was minutes away.

The student leaders looked shell-shocked. "We know you are going to Council to establish first year residences," they said, and then started to plead that I change my mind. I was not in the mood for this kind of retraction, remembering all too well the recent hardships suffered by first-year students and the great damage caused to the university in the media. They must have sensed a managerial body language that was not persuaded by these last-minute antics. But I watched them carefully and by now could distinguish fake remorse from genuine commitment to change behaviour on the part of students. One or two had tears in their eyes and I sensed sincerity on their part.

"Okay, but mess this up and we go back to the original proposal." They jumped up and after hugs all round, left the office elated. I went to my chairman and asked that he withdraw the proposal for first-year residences. From that day onwards, *Huis Karee* would gradually become the most impressive male residence in terms of the treatment of first-year students. What was much more important was that they had learnt they could change a management decision even on such a crucial matter as the design and character of residential accommodation.

There is another unacceptable assumption in the "inherently unequal argument", and it is that it portrays the leader as all powerful and the staff member or student as powerless. I do not accept this, as already demonstrated in the reflections on the Reitz women. In a democracy, the leader is both formally accountable through the rules of conduct and routine elections but also through the capacity of individuals to be represented and to mobilise against unethical or authoritarian leaders. As a young democracy, South African citizens are very alert to the abuse of power and privilege and it is the unusual case where leaders inside public universities are able to abuse authority without consequences. Still, the primary route to achieving genuine consent is through humane leadership, especially under challenge.

This challenge is most intense when it comes to leading colleagues in a former white university. Most staff are found to be warmly in support of your leadership on the basis of position, competence and a shared humanity. There is a significant "middle" group that, while cautious, will follow the leadership given and deliver on the tasks required; in a beautiful turn of phrase in the Afrikaans language, "*ons kyk die kat uit die boom uit*" (we'll take a detached, distant view for now until we figure out whether to commit). And then there is a third group that no matter what you do will resent your leadership for no other reason than *who you are*.

I have learnt to appreciate the acceptance and camaraderie of the first group; I have also understood and even accepted the reticence of the second group given their own racial socialisation; this was, after all, the first time they were to be led at this level by a black academic personality and rector; but I had to learn how to manage my emotions and conceal my irritation with the third group.

Bare-knuckled prejudice can get under your skin.

Communicate clearly the messiness of change

Our greatest challenge has been to downplay the overly positive media hype from certain quarters in the press about what was happening at the university. This is important since the most important lesson that must be communicated about transformation is that it is not a straight line of progress. Transformation by its very nature is contentious – it upsets settled interests, it mobilises desperate groups into counteractions, it drives people to the local media, and it generates alibi complaints about everything from those who feel the ground has shifted from under them.

Inevitably, the more conservative elements leave the university either as staff or governors, and the more unscrupulous among them will make abstract claims about some sense of moral duty; but the real reason some leave is because they do not like the pace and direction of transformation. There will be setbacks. No matter how much has been achieved in terms of racial desegregation, on the one hand, and human integration, on the other, there will be regular incidents of racial abuse often in the form of invisible micro-aggressions but also the occasional public incident.

It is important to communicate this sense of the non-linearity of change, both to keep the troopers encouraged, those who work at the coalface of this difficult process, and also to convey a realistic sense of the long path towards racial inclusion and social justice inside century-old institutions.

Create opportunities for nearness

"It is not good for Man to be alone."[17]

Now to the heart of the book. Humans are warm-blooded animals. In the segregation wrought by history and the isolation amplified by technology, more than ever students (and staff) desire a sense of closeness to each other and to their leaders. It is perhaps the primary task of the leader (plural) in divided communities to constantly seek ways of breaking down barriers to interracial communion, from the design of urban spaces to the planning of the student residence experience. Human beings are emotionally wired for closeness, not distance, and the architects of social and educational change need to recognise that simple but profound fact in a twenty-first-century leadership approach.

The notion of a distant leader issuing instructions from on high belongs in another century. Students appreciate leadership presence among them. They need to experience an emotional attachment to the vision for change. In a tactile culture, anxious white students need to interact closely with open-hearted black leaders. White leaders need to convey a sense of commitment to wary black students. That cannot be done from a distance but from the network of formal and informal interactions that break through those sticky, invisible spider webs of distrust that tie up our capacity to see the other in ourselves. The building of trust through intimate relationships is best done during periods of stability so that when crises do emerge – and they will – there is a solid cross-racial solidarity that prevents a falling back into racial blocks that not only inflame conflict but reinforce racial distancing from each other.

Despite all, surprised by joy

The labour of leadership is costly. I now understand how the body becomes compromised under opposing pressures from those who resist the deep transformation of our treasured institutions and those with a retributive bent who seem to disregard the fragile human relations needed to transform intimacy into nearness.

As leaders, we take on these jobs because we anticipate the costs of helping to undo three centuries of injustice and inequality while trying to keep our students and the surrounding communities in communion. The costs, however, are but one side of the human equation called leadership.

Nothing can outweigh the sheer elation of living among and learning from young South African students and their peers from the region and beyond. Time after time I would find myself, over these years of leadership, surprised by joy.[18] I bore witness to the transformation of tens of thousands of students from entry positions of anger, fear and anxiety towards something as elusive as human togetherness. Many have made that transition from physical proximity to emotional embrace, and simply to have been part of their journey as students remains an unspeakable joy.

Notes

1. Chris Brink, a distinguished mathematician and competent leader, who served Stellenbosch University from 2002–07, was asked to leave shortly after his reappointment for a second term, and under relentless pressure from alumni and the press on, among other things, the never-ending complaint about the plight of Afrikaans at the university. "Did the "heat and emotion" – Brink's phrase – generated by the language debate at Stellenbosch [impose] too great a toll on him?" was the rhetorical question posed by the *Mail & Guardian* (11–17 August 2006, p. 178) newspaper as he departed the university after six years. See also the chapter by Brink's wife on the impacts on his life of leading Stellenbosch: Brink, T. 2007. What happened with Chris? In Botha, A. (ed.) *Chris Brink; Anatomy of a transformer*. Stellenbosch: SUN MEDIA. pp. 282–3.
2. de Vos, P. 2013. Why an attempt to stop the racial integration of residences at Maties is legally untenable. *Constitutionally Speaking*, 11 March. Available from: http://constitutionallyspeaking.co.za/why-an-attempt-to-stop-the-racial-integration-of-residences-at-maties-is-legally-untenable/
3. See Keet, A. 2014. *The 'Flesh' of Ghosts: Heritage, Memory and Identity in Stellenbosch*. Heritage Lecture, 18 September, University of Stellenbosch; Chet. Fransch, J.P. 2010. "We Would Have No Name": The porosity of locational and racial identities amongst the "Coloured Communities" of Stellenbosch, c. 1890–1960s. *African Studies* 69(3), 419–22; Giliomee, H. 2007. *Nog Altyd Hier Gewees: Die storie van 'n Stellenbosse gemeenskap*. Cape Town: Tafelberg; Biscombe, H. 2006. *In Ons Bloed*. Stellenbosch, Sun Press.

    This Open Letter to Professor Botman further captures, in some powerful observations, the troubled racial history of the town and the university, and its legacies into the present:

    Odendaal, P. 2012. Open letter to Professor Botman, Vice-Chancellor and Rector of Stellenbosch University. *Bonfiire*, 6 August. Available from: http://bonfiire.com/stellenbosch/2012/08/06/open-letter-to-professor-botman-vice-chancellor-and-rector-of-stellenbosch-university/
4. Newling, D. 2013. Debate over Nazi 'race index' tools found at Stellenbosch. *Times Higher Education (THE)*, 31 October. Available from: www.timeshighereducation.co.uk/news/debate-over-nazi-race-index-tools-found-at-stellenbosch/2/2008477.article#.Uq9mLYib_rM.twitter
5. The *Journal of Social Science and Medicine* is published by Elsevier.
6. There is only one thing worse for the Afrikaans language activists at the University of Stellenbosch than non-Afrikaans speaking "Africans", and that is the trend over recent years for white English-speaking students from the former British colony of Natal (now KwaZulu Natal province in the new South Africa) to abandon the virulently ethnic African politics of their nearby university (the University of KwaZulu Natal, formerly the white English University of Natal, which was now, by a large majority, black) and seek out the pure, white campus of the idyllic Stellenbosch wine lands in the beautiful Cape. The only acceptable "Other" here was the so-called Coloured student, regarded as a distant [*sic*] cousin but whose language, for the majority who spoke it, was close enough and whose numbers were small enough not to upset the ethnic apple cart of the pristine white campus. "Even the buildings are white," moaned a Coloured academic quoting the experiences of a black Stellenbosch student on this campus.
7. Thamm, M. 2014. Revealed: Professor Botman's torrid final week. *Daily Maverick*, 2 July. Available from: www.dailymaverick.co.za/article/2014-07-02-revealed-professor-botmans-torrid-final-week/; and Thamm, M. 2014, July 8. Russell Botman's Legacy: Time for progressive voices to emerge. *Daily Maverick*. Available from: www.dailymaverick.co.za/article/2014-07-08-russel-botmans-legacy-time-for-progressive-voices-to-emerge/#.VOJzl_mUc7k; see also Jansen, J.D. 2014, July 11.

Who Killed Russell Botman? *The Times*. Available from: www.timeslive.co.za/thetimes/2014/07/11/the-big-read-who-killed-russel-botman
8 Allport, G. 1954. *The Nature of Prejudice*. New York: Perseus Books; and Aboud, F.E. 2005. The development of prejudice in childhood and adolescence. In Dovidio, J. F., Glick, P. and Rudman, L.A. (eds) *On the Nature of Prejudice: Fifty years after Allport*. Malden, MA: Blackwell Publishing Ltd, pp. 310–26.
9 Abrams, D. and Killen, M. 2014. Social Exclusion of Children: Developmental origins of prejudice. *Journal of Social Issues* 70(1), 1–11.
10 Sizer, T.R. and Sizer, N.F. 1999. *The Students Are Watching: Schools and the moral contract*. Boston, MA: Beacon Press.
11 Thagard, P. 2006. *Hot Thought: Mechanisms and application of emotional cognition*. Boston, MA: MIT Press.
12 2 Corinthians 12: 10. Bible. 1986. *The Holy Bible: New International version*. Cape Town: Bible Society of South Africa.
13 See Jansen, J.D. 2005. Black Dean: Race, reconciliation and the emotions of deanship. *Harvard Educational Review* 75(3), 306–26.
14 See O' Meara, D. 1983. Volkskapitalisme: Class, capital, and ideology in the development of Afrikaner nationalism 1934–48. Cambridge: Cambridge University Press.
15 Spillane, J. 2006. *Distributed Leadership*. San Francisco, CA: Jossey Bass; see also Harris, A. 2014. *Distributed Leadership Matters: Perspectives, practicalities and potential*. Thousand Oaks, CA: Corwin Press.
16 Ibid.
17 Genesis 2: 18, the Divine observation that led to the creation of Adam's companion. Bible. 1986. *The Holy Bible: New International version*. Cape Town: Bible Society of South Africa.
18 The phrase "Surprised by Joy" is borrowed, of course, from C.S. Lewis, who has a book by that name: Lewis, C.S. 1955. *Surprised by Joy: The shape of my early life*. New York: HarperCollins.

Index

Italics are used to indicate pages containing photographs.

50:50 policy (integration) 79–81, 126, 135

Abdurahman, Dr Abdullah 39–40
abuse: of authority 215–16; of first year students 94; intimacy 58, 164; Reitz case 22–3, 27, 33–5, 182; and social media 128, 162
academic standards 53, 98–100, 193
acting, Reitz video 21, 22, 32
Aden, Roger 194
admissions: medical schools 109–12, 183–4; University of the Free State 80–1, 98–9
affirmative action 97, 98, 109–11; white opposition to 179, 183–6, 191–3
African National Congress (ANC) 76, 91–2
African People's Organisation (APO) 39s
Afrikaans language: classes 77, 135–6, 188; nationalism 148; University of Stellenbosch 201–2; vs common language 54, 83–9, 183
Afrikaner Nationalist Party 186
Afrikaners: Boer War 41, 43, 52; media 5, 53, 74, 163, 173–95; nationalism 75, 83; *Volkskongres* 61; *see also Volksblad* (newspaper)
age 23, 30, 138, 143
aggression in romantic relationships 58
agnotology 119; *see also* ignorance, about racism
Akasia (residence) 127
alcohol 23–4, 94

Allport, Gordon 140, 146
Ally, Shireen 67, 68
alumni: cultural heritage 87, 160, 174, 175–6, 194, 202; fun vs racism 181–2; name changes 100, 207–8; *Vryfees* festival 46
America: *see* United States (USA)
Anderson, Elizabeth 12
anti-ras (Letters) 180–1
apartheid: blacks 43–4, 165; in curriculum 108, 111–17; domestic labour 64–6; Group Areas Act 50; identities 96–7, 164–5; ignorance of 106, 117–20; opposition 51–3; over-exposure 113, 180–1; and Reitz case 29; scholarship 102–3, 105; whites 51–3, 189, 195
Apartheid Archive 65, 67
Aron, Arthur 142
art symbols 101
assault cases 153–9, 160, 161–4, 177, 209–10
attachments (intimacy) 58–9
authority 2, 30, 138–9; leadership 214, 215–17
autoethnography 2

babies, apartheid 64–5
bakkie (pick-up truck) 153–4, 163, 177
balance, in leadership 210
barbarism 61, 187
Basothos: history 41–2; nationalism 75, 137
Benzien, Jeffrey 59
Bethlehem, Free State 42

Bible 7–8, 78, 100
Bible School, Bloemfontein 41
bigotry 43, 78, 205
Black Consciousness Movement 165
Blackface incidents 117–18
blacks: under apartheid 43–4, 165; black racism 8–9; classes 77, 135–6; education system 47–8, 84–5; employment 48–50, 61, 64–6, 138–9, 188; history and customs 46, 47, 50–1, 74–5; middles classes 48, 74–5, 146; nationalism 148, 191; Reitz case 17–18, 22–4, 29, 31–2, 182; residences 57–8, 76–7, 127, 166–8; victimhood 43, 160, 168
Bloemfontein 40–3; Community Revival Church 139; politics 74–5; social class 50–1; *Volkskongres* of 1956 61
Boeremusiek 46
Boerseun (Letters) 178–9, 189
Boer War *vi*, 5, 39; Museum 41–2, 52; as part of curriculum 107–8; present day reminders 41–3
Botman, Russell Hayman 201–3
braai (barbeque) 130
Brawley, Tawana 163
brokenness, leadership 209–10
Burger, Die (newspaper) 45, 174–5, 186
bursaries 141–2
Buys, Rudi 153

Cape Flats 91
Cape Town xiii–xiv, 129–30
children, apartheid 64–5
choirs 136–7
Christianity 8; Bible School, Bloemfontein 41; missions 61–2, 144–5; in public sphere 100, 101; racial segregation 44–5, 61–2, 75, 78, 139; role in transformation 137, 169–71, *170*, 172
churches: missions 61–2, 144–5; racial segregation 44–5, 61–2, 75, 139; role in transformation 169–71, 172
City of Oaks (*Eikestad*) 201
civil service 191
class: *see* social class
classes/ lectures 77, 135–6, 188; history education (UFS 101) 107–17, 181

cleaners, Reitz case 17–18, 22–4, 29, 31–2, 182
closeness: *see* nearness
coercion, Reitz case 24, 27, 31
Coloured, as racial category 164–5
common language 54, 83–9, 183
communion 130–1
Community Revival Church, Bloemfontein 139
concentration camps, Boer War 41, 42
contact theory 140–1, 145–6, 206
content analysis, newspapers 5, 176, 178
Coolies (slang) xiv
court cases 163, 168
culture evening, Reitz 20–1, 33
curriculum (education system) 105–6
curriculum, University of the Free State 105, 106–17, 205

death threat 91
de Kock, Eugene 46
democracy 108, 186–7, 188–9, 215–16
demographics: Free State 50–3; social class 50–1, 74–5, 146; universities 160–1; University of the Free State 10–11, 76, 79–82, 188
desegregation 147, 212; *see also* integration
de Vos, Pierre 19–20
Diep Seun (Letters) 189
distributed leadership 212–14
diversity 77–80; initiatives 95, 96; of religion 100, 101; songs 101–2
domestic labour 64–6, 67, 117–18
domestic violence 58
dominees (ministers) 44–5, 62
du Pisanie, Johan 190
Dutch Reformed Church (DRC) 44–5, 61, 75, 144
du Toit, Andrew 62
du Toit, Jannie 186

Eastern Free State 9–10, 42
economics: financial support 141–2, 211–12; and intimacy 61, 63; racial segregation 61, 146
education system 1–2; competence of 98–9; curriculum 105–6; history 113,

117, 120; racial segregation 47–8, 47–9, 84–5, 139
Eikestad (City of Oaks) 201
emblems, of universities 100–1
Emily (residence) 77, 81
employment: domestic 64–6, 67, 117–18; racial segregation 48–50, 61, 138–9, 188; University of the Free State 76, 191–2; working students 136
English language: classes 77, 135–6; as common language 54, 84–5, 86–7; imposition of 183
entanglement 5–8, 62
entitlement 160–1, 191–3
equality 39, 61–2
ethnocentrism 178–9
ethnography 2
Evans, Ivan 28
examinations, University of the Free State 99
exhaustion, about race 113, 180–1

F1 'Leadership for Change' initiative 95
Facebook 7
farming communities 30, 49–50, 62
festivals: *Macufe* 46; *Vryfees* 45–7
Figueroa, Monica Moreno 4
financial support, at university 141–2, 211–12; No Student Hungry Campaign 97, 133–4, 137–8
first year students, University of the Free State 34, 93–4, 204
Fleming, Leonard 41
food: cultural significance of 130–1; No Student Hungry Campaign 97, 133–4, 137–8
forced integration (*gedwonge integrasie*) 77–8, 125; *see also* integration
free association 77, 179–80
Freedom Front Plus (FF+) 76
Free State: province 39–53; churches 44–5; festivals 45–6; labour 48–50; living 50–3; meals 130; politics 74–5; schools 47–8; sports 46–7
Free State, University of the 9–11; assault cases 153–9, 160, 161–4, 177, 209–10; core curriculum 105, 106–17, 205; jobs 76, 191–2; language use 77, 83–7; public relations 18–19, 128–9, 195;

racial segregation 11–12, 53–4, 57–8, 75–6, 125–6; symbolism 100–1; transformation 93–5, 125–7, 168–72, 203–17; *see also* integration; Reitz case
Friend, The (newspaper) 74

gedwonge integrasie (forced integration) 77–8, 125; *see also* integration
Georgia (USA) 63–4
Gobodo-Madikizela, Pumla 46
God: in motto 101; Reitz case 27
Gordon-Reed, Annette 63
government 108, 186–7, 188–9, 215–16
Group Areas Act 50

Halling, Steen 143, 144
Hancock County, Georgia 63–4
helpless victim narratives 31, 64, 146
Herzog, J.B.M. (Prime Minister) 73
history education, schools 113, 117, 120
history education (UFS 101) 107–17, 181
Hodges, Martha 62–3
hoer (whore) 18, 27, 31
Hotnot (slang) 50, 191
house committees (HKs) 81
Huis Karee (residence) 215
human project, University of the Free State 96–8
humour, racial 117–19
hypersensitivity 113, 116

identity 41, 42, 95, 96–7, 142–3
ignorance, about racism 106, 117–20, 150
independence of South Africa 6, 188–9
infants, apartheid 64–5
initiation rituals, University of the Free State 94; Reitz case 17–18, 19, 21, 27, 34–5; *Villa Bravado* residence 166–7, 168
institutions 3
insults: Reitz case 18, 25–6, 27, 31; *see also* racist terms
integration, schools 139
integration, University of the Free State 11–13; 50:50 policy 79–81, 126, 135; and leadership 81, 125–7, 217; and nearness 134–5, 147–8; opposition to 17–18, 26–7, 57–8, 77–82, 125–6, 178–9; Reitz case 17–18, 26–7

interpretive autoethnography 2
interracial marriage 8–9, 58, 63–4
interracial sexual intimacy 60–6
interracial solidarity 127, 133–4, 137–8, 206–7, 210–12
intimacy 1–5, 58–62; dark side 164–6, 167–72; and knowledge 105–6, 117; leadership 169, 203–17; meaning of 134; portraits of 123–31, *124*, *126*; and transformation 68–9, 93–5, 167–72; *see also* nearness

Jansen, Jonathan: "Kill the Rector" campaign 91–2, 93; marriage 8–9; in the media 155–6, 162, 183, 186; 190–1
JBM Herzog (residence) 127
Jefferson, Thomas (President of USA) 63, 64
Jews 73
jobs: *see* employment
'juggy' drink (initiation ritual) 21–3, 24–5
junior students, University of the Free State 34, 93–4, 204

kaffir (slang) 162
Kathrada, Ahmed 43–4
"Kill the Rector" campaign 91–2, 93
Kimberley 39–40
Kliptown People's Congress of 1955 61
knowledge, and intimacy 105–6, 117
Knowledge in the Blood (Jansen) 3, 113, 141

labour: *see* employment
language: and authority 138; common language 54, 83–9, 183; and leadership 81; of lectures 77; scholarship 1, 86–7, 88–9; *see also* racist terms
laws, racial 43, 60
leadership 4; and assault case 154, 157–9; authority 214, 215–17; initiation rituals 167, integration 81, 82; nearness 149, 169, 203–17; opposing racism 93–6, 204–5; orientation sessions 78–9; Reitz case 92–3; student leaders *126*, 126–7, 149, 171–2, 206, 207–9, 215;

transformation 125–7, 203–17; University of Stellenbosch 201–3; *Villa Bravado* 168–9
'Leadership for Change' initiative 95
lectures/ classes 77, 135–6, 188; history education (UFS 101) 107–17, 181
Letters to the Editor: see Volksblad (newspaper)
Lewis, C. S. 134, 217
liquor 23–4, 94
living arrangements, Bloemfontein 50–3
living arrangements, University of the Free State: *see* residences
love, interracial 67–9; nannies-children 65, 67, 150; Reitz case 23; sexual intimacy 63, 64, 68–9

Macufe (black festival) 46
Mahlangu, Solomon 108
Malan, D. F. (Prime Minister) 201
Maljan (Mad John) 17, 32
Mandela, Nelson 29; and food 131; government 29, 186–7, 188–9; language 88; as national icon 100; as part of curriculum 108
marriage, interracial 8–9, 58, 63–4
Marxian analyses 66
Mda, Zakes 66, 68
Mead, Jane 2
mealtimes, cultural significance of 130–1
media: assault cases 155, 156, 162, 163–4; Donald Sterling 59–60; Jonathan Jansen 155–6, 162, 183, 186; 190–1; "Kill the Rector" campaign 91–2, 93; Reitz case 18, 29; transformation of University of the Free State 161, 175; *see also* newspapers; *Volksblad*
medical schools, admissions 109–12, 183–4
Meeko, Thabo 91–2
middle classes: blacks 48, 74–5, 146; whites 30, 109–10, 146
military training 34, 35–6
Mills, Charles 119
Minister of Education, South Africa 17
Missing (play) 46
missions, Christian 61–2, 144–5
mistresses 60, 64, 68
Mohammed, Justice Ismail 43

Moshoeshoe, King 42
mottos, of universities 101
multiculturalism 54, 136, 142–3
music: *Boeremusiek* 46; racial diversity 101–2; racial segregation 77, 136–7

names, university buildings 100, 207–8
nannies 65, 67, 150
narratives 2–5, 141
nationalism 75, 83, 97, 137, 148–9
natives 6, 39, 50, 60–1
nearness 4; capacity for 138–50; leadership 149, 169, 203–17; meaning 134; portraits of 123–31, *124*, *126*; spiritual 134, 136–8; strategic 134–6; *see also* intimacy
Neethling, Ben 184
Netherlands, the 5–6
newspapers 173; assault case 156, 163; *Die Burger* 45, 174–5, 186; *The Friend* 74; *The Star* 162; *The Times* 4, 5; *see also Volksblad*
North West, University of 87, 123–4, 171–2, 194
nostalgia 182, 193–4
No Student Hungry campaign 97, 133–4, 137–8

openness and intimacy 143–5
oppression and intimacy 62–4, 66
Orange, Donna 88
Orange Free State 17, 39–40, 49–50
orientation sessions: in churches 75; leadership 78–9, 205
over-exposure, to race 113, 180–1

pacifism 109–10
Perkins-Valdez, Dolen 68
personalism 63–4
perspective/ proportion, sense of 19, 27–8, 182
photography 4–5; Boer War *vi*, 5; prayer *170*; rugby game *124*; student leaders *126*
physical proximity 129–30, 134
Plaatje, Sol 39
playfulness/ *studentepret* 27, 28, 181–2
policy: 50:50 integration 79–81, 126, 135; laws 43, 60

politics: democracy 108, 186–7, 188–9, 215–16; Free State (province) 74–5; nationalism 75, 83, 97, 137, 148–9; reconciliation politics 29; University of the Free State 76
"Potch" (University of the North West) 123–4
poverty 61, 63, 146; financial support 141–2, 211–12; No Student Hungry Campaign 97, 133–4, 137–8
power relations 3; leadership 167, 212, 214, 215; sexual intimacy 66, 68
prayer: racial segregation 44–5, 75; role in transformation 137, 169–71, *170*, 172
Prestige Scholars Programme 102–3
Pretoria, University of 87, 100–1, 117–18, 141–2; newspapers 174, 175
Pretorius, Tokkie 52
Proctor, Robert Neel 119
proportion/ perspective, sense of 19, 27–8, 182
'prostitute', as insult 18, 25, 26, 27, 31
protest march, Red Square 157
Proverbs (Bible) 7–8
public relations, University of the Free State 18–19, 128–9, 177–8, 195
public sector 191

qualifications 106
quotas, racial 179, 193
Qwa Qwa campus 9–10

race, as category 145, 164–5
racial segregation: Boer War *vi*, 5; Christianity 44–5, 61–2, 75, 78, 139; employment 48–50, 61, 138–9, 191–2; festivals 45–6; Free State province 40, 43–4, 50–3; laws 43, 60; music 77, 136–7; and nearness 150; residences 57–8, 76, 79–82, 125–7, 207–9; schools 47–8, 139; sports 46–7, 123–5, *124*, 171–2; University of the Free State 11–12, 26–7, 53–4, 57–8, 75–82, 125–6
racist terms xiv; *Coolies* xiv; farming communities 49–50; *Hotnot* 50, 191; *kaffir* 162; laws 43; *Maljan* 17, 32; *squeezas* 17, 22, 26, 33
rape 185–6

recidivism 4
reconciliation politics 29, 188–9, 210
recruitment, University of the Free State 53, 81, 98–9
Reformed churches 44–5
Reitz case, University of the Free State 10–11, 17–18; defence of 18–27; interpretations 27–36, 181–2, 184–5, 186; media 18, 29; repercussions 92–3, 166–7
religion: diversity of 100, 101; role in transformation 169–71, *170*, 172; *see also* Christianity
residences: *Akasia* 127; alcohol consumption 23–4, 94; *Emily* 77, 81; free association 77, 179–80; *Huis Karee* 215; *JBM Herzog* 127; racial segregation 57–8, 76, 79–82, 125–7, 207–9; roommates 78, 135, 140, 180; *Tswelopele* 82; *Villa Bravado* 166–7, 168–9; *Welwitschia* 80–1; *see also* Reitz case
romantic intimacy 58–9
roommates 78, 135, 140, 180
rugby 46–7, 123–5, *124*, 143
rural areas 74, 84–5, 148, 153; farming communities 30, 49–50, 62

sadness, Bloemfontein 41–3
Saldanha, Arun 145
scholarship 1–4; academic standards 99–100, 192; apartheid 102–3, 105; intimacy 58; language of 1, 86–7, 88–9; storytelling 2–4
schools: *see* education system
Schultz, Mark 63–4
scriptures 7–8
segregation: *see* racial segregation
senior leaders 135, 149, 154, 203–17
senior students 34, 93–4, 204
sensitivity, to apartheid 113, 116
Serenade events 77, 101–2
serfdom 39
settlers 6
sexism: Reitz case 22, 29–32; *squeezas* (slang) 17, 22, 26, 33; *tiekie* case 159–60
sexual intimacy, interracial 60–6
Shimlas (rugby team) 123–5, *124*

slavery: American South 63–4; and intimacy 62–3, 68
soccer 46
social class: demographics 50–1, 74–5, 146; and intimacy 61; lecture times 136; living arrangements 50–1; middles classes 30, 48, 74–5, 109–10, 146; Reitz case 30
social closure 12; *see also* racial segregation
social media: assault case 153, 155; connecting students with senior leaders 128–9; racism among students 117–18; vandalism case 7
songs: racial diversity 101–2; racial segregation 77, 136–7
South African Human Rights Commission (SAHRC) 162, 178
South African Qualifications Authority (SAQA) 106
Spelman College, USA 82
spirituality: *see* Christianity; religion
spiritual nearness 134, 136–8
sports 46–7; rugby match 123–5, *124*, 143; varsity competition 171–2
squeezas (slang) 17, 22, 26, 33
standards, academic 98–100, 193
Star, The (newspaper) 162
Stellenbosch, University of 118, 174–5, 201–3
Sterling, Donald 59–60
Steyn, Jaap 183
Steyn, Melissa 119–20
Steyn, M. T. statue 42
storytelling 2–5, 141
strategic nearness 134–6
studentepret (student fun) 27, 28, 181–2
Student Representative Council (SRC) 95, 157
students: first years vs seniors 93–4, 204; leadership *126*, 126–7, 149, 171–2, 206, 207–9, 215; views on UFS 101 (core curriculum) 112–17; working students 136; *see also* traditions, of students
Study Abroad programme 95, 139
swastika 73–4
symbolism 100–2, 206

"Talk to me" sessions 129–30
teaching staff, University of the Free State 102–3
technology 59, 128–9
theft case 184–5
tiekie (student tradition) 159–60
Times, The (newspaper) 4, 5
togetherness: *see* integration
tolerance (racial) 147
torture 59
traditions, of students: initiation rituals 17–19, 21, 27, 34–5, 94; threats to 181–2, 190; *tiekie* 159–60
transcendence (intimacy) 134, 137–8, 143–4
transformation xiii, 3–5; and intimacy 68–9, 93–5, 167–72; leadership 125–7, 203–17; and media coverage 161, 175, 177–8; role of Christianity 137, 169–71, *170*, 172; University of Stellenbosch 201–3
trauma, Reitz case 19–20
trivialisation of racism 182
Tswelopele (residence) 82
Tutu, Desmond (Archbishop) 29, 93
Twitter (social media) 128–9; assault case 153, 155

UFS 101 (core curriculum) 105, 106–12, 181; student opinions 112–17
undergraduates: *see* students
United States (USA) 3; assault case 163; interracial sex 62–3; slavery 63–4; universities 95
universities, South Africa 3, 5; academic standards 98–9, 192; demographics 160–1; history 83, 123; newspapers 173–8; racial segregation 48, 49, 53–4; studying abroad 95; transformation of 203; white privilege 188
universities, United States 95
University of... *see individual named institutions e.g. Free State, Pretoria*

vandalism 7, 184
van Onselen, Charles 6

van Tonder, Gerrit 192
van Zyl, Andre 179
varsity competitions 123, 171–2, 182, 190
veterans, military 34
victimhood: of blacks 43, 160, 168; of whites 182–6, 188–93, 194
video, Reitz case 20–1, 22, 26, 29, 32
video, *Villa Bravado* 166–7, 168
Villa Bravado (residence) 166–7, 168–9
violence 7, 153–64, 177, 184
Vista campus, University of the Free State 10
visual narratives 4–5
Volf, Miroslav 142–3
Volksblad (newspaper) 5, 173–95; government 186–7; integration 78, 178–80; over-exposure to race 180–1; residences 74, 78, 208; rugby 47; student fun 181–2; whites as victims 182–6, 188–93; worship 45
Volkskongres of 1956 61
Vryfees (festival) 45–7
Vrygrond, Cape Town 129–30

Wasserman, Herman 182
Welwitschia (residence) 80–1
white privilege 188, 195
whites: under apartheid 51–3, 189, 195; employment 48–50, 191–2; history and customs 43–8, 50–4, 74, 76; middles classes 30, 109–10, 146; victimhood 182–6, 188–93, 194
white supremacy, United States 63–4
whore, as insult 18, 25, 26, 27, 31
women: Boer War 40–1; Reitz case 17, 22, 29–32; *tiekie* case 159–60
work: *see* employment
working students 136
worship: racial segregation 44–5, 75; role in transformation 137, 169–71, *170*, 172

Yengeni, Tony 59

Zimbabwe 6

eBooks
from Taylor & Francis

Helping you to choose the right eBooks for your Library

Add to your library's digital collection today with Taylor & Francis eBooks. We have over 50,000 eBooks in the Humanities, Social Sciences, Behavioural Sciences, Built Environment and Law, from leading imprints, including Routledge, Focal Press and Psychology Press.

Choose from a range of subject packages or create your own!

Benefits for you
- Free MARC records
- COUNTER-compliant usage statistics
- Flexible purchase and pricing options
- All titles DRM-free.

Benefits for your user
- Off-site, anytime access via Athens or referring URL
- Print or copy pages or chapters
- Full content search
- Bookmark, highlight and annotate text
- Access to thousands of pages of quality research at the click of a button.

Free Trials Available
We offer free trials to qualifying academic, corporate and government customers.

eCollections

Choose from over 30 subject eCollections, including:

Archaeology	Language Learning
Architecture	Law
Asian Studies	Literature
Business & Management	Media & Communication
Classical Studies	Middle East Studies
Construction	Music
Creative & Media Arts	Philosophy
Criminology & Criminal Justice	Planning
Economics	Politics
Education	Psychology & Mental Health
Energy	Religion
Engineering	Security
English Language & Linguistics	Social Work
Environment & Sustainability	Sociology
Geography	Sport
Health Studies	Theatre & Performance
History	Tourism, Hospitality & Events

For more information, pricing enquiries or to order a free trial, please contact your local sales team:
www.tandfebooks.com/page/sales

www.tandfebooks.com

CPSIA information can be obtained
at www.ICGtesting.com
Printed in the USA
BVHW04*2043280918
528314BV00004B/30/P